BATTLETECH™

COMBAT MANUAL: MERCENARIES

MRB

TABLE OF CONTENTS

- FILTHY PLIGHT 5
- SOLDIERS OF FORTUNE 11
  - **MERCENARY HISTORY** 12
    - Star League 12
    - The Succession Wars 13
    - Present 14
  - **HIRING HALLS** 16
    - Galatea 16
    - Outreach 16
    - Solaris VII 17
    - Lesser Hiring Halls 18
      - Antallos 18
      - Astrokaszy 19
      - Herotitus 19
      - Noisiel 19
      - Westerhand 19
  - **THE BUSINESS OF WAR** 20
    - Contracts 20
    - Necessities 20
    - Survival 21
    - Oversight 21
- MERCENARY COMBAT COMMANDS 23
  - Combat Command Briefs 23
  - **BLUE STAR IRREGULARS** 24
    - 1894th Light Horse 24
    - Avatars of Painful Death 25
    - Twenty-first Rim Worlds 25
  - **BRION'S LEGION** 26
  - **21ST CENTAURI LANCERS** 27
    - Lancers Command 27
    - 17th Armored Recon Company 27
    - 21st Centauri Armored Lancers 27
    - 21st Centauri Security Lancers 27
  - **CRANSTON SNORD'S IRREGULARS** 28
    - Rhonda's Irregulars 28
    - H'Chu's Diggers 28
    - Shorty's Scavengers 28
  - **CRESCENT HAWKS** 29
  - **DEREK'S DEVILS** 30
    - Void Devils 30
    - Pit Fiends 30
  - **THE DIOSCURI** 31
    - Castor 31
    - Pollux 31
    - The Brotherhood 31
  - **DISMAL DISINHERITED** 32
    - First Dismal Disinherited 32
    - Second Dismal Disinherited 32
    - Third Dismal Disinherited 33
    - ***The Battle for Dromini VI*** 33
  - **15TH DRACON** 34
    - First Battalion 35
    - Second Battalion 35
    - Third Battalion 35
    - Fourth Battalion 35
    - ***The Battle for Ares*** 35
  - **ERIDANI LIGHT HORSE** 36
    - Light Horse Command 37
    - Twenty-first Striker 37
    - Seventy-first Light Horse 37
    - 151st Light Horse "Dark Horse Regiment" 37
  - **THE FILTHY LUCRE** 38
    - Blood Money 38
    - Weregilt 38
  - **FUCHIDA'S FUSILIERS** 39
  - **GLORY WARRIORS** 40
    - Second Skallevoll People's Mechanized 40
  - **GRAVE WALKERS** 41
    - First Grave Walkers 41
    - Second Grave Walkers 41
  - **GRAY DEATH LEGION** 42
    - Headquarters Company 42
    - Armored Scouts 42
    - Death Eagles 42
    - Gray Death Infantry 42
  - **GRIM DETERMINATION** 43
    - ***Plain Determination*** 43
  - **HANSEN'S ROUGHRIDERS** 44
    - Roughriders Air Support 44
    - Roughriders Armor Support 45
    - Roughriders Infantry Support 45
    - ***Death in the Arroyo*** 45
  - **ILLICIAN LANCERS** 46
    - Lancers Command 46
    - 59th Strike Regiment 47
    - 4th Illician Rangers 47
    - 9th Illician Rangers 47
    - 21st Illician Rangers 47
  - **KELL HOUNDS** 48
    - Kell Hounds Command Lance 48
    - First Kell Hounds 48
    - Second Kell Hounds 48
    - ***Hard Place on the Rock*** 49
  - **KILLER BEES** 50
    - Stinger Company 50
    - Yellowjacket Squadron 50
    - Swarm Company 50
    - Bumblebee Company 50
  - **LANGENDORF LANCERS** 51
  - **LEXINGTON COMBAT GROUP** 52
    - Lexington Combat Group Command 52
    - 32nd Recon Combat Group 52
    - 180th Dragoon Combat Group 53
    - 241st Battle Combat Group 53
  - **LINDON'S COMPANY** 54
    - Lindon's Air Wing 54
  - **LITTLE RICHARD'S PANZER BRIGADE** 55
  - **LONE WOLVES** 56
  - **MARSHIGAMA'S LEGIONNAIRES** 57
    - Ju-Lei's Queens 57
    - The Pretty-Boys 57
  - **NORTHWIND HIGHLANDERS** 58
    - First Kearny Highlanders 58
    - Second Kearny Highlanders 59
    - MacLeod's Highlanders 59
    - Stirling's Fusiliers 59
  - **RAMILIE'S RAIDERS** 60
    - Command Lance 60
    - Command Battalion 60
    - Assault Battalion 60
    - Sky Pirates 60
  - **SEVENTEENTH RECON REGIMENT** 61
    - Scout Company 61
  - **SCREAMING EAGLES** 62
    - First Screaming Eagles 62
    - Second Screaming Eagles 63
    - Diving Eagles 63
    - 77th Heavy Armor 63
    - Nested Eagles 63
  - **SIMONSON'S CUTTHROATS** 64
  - **SMITHSON'S CHINESE BANDITS** 65
    - First Smithson's Chinese Bandits 65
    - Second Smithson's Chinese Bandits 65
  - **12TH STAR GUARDS** 66
    - Guard Primary 66
    - First Regiment "Rivers Gamblers" 66
    - Second Regiment "Ohell's Heavies" 66
    - Third Regiment "Paget's War Ponies" 67
    - Seventh Regiment "Scovy's Ironmen" 67
    - ***Valley of Despair*** 67
  - **4TH TAU CETI RANGERS** 68
    - Hard Air 68
  - **WACO'S RANGERS** 69
    - Ranger Command 69
    - Air Rangers 69
  - **12TH VEGAN RANGERS** 70
    - Alpha Regiment 71
    - Beta Regiment 71
    - Gamma Regiment 71
    - Delta Regiment 71
  - **WILSON'S HUSSARS** 72
    - ***Escape from Kimball VI*** 72
  - **WYLIE'S COYOTES** 73
  - **WOLF'S DRAGOONS** 74
    - Alpha Regiment 75
    - Beta Regiment 75
    - Gamma Regiment 75
    - Delta Regiment 75
    - Epsilon Regiment 75
    - Zeta Battalion 75
    - Independant Units (Operational Commands) 76
    - Black Widow Company 75
- RULES ADDENDUM 79
  - **FORCE BUILDING** 80
    - Force Building Terms 80
  - **SELECT POINT VALUE TOTAL** 80
  - **CHOOSE AN ERA** 80
  - **CHOOSE A FACTION** 80
  - **CHOOSE A COMBAT COMMAND** 81
    - Unit Organizations 82
      - BattleMech Organization 82
      - Aerospace Organization 82
      - Armor Organization 82
      - Infantry Organization 82
      - Artillery Organization 83
      - Aviation Organization 83

BUILD A COMPANY 83
BUILD FORMATIONS 84
- Step 1: Choose Formation Type 84
- Step 2: Choose Units for the Formation 84
  - Standard Lances 84
  - Availability Lists 84
  - What if I Just Want to Start Playing? 85
- Step 3: Select Skill and Modify PV 86
- Step 4: Assign Special Pilot Abilities 86

ASSIGNING SPECIAL COMMAND ABILITIES 87
- Determine Force Experience Rating 87
- Determine Number of Special Command Abilities 87
- Assign Special Command Abilities 87

SUPPLEMENTAL MERCENARIES 87
MERCENARY SPECIAL COMMAND ABILITIES 90
- Environmental Specializations 90
  - Optional Game Setup: Environment Conditions 90
- Enemy Specializations 90
- New Special Command Abilities 91

PLAYER-GENERATED COMBAT COMMANDS 94
- Force Composition 94
- Skill Rating and Special Command Abilities 94
- Availability Lists 94
- Special Rules 94
- Unique Character 94

MERCENARY OPFOR (OPTIONAL) 95
- Select Formations 95

MERCENARY LANCES (FORMATIONS) 94
- New Lance (Formation) Types 94
- Standard Lances 94

UNAFFILIATED MECHWARRIORS 98
TECHNICAL READOUT 99
- LCT-1V Locust 100
- OTT-7J Ostscout 102
- SHD-2H Shadow Hawk 104
- WHM-6R Warhammer 106

GUNS FOR HIRE 108

MERCENARY FACTION LISTS 114

Special Thanks to our Review Team
Alex Aguila, Miguel Alvarez, Joel Bancroft-Connors, Roy Carl, Rich Cencarik, Brent Enzel, Stephan Frabartolo, William Gauthier, Keith Hann, Jason Hansa, John Haward, Ross Hines, Alex Kaempen, Chris Marti, Josh McCarthy, Mike Miller, Chris Negelein, William J. Pennington, Joshua Perian, Luke Robertson, Andreas Rudolph, Rick Sardiñas, Jason Schmetzer, Colin Toenjes, Chris Wheeler, Matthew Wilsbacher, Peter Wort.

Miniatures Painting & Photography
Todd Farnholtz, Joel Hardwick, Phil Hays, Michael Holzapfel, Ryan Peterson, Peter Wort.
CamosSpecs Online: Ray Arrastia, George Bluoin, William Burt, Roy Carl, Chris Dolega, Paul Eckes, Matt Edwards, Dave Fanjoy, Todd Farnholtz, Matt Frederiksen, Joel Hardwick, Phil Hays, Ross Hines, Michael Holzapfel, David Kerber, Frederic Lagoanere, Steve Livingston, Mark Maestas, Ryan Peterson, Brian Plunkitt, Mike Raper, Ben Rome, Lance Scarinci, Paul Sjardijn, Edward Smith, Allen Soles, Drew Williams, and Peter Wort.

Printed in USA.

Published by Catalyst Game Labs, an imprint of InMediaRes Productions, LLC.
PMB 202 303 91st Ave NE E502 • Lake Stevens, WA 98258

FIND US ONLINE:
Web Site: bg.battletech.com/ • CatalystGameLabs.com
Online Store: battlecorps.com/catalog
Facebook: fb.com/battletechgame • **Twitter:** @CGL_BattleTech

CREDITS

Development
Ray Arrastia

Development Assistance
Joshua Franklin

Writing
Geoff Swift

Rules and Additional Writing
Ray Arrastia
Joshua Franklin

Editing
Aaron Cahall

BattleTech Line Developer
Randall Bills
Assistant Line Developer
Ben H. Rome
Products Developer
Ray Arrastia

Art Direction
Brent Evans

Cover Art
Anthony Scroggins

Illustrations
Ray Arrastia
Ken Fairclough
Mark Hayden
Alexander Immerzeel
David Allen Kerber
Chris Lewis
Marco Mazzoni
Florian Mellies
Jeff Porter
Anthony Scroggins
Eric Williams

Design and Layout
Ray Arrastia

Evolved Faction Logos Design
Ray Arrastia, Matt Heerdt, Jason Vargas

FILTHY PLIGHT

Major Myron Carpathia squinted at his viewscreen, cursing the enemy missile that had hit his 'Mech's head and damaged his sensors. Static-filled monitors and a targeting reticle that fuzzed in and out on his HUD mocked his need to target the enemy accurately. Aiming as best he could, he tightened his grip on the control sticks of his grandfather's *Warhammer* and pressed the firing studs for its twin PPCs. He swooned in the sudden wash of oppressive heat and struggled to observe the effect of his weapons fire. Coruscating blue bolts traced their way through air made dusty by the tread of BattleMechs. The left beam passed harmlessly over the fleeing enemy *Grasshopper*'s shoulder, while the right made a ruin of its left arm. The damage was insignificant, though. The Langendorf Lancer 'Mech poured on the speed and left Carpathia's *Warhammer* behind. The *Grasshopper* was one of the slower raiders, but now it joined their ranks in the city's edge, disappearing from view behind the homes and apartment buildings of the city's residential quarter.

Almost in unison, Carpathia's comrades in the Filthy Lucre slowed their 'Mechs to a halt outside the city and beyond enemy range. Their garrison contract required them to protect the world of Dixie from Free Worlds League raiders like these fellow mercs. Pursuing the enemy into the city, especially the nearby civilian district, would go against their pledge to safeguard the locals. The raiders had grounded their DropShips on the far side of New Wichita before making an end run at the supply depot in the old Castle Brian. Once the Filthy Lucre Battalion had repulsed the raiders, the retreating enemy had walked right into the clutches of Carpathia's own Blood Money Battalion. Unfortunately, the speedy raiders evaded his heavier battalion's weapons. The lucky shot on the *Grasshopper*'s arm was the only damage he had managed to inflict, and that was less meaningful than the *Grasshopper*'s own missile shot to the *Warhammer*'s head.

Luxuriating in the rapidly cooling air of his cockpit, Carpathia toggled his comm system to the command channel. "Colonel, Carpathia here, over."

"Major Carpathia, why have you and your command ceased pursuit?" The voice that crackled through his comm was not the stern tones of Colonel Karl Timson. This voice was higher pitched and carried the whining tone of someone used to getting his own way at all times suddenly faced with disappointment. It was the voice of Kommandant Mandingo Gluck. With Hauptmann-General Miguel James and his XO Leutnant-General Jean Andrews in the arctic on a training operation with the Dixie TMM, Gluck was the senior officer in the area. He had not let the Lucre officers forget that fact.

Carpathia took a steadying breath before answering to avoid saying something he'd regret. "The Lancers entered the city, *sir*." The last word came out as a growl, despite his best efforts.

"I fail to see the reasoning, *Major*." Gluck's tone was condescending at best.

"Civilian homes fill this entire district." He didn't elaborate. Clearly that said it all.

"I don't care about who lives where, Major. You were ordered to prevent the escape of the raiders. Move in and end their retreat!"

"You can't be serious, sir." *Where is the Colonel? Why is Gluck the only one on the channel?*

"I am absolutely serious, Major."

"It's too risky. Better to let them go. We'll get 'em next time."

"Next time? So rather than do your duty, you push your job off on your successor?"

The Filthy Lucre's contract on Dixie was up at midnight, and an extension had not been offered by the Commonwealth. Carpathia knew from the colonel that a new offer was on the table. He had asked everyone's opinion on the contract, which would take the Lucre out of Lyran employ for the first time in almost two centuries. The kommandant was making the choice easier, though nothing had been finalized yet.

"How can you care so little about your own people?"

"How can you care so little about your honor?"

"It's our honor that keeps us from risking the lives of your people!" Carpathia could not help it. He was frustrated at his failure to contain the Lancers, and now he was angry at the ridiculous order being issued over the battalion's comm channel. His fellow MechWarriors were keeping quiet, but he knew they could all hear.

"I'm warning you, Major..." The tone in Gluck's voice had changed from one of outrage to cold fury.

"Warn all you want. We're returning to base." Carpathia clicked off his comm rather than listen to the kommandant's reply. He wheeled his *Warhammer* about and proceeded around the city to the Blood Money Battalion's base on the edge of the spaceport. An hour later, he climbed down the ladder from his cockpit to the sound of cooling metal pinging throughout the 'Mechbay. As he hailed the head technician, a quartet of hovercraft pulled into the bay entrance in a swirl of dust. Coughing, and waving his hands to clear the air, he could barely make out the squads of security troops dismounting in full kit and surrounding him and his MechWarriors.

"Major Carpathia?" the helmeted master sergeant asked politely.

"Yes, what's this about?"

The sergeant sounded apologetic as he answered. "You're under arrest, sir."

"Arrest?! For what?" Carpathia clenched his fists—but kept them clear of his sidearm as the squad trained their rifles on him. His fellow mercenaries wisely kept their own arms held out to their sides.

"Kommandant's orders, sir. You're accused of dereliction of duty, breach of contract, and cowardice. I'm afraid you and your command are ordered to surrender peacefully, sir."

Wide-eyed, Carpathia felt the blood drain from his face. No one had ever called him a coward. He wanted to kill someone. He looked around. The looks on his fellows' faces made it clear they felt like he did. But none of them had their weapons drawn, and all were clad just in cooling vests and undergarments. The security troops wore body armor and held their rifles in steady grips.

Carpathia swallowed hard, but could not clear the lump in his throat to form a response. He nodded, and was quickly placed in restraints before being hustled gently into the waiting hovercraft along with his men.

▲▼▲

Colonel Karl Timson was not in a pleasant mood. He swung down the ladder from his *Marauder* and stalked into the headquarters of the Dixie TMM. He glared down the troopers who considered slowing his progress, cowing each of them into silence. He burst into Kommandant Gluck's office without bothering to knock.

"What in the hell have you done?" Timson managed not to shout, instead growling out the question.

Gluck didn't even bother to turn and face his uninvited guest. He remained at the large picture window overlooking the spaceport grounds.

In the distance were the barracks and 'Mechbays of the Blood Money Battalion. Instead of the normal activity, the windows were dark and the bay empty. Guards were visible at the bay doors. Everyone in the battalion had been arrested, even the technicians and supply clerks.

"Your men failed to carry out a lawful order by their commanding officer."

"*I* am their commander and they have never failed to—"

"You answer to me, do you not?" The calm way he interrupted Timson's building tirade was unsettling, almost rehearsed.

"For the moment, yes."

"And I gave them an order in your absence. They disobeyed and so were arrested accordingly."

"Chain of command requires you to issue orders to *me*, and I pass them to my men, dammit!"

"And in your absence I cannot issue orders to a subordinate? You and I both know that's not how things work."

"Is that why you jammed my comms when Carpathia tried to report in?"

Gluck tried but failed to cover a brief smirk as it flashed across his face. "Jamming? Why, whatever do you mean? Surely you're not accusing me of something, Colonel?" Now the smirk opened wide and shameless on Gluck's face.

"What's this really about, Gluck?"

Gluck smiled and sat in the large synth-leather chair behind the DropShip-sized oak desk. He steepled his fingers and rested his elbows on the massive polished surface. "Colonel, it's been brought to my attention that your contract expires with the current year."

Timson narrowed his eyes but said nothing.

"And no extension has been negotiated. Yet you still owe a significant debt to the Commonwealth for..." Gluck paused and slid a file from the edge of the desk to its center, then opened it and read from its contents, "ammunition, armor, fuel, JumpShip transport to present duty station, housing for your dependents... Well, the list goes on. Perhaps you'd like to verify these amounts?" Gluck slid the file across the desk toward Timson.

Timson didn't move. "So what? Arresting my men is some tactic to—what? Force us further into the company store?"

"Why, I never would have considered such a thing, Colonel. Your men will be prosecuted for their crimes. Of course, the charges might be suspended if we can come to, shall we say, a favorable agreement for your continued service?" The largest shit-eating grin Timson had ever seen alit on the kommandant's face. Timson wanted nothing more than to wipe it off, permanently. "Are we clear?"

Gluck was waiting for a response. Instead, Timson wheeled about and left the office as abruptly as he had entered it. As soon as the door closed behind him, he pulled his pocket comm and spoke into it. "Deeley, come in." Deeley was the Lucre's closest thing to a negotiator, having run a succession of small side businesses during his service with the mercenary command.

Deeley's voice crackled tinnily through the speaker. "Deeley here, sir."

"You at the HPG with our MRB friend?"

"Roger that, boss."

"Sign the contract, and send out Condition Dragoon."

"Done and done, boss."

Timson hurried back to his waiting 'Mech, glad to see there were no guards around it like those in the Blood Money 'Mechbay. He hated what he was about to do, but this was the last straw. In four hours the Filthy Lucre's time with the Lyran Commonwealth would end.

Colonel Karl Timson presented a very different figure as he re-entered the Dixie TMM's headquarters a few hours later. Replacing the cooling vest and briefs was his nicely-pressed and rarely-worn dress uniform. Modeled after the old LCAF uniform in use when the Lucre first signed on with the Commonwealth, it was plain of the gaudy medals and campaign awards common on Lyran officer uniforms. Only the blue sash showing his graduation from the prestigious Nagelring and the white C-bill symbol of the Filthy Lucre broke up the otherwise dull gray affair. His sidearm was holstered on the left as always for easy cross-draw with his right hand. No one challenged him carrying it. They thought he was contrite and defeated.

He nodded politely to those guards who were present and knocked gently on the kommandant's door. An aide opened the door and nodded Timson inside. The aide stepped outside and closed the door behind him. Timson marshalled his will and forced outward calmness to his face. All he wanted was for this meeting to end better than he expected.

"What can I do for you, Colonel?" the kommandant asked without looking up from the files he was reading.

"Thank you for seeing me."

Gluck looked up from the desk and closed the folder in front of him. "I didn't think our business was finished, Colonel. I've been expecting you to call again." A perfect smile of gleaming teeth shone at Timson.

Timson nodded. "I apologize for my earlier behavior, Kommandant. The trip from the Castle Brian left me weary. I would like to discuss the release of my men."

"Of course. Allow me to reiterate my earlier offer. The charges will be dropped if you can settle your debt to the Lyran people. Since your accounts lack the funds, this can be accomplished by finally joining your long time comrades in the AFFC, bringing your regiment of 'Mechs and trio of *Overlords* along."

Timson sighed. "Is that really your only offer?"

"The alternative is to watch your men get court-martialed, and their 'Mechs be sold to pay for their legal defense. Surely you don't want that?" That grin reappeared. The man was clearly enjoying himself.

"Actually, kommandant, there is a third option."

"Oh? And what might that be?" He sounded as if he was talking to a small, slow child.

"You could release my men, and their confiscated equipment, to me. Right now. Without any prejudice or charges to follow. The debt will be paid in full at midnight."

Gluck scoffed and disbelief showed clearly on his face. "And what precisely would motivate me to agree to such a ludicrous offer?"

Timson drew his pistol. "What value do you place on your own life, Kommandant? Surely that should go far toward leveling our debt?"

"You realize I could simply call out, and a squad of troops would arrive and toss you in with your men?" Gluck's composure started to break. A sheen of sweat formed on his forehead.

Timson checked his wristchron. *Thirty seconds to midnight.* "I don't think that will make any difference anymore."

On cue, as the hour ticked over, the city launched its fireworks display. Sparkles lit the sky to explosive reports.

"I love fireworks, don't you, Kommandant? They provide such excellent cover for unauthorized operations."

Dimly, below the series of explosions in the sky, came the sound of small arms fire. A distinctly close explosion rattled the large window pane and shook the office.

Gluck's face paled and his jaw tightened. Through clenched teeth he growled out, "You cannot seriously have—"

"You didn't really leave me much choice, did you? Arresting my men for not starting a melee in the residential quarter? Threatening to sell off their equipment unless we signed on to be your stooges, all so you can get a promotion for extorting us into the state military?"

Gluck rose and opened his mouth to shout.

"Go ahead. Call them. See what happens." His pistol was steady, its barrel not wavering in the slightest from the kommandant's face. Gluck sat back down, his knuckles whitening on the arms of his chair.

"So now what? All you've done is make yourselves criminals one and all. You'll be hunted down anywhere in the FedCom."

"Then I guess it's a good thing we just got hired by the Free Worlds League."

"What?!"

"Yes. I was serious about the money being in our accounts at midnight. We requested a signing bonus to leave the Commonwealth, an amount equal to the debt we owe. We directed the MRB to transfer the funds at midnight when they became available. Our debt is being settled even now."

"That doesn't absolve your men of their criminal charges."

"Perhaps not to you. But no one would condemn my men for refusing an order to put innocent lives on the line to chase down raiders who were already defeated."

"I see. I didn't want to do this, but I will detain your dependents to prevent this."

"Oh,you can try. When I signed the contract I issued a long-standing order. Condition Dragoon, we call it."

"Dragoon?"

"Yep. See, every merc in the business knows what happened to Wolf's Dragoons' civilians when the Combine betrayed them. Mercs everywhere laid contingency plans to avoid the exact same thing. We've drilled many times on evacuating a base quickly, taking only what we truly need. Knowing the sort of," Timson flicked his gaze distastefully over Gluck, "*man* you are, our families packed up and boarded our DropShips as soon as I left our last meeting. Weregilt Battalion is already on the way to the zenith jump point. Our new comrades in the Langendorf Lancers are waiting for us. Lucre Battalion is just outside the city waiting for me and the men from Blood Money Battalion. They're sort of an insurance package. We might not want to fight in the civilian area, but this spaceport and your headquarters are an entirely different target. *Are we clear?*"

Gluck stared daggers. Without moving his gaze, he reached for the comm panel on his desk. His fingers keyed a brief sequence.

"Yes, Kommandant?" a voice issued from the speaker grille.

"Release the prisoners."

Timson cleared his throat and tightened his eyes.

Gluck scowled. "And their 'Mechs. Immediately."

Silence reigned for a pregnant ten seconds. "Acknowledge!" Gluck was losing his composure.

"Yes, Kommandant. Prisoners are being released.

Timson calmly pulled his portable comm from a pocket and spoke into it. "Report." A sibilant hiss of response answered him. "Good." He returned the comm to his pocket, but kept the pistol on the kommandant. He smiled like a crocodile after a meal. "Take care. *Sir*."

Timson kept his pistol on the kommandant as he backed toward the door. He opened it and stepped through before lowering his weapon. He turned a parade-worthy about-face and holstered his sidearm, departing the headquarters at a fast pace. The Lucre was free, but he did not smile. He whispered his thought to the empty courtyard. "No one won here today."

SOLDIERS OF FORTUNE

Mercenaries are ubiquitous in the Inner Sphere, and have factored into nearly every conflict throughout interstellar history in some way. Their role is an important one, and their presence alongside the national militaries of the Successor States makes them well-known figures. Many are reviled as honorless money-grubbers seeking a payday from the highest bidder, but a select few are idolized by those they fight for or against. The role mercenaries play on the battlefield is usually influential and necessary for victory, making them the focus of intense scrutiny and publicity.

The centuries-long series of conflicts dubbed the Succession Wars killed billions as the Successor States vied with their neighbors for dominion over the Inner Sphere—and provided mercenaries with no shortage of work. But while they were focused on one another, a greater threat was forming beyond the Periphery. The Clans are unlike anything the Inner Sphere has ever seen and their invasion will force a true test upon its mercenaries, who must pit their mettle and superior numbers against overwhelmingly superior technology. Many will fail that test, while others will triumph thanks to the inimitable ingenuity and tenacity for which mercenaries are renowned.

Welcome to the first volume in a new series of *BattleTech* game supplements. This installment, *Combat Manual: Mercenaries,* provides crucial information and rules for the soldiers of fortune of the *BattleTech* universe. With the information contained in this volume, players will be able to create a mercenary Force for use in their *Alpha Strike* games.

Combat Manual: Mercenaries covers just a sample of the mercenary Combat Commands in the Inner Sphere. Because so many mercenary Combat Commands are formed and disbanded for various reasons, their role is ever-changing. Players should feel free to modify what they read here to suit the needs of their game. Nothing contained in these pages should be considered so restrictive as to reduce or eliminate the fun of the *Alpha Strike* game itself.

HOW TO USE THIS BOOK

This chapter, ***Soldiers of Fortune***, and sidebars located throughout this *Combat Manual*, will ground players in the history of mercenaries in the Inner Sphere and their significant contribution to the development of the Successor States. Following this brief history is information on mercenary hiring practices, including everything from how they are employed by various Successor States to where they congregate to find work, as well as typical contract requirements and performance stipulations.

The ***Mercenary Combat Commands*** present information about many specific mercenary Combat Commands, large and small. Due to the number of mercenary outfits, however, these represent a mere cross-section of the profession. Included are their personal histories and Force composition, along with particularly noteworthy moments from their past and notable warriors from their ranks.

The ***Rules Addendum*** introduces special rules for *Alpha Strike* games which include mercenary Forces. This chapter provides Force Building rules for mercenaries and includes a review of mercenary Special Command Abilities. Pre-made mercenary Standard Lances, as well as Unaffiliated MechWarriors, are supplied for players who simply want to jump straight into a game. Finally, the Technical Readout section details four venerable BattleMechs in service to mercenary and Great House Combat Commands throughout the Inner Sphere.

Guns For Hire showcases the myriad mercenary paint schemes. Players may use this section as a reference if they choose to paint their miniatures to match one or more of the mercenary Combat Commands presented in this *Combat Manual*. Additional examples of many other mercenary paint schemes can be found on the CamoSpecs website at CamoSpecs.com.

Finally, ***Mercenary Faction Lists*** offers detailed Unit listings available to mercenary Combat Commands. These should be used as a guideline when constructing a Force based on the mercenaries featured in this *Combat Manual*.

MERCENARY HISTORY

STAR LEAGUE

Under the Star League, mercenaries were largely relegated to the same supporting role they occupied for centuries, dating back to pre-spaceflight Terra. BattleMechs only reached mercenary hands through leases offered by their employers, as they were simply too rare and expensive for private owners to maintain. Only the House militaries and the Star League Defense Force had the technical experts and logistics chains required for such work. Some mercenaries managed to find a role as deniable forces in the battles between rival House Lords. As the House Lords pushed the limits of their agreements with the Star League in the 2700s, more mercenaries found themselves equipped with BattleMechs. Things changed forever when Stefan Amaris assassinated the First Lord of the Star League and declared himself Emperor.

The resulting Amaris Civil War was the greatest conflict in human history to that point. General Aleksandr Kerensky led the SLDF to retake Terra and overthrow Stefan the Usurper; the conflict consumed billions of lives and left entire worlds in ruins. It was Amaris who provided the first true influx of BattleMechs to the mercenary profession, equipping those under his employ with the war machines. These 'Mech-equipped Amaris mercenaries committed a litany of war crimes. The poor regard for mercenaries among civilian populations of the Inner Sphere since that time stem almost entirely from the dishonorable conduct of these troops.

Following the war, common wisdom held that Kerensky could have become a king or a kingmaker. Had he seized power, none of the House Lords could have opposed him, though politics would have made it far from simple. Alternatively, Kerensky could have selected one of the five House Lords to back as the new First Lord. Just as Amaris' massive army could not withstand the SLDF, neither could the combined might of all the House Lords. Instead Kerensky chose a third option, intended to lessen the damage of the war of succession he foresaw.

In 2784, Kerensky left behind the squabbling member states of the former Star League and departed the Inner Sphere, taking 80 percent of the SLDF into Exodus beyond the trackless Periphery. Many of the SLDF troops who remained joined House militaries, but a great number elected to sell their extensive skills and equipment to the highest bidder, forming the core of the new mercenary profession. Several of these would stand among the greatest of all mercenary commands, including some that have survived to the present day. Unlike the dregs that once served Amaris, these crack troops possessed a sense of honor along with vast experience, and the exemplary manner in which they comported themselves in and out of battle began to change the public perception of mercenaries for the better. The change was slow, however, and these honorable commands were few and far between—too many mercenary outfits were little more than marauding criminals as likely to raid their employers as to attack the enemy.

THE SUCCESSION WARS

Kerensky's Exodus spawned the first reputable 'Mech-equipped mercenaries with sufficient skill and appropriate equipment to survive in the Inner Sphere of the late 28th century. But the departure of the bulk of the SLDF also removed the restraint that had prevented the House militaries from warring openly with one another. Coordinator Minoru Kurita and the other House Lords each declared themselves First Lord of the Star League, and chose warfare to settle their dispute. Thus began the Succession Wars, ensuring stable and long-term employment for mercenaries regardless of which House they signed a contract with.

The mercenary trade flourished during the Succession Wars as the constant state of warfare—in varying degrees of intensity—made for profitable times. However, the sheer destruction and the concomitant loss of technology punished mercenaries to an even greater degree than House militaries. The First Succession War saw some of the greatest atrocities of all time, foremost among them the Kentares Massacre in 2796. The indiscriminate murder of some 52 million civilians shocked the whole of humanity. While the horror motivated the Federated Suns to blunt an ongoing Draconis Combine invasion, the conduct of war was not curtailed in the least. After less than a decade of fitful peace, the Second Succession War brought another thirty-plus years of unremitting warfare between the Successor States.

The continued erosion of civilization threatened to prevent the very warfare that kept mercenaries employed. It fell to those mercenaries of former SLDF extraction to

THE STAR LEAGUE

The Star League was founded in 2571 when the Terran Hegemony and the Five Great Houses united. This stopped the warfare between the Houses, but only by focusing military efforts elsewhere. One of the League's first orders of business was to launch the Reunification War against the Periphery nations. Through force of arms, the Magistracy of Canopus, Outworlds Alliance, the Rim Worlds Republic, and the Taurian Concordat were conquered.

The Star League Era is often referred to as humanity's Golden Age. Technology, especially military hardware but also medical, manufacturing, and scientific applications, reached its zenith under the Star League. Despite the great advances, humanity remained ever the same: those seeking power worked to foment rebellions and internecine warfare, culminating with the assassination of the last in the Cameron line of First Lords. The League fell as it ascended: in bloody ruin.

restore some semblance of civility to war. While House military leaders no longer bothered with the Ares Conventions, some mercenary commands began to refuse missions which required violating the accords. Mercenaries also revived the ancient concept of allowing surrendered opponents to be ransomed back to their comrades, thus reducing—but not eliminating—the terrible war of attrition that degraded the military readiness of all sides. Augmenting the efforts of these too-few honorable commands was the ComStar-created Mercenary Review Board. The MRB sought to legitimize the mercenary profession and standardize the means by which they were treated. The Board's establishment had some effect, but there was no true means of enforcement to punish those who sullied mercenary work with criminal conduct. While one House might brand a mercenary command as criminals, another House would hail them as allies against a common foe and actually reward them for their atrocities.

Another all-too-brief peace was shattered by the Third Succession War. While the first two Succession Wars each endured for more than three decades, the Third lasted more than a century—though at an incredibly reduced scale. As the Houses waged wholesale warfare against each other's industrial bases, technology was lost in the fires of war. Entire cities where factory workers built the weapons of war were transformed into wastelands, their products regarded as precious beyond measure. While the Houses hoarded their educated persons and precious technology, mercenaries were largely left to their own devices. This led to the salvage clauses so prevalent in mercenary contracts, allowing the paid warfighters to rebuild their battered equipment from the flotsam of warfare.

The Third Succession War finally ground to a halt a quarter of the way into the 31st century. Again, a mere three years of peace lingered before the brief Fourth Succession War ripped the Inner Sphere apart. The Fourth War saw large-scale invasions and attempts to outright eliminate rival Houses for the first time in well over a century. This was aided by the incipient recovery or rediscovery of lost technology. Mercenaries factored once more in the prosecution of the new conflict, perhaps to a greater degree than in any of the prior Succession Wars. This was most obvious in the personal war between the Coordinator of the Draconis Combine and the mercenary Wolf's Dragoons. The nigh-genocidal warfare between the Draconis Combine Mustered Soldiery and the Dragoons regiments laid waste to vast stretches of multiple worlds. This duel blunted the DCMS and allowed the Federated Suns to concentrate on conquering the Capellan Confederation. It fell to ComStar to prevent the complete collapse of House Liao, but the map of the Inner Sphere was redrawn significantly for the first time since the Star League era. Because of their crucial presence among the Davion forces, the profile and regard of mercenaries was at its highest level ever during and after the war.

PRESENT

The aftermath of the Fourth Succession War, and to a lesser extent the War of 3039, saw many mercenaries considered heroes worthy of worship—especially compared to the profession's unsavory past. Still, there were no shortage of disreputable commands that lived down to that reputation. Some Inner Sphere powers had new reasons to disdain soldiers of fortune; in the Draconis Combine, mercenaries were all labeled criminals and condemned.

The number of mercenaries for hire swelled, drawing from retired MechWarriors who craved the taste of combat, disaffected troops unhappy with the orders they were forced to carry out, young academy graduates upset they missed the great war of their lives, and defeated troops refusing to return to the nation that abandoned them.

The exploding number of mercenary units forced a new emphasis on self-policing in the profession. Despite great strides made by the most honorable commands, many mercenaries exemplified the worst stereotypes of the profession. These groups often committed heinous crimes on the populace they were hired to protect, disobeyed orders, or switched sides in the middle of a conflict after receiving an offer for higher pay. For some commands, bounty hunting of those accused of these actions became a means of support, as it had long been for the famed Bounty Hunter. The Mercenary Review Board, established by Jerome Blake shortly after ComStar's own founding as an impartial broker for mercenary contracts, found itself more in demand than ever before.

The Federated Commonwealth regards mercenaries with great respect. This is especially true in the Davion portion of the Commonwealth, long the home of the Inner Sphere's largest military. This massive force remains augmented with the greatest number of mercenary commands under contract anywhere in the Inner Sphere. The Steiner portion of the nation made do with a smaller military, but faced Periphery border which was filled with more bandit kingdoms than that of the Federated Suns. As a result, mercenaries were always a critical component of safeguarding shipping routes and hunting pirates.

The Draconis Combine is the only nation which holds a particular enmity for mercenaries. After his effort to destroy Wolf's Dragoons allowed Coordinator Takashi Kurita's hated Davion enemies to conquer vast stretches of Combine territory almost without effort, the Dragon instituted the infamous Death to Mercenaries policy. Hired soldiers were no longer allowed in the Combine. Those who managed to escape the nation's borders with their lives were the lucky ones—not all were so fortunate.

The Free Rasalhague Republic relies heavily on mercenaries to defend its small territory. Most of these mercenaries help train the growing KungsArmé, with a significant portion guarding the tough civilian population from pirates and constant raids from their former Combine countrymen.

The Free Worlds League employs a number of mercenaries, but most are relegated to pirate hunting on the Periphery border. Tentative peace reigns along the Federated Commonwealth border, thanks to the efforts of the New Avalon Institute of Science in treating the Captain-General's heir. With his son on New Avalon, Thomas Marik is essentially restrained from any hostility towards the Federated Commonwealth.

The Capellan Confederation largely distrusts mercenaries, stemming from the betrayal and departure of the Northwind Highlanders during the Fourth Succession War. The Highlanders left their centuries-long employer to return to their ancestral homeworld, offered to them by First Prince Hanse Davion in exchange for their loyalty to the Suns. At the same time, however, McCarron's Armored Cavalry provided some of the stiffest resistance against the Davion invaders along the entire Capellan front. The splinter St. Ives Compact views mercenaries far more favorably than their former Capellan countrymen, both because the Compact cleaves closely to the Federated Commonwealth, and because it depends on mercenaries to defend it from the Capellan Chancellor's hateful efforts to reclaim her lost worlds.

The nations of the Periphery have increased their hiring of mercenaries since the Fourth Succession War due to the greater numbers of pirates infesting the region. Many of these pirates are disgraced House troops or deserters who saw a means to live free and fled with their equipment. Others simply hated the new status quo and refused to live under the thumb of new masters. No matter their origin, the need for easily-deployed troops keeps mercenaries as busy in the Periphery as in the Inner Sphere.

FEDERATED COMMONWEALTH

The Federated Commonwealth was born on Terra on 20 August 3028, when First Prince Hanse Davion of the Federated Suns married Archon-Designate Melissa Davion, heir to the Lyran Commonwealth. The First Prince launched the Fourth Succession War when he toasted his wife by saying, "I give you the Capellan Confederation!" Seventeen months later, the war ended, with the Federated Suns in possession of nearly a third of the Confederation, plus a number of worlds from the Free Worlds League and Draconis Combine.

Uniting the nations has proved more difficult than uniting the two ruling families. The Lyran military has greatly benefited from "Davionization," but many Lyrans dislike the Davion influence. The allies' defeat in the War of 3039 showed that coordination of the two nations' militaries had a long way to go. The last decade has seen further integration, including new FedCom RCTs intended to foster unification as new troops lacking affiliation to one nation over the other.

HOUSE DAVION

The Federated Suns has long been the promised land for mercenary employment. The realm would not have endured intact for so long without mercenaries; even though the Federated Suns has long had the largest House military, it also has the most territory to secure. This requires more troops than the House can adequately support via its academies and militia training efforts.

The Suns has generally treated mercenaries generously and fairly, despite a few isolated cases of mercenary units nearly falling under the Company Store, and thus is the first choice for mercenaries without a personal objection to serving there. Because the Suns has always employed so many mercenaries, paying them all poses a problem. Federated Suns contract negotiators solved this dilemma by always offering generous salvage terms in exchange for lower outright payment. This ensures their contracted mercenaries are eager for combat assignments, and less so for garrison or cadre duties.

HIRING HALLS

To some extent, every world can potentially serve as a "hiring hall"—all that is needed is an official House representative, a mercenary command's officer, and preferably a broker from the Mercenary Review Board. However, mercenaries began to congregate in large numbers on a select few worlds for convenience. Choosing high-traffic worlds reduced their transport issues, since dedicated JumpShip assets have always been rare among mercenaries. Employers also preferred mercenaries to congregate at a single site, as it enabled them to send fewer representatives to secure the troops they required. Even when the hiring hall is found within the borders of a particular House, agents of all Houses are usually allowed to operate freely and openly to hire troops. Perhaps foolish at first blush, keeping mercenary hiring a non-secret process ensured that each side knew which units were hired by their rivals. With their contract known to all, mercenaries were less likely to commit war crimes which would reflect poorly on their employers, and those employers were likely to keep tighter leashes on lesser-known commands who had yet to cement their reputations.

GALATEA

A largely barren world in the Lyran Commonwealth just three jumps from Terra, Galatea was a major training world for the SLDF and the Lyran Commonwealth Armed Forces for centuries. The constant presence of large military formations maintained a strong economy, and Galatea became a major trading port along the route from Terra into the Commonwealth. However, when the League fell, the world collapsed into economic depression. Without any industry or agriculture to support itself, Galatea might have become depopulated save for the influx of unemployed mercenaries seeking work. Had the world not suffered economic collapse, the mercenaries might have been turned away. Instead, the desperate need for some manner of industry allowed the growing profession to flourish on Galatea. Centuries of brisk trade in mercenary hiring by all nations earned the world the nickname of "the Mercenary's Star." The emergence of Outreach under Jaime Wolf's rule saw Galatea's fortunes wane. Nonetheless, for many the world is still the Mercenary's Star, even if its light has faded in recent years.

Mercenaries typically arrive in Galaport, an immense spaceport able to accommodate terrific numbers of DropShips at one time. Southeast of Galaport lies Galatean City, the center of the mercenary trade. This huge, sprawling city exhibits all the hallmarks of its birth during the Golden Age of the Star League, while the boom and bust cycles that followed the League's fall are evident in the chaotic layout of the city itself. The city is defended by a dedicated and tough defense force, often augmented by desperate mercenaries seeking pay of any sort. If not for large abandoned sectors of housing, the effect of Outreach on the world might not be noticed. As it is, if the outflux of mercenary hiring continues to ebb toward the Dragoons' homeworld, Galatea's economy will likely collapse again.

OUTREACH

Outreach is a pleasant world with huge oceans covering most of the surface and only the two small continents of Romulus and Remus to interrupt the tides. Once the site of the Star League Martial Olympiad, Outreach is no stranger to hosting 'Mech forces of various extraction. Hanse Davion gave the world to Jaime Wolf as a gift in 3030, in appreciation for the Dragoons' efforts and terrible losses in the Fourth Succession War.

The Dragoons set aside Remus as their personal holding, while establishing and upgrading numerous facilities on Romulus. The capital, Harlech, soon became the mercenary capital of the Inner Sphere offering an array of services: a grand Hiring Hall, primarily for aiding the Dragoons' mercenary comrades in obtaining legitimate employment; seemingly-endless warehouses and repair bays for all manner of combat machines; and training facilities of the highest caliber. The Harlech spaceport is one of the largest in the Inner Sphere, and is the only location on Outreach at which the Dragoons allow non-Dragoons personnel to land.

The mercenary trade on Outreach is very forgiving; only those mercenaries labeled renegades and criminals are prohibited from doing business there. No matter a command's background or recent battlefield performance, they have a (temporary) home on Outreach. In fact, so many down-and-out mercenaries pass through Harlech that the southeast quarter of the city has greatly expanded to accommodate them. The shabby conditions in the area, known as TempTown, reflect the mercenaries who inhabit it, and so many are unable to find work that they have become de facto residents of the city. Crime is rife in TempTown, as tempers flare when alcohol and depression mix too freely. The bad reputation of the area only further prevents its residents from obtaining gainful employment.

SOLARIS VII

Solaris VII is a largely unexplored and unexploited world, with huge oceans surrounding small continents filled with jungles that have never known the tread of man. This Lyran world near the Free Worlds League border grew wealthy first from the BattleMech factories churning out war machines for the Star League, and later from its BattleMech games.

Solaris VII is known as the Game World thanks to the massive gambling industry that powers the local economy. The games grew out of the need for manufacturers to test their weapons in real combat conditions. Soon, sideline betting to make the contests interesting became formalized, and the world's economy further boomed. Solaris City, the capital, is divided into districts representing each of the Successor States. Each House

HOUSE STEINER

The Lyran Commonwealth has always been known for dealing fairly and generously toward mercenaries. This stems from the mercantile nation viewing mercenary commands as businesses and treating them accordingly.

However, the long period of military decay in the Commonwealth caused by the favoring of political appointees over military adepts placed an undue reliance on mercenaries over House troops in many instances. This has already been alleviated thanks to the Federated Commonwealth alliance improving the Lyran portion of the new state's military.

The need for mercenaries to take up the slack for inferior House troops has been lessed, but mercenaries share a great deal of the burden in protecting the Periphery border from pirate raiders. Meanwhile, the Free Rasalhague Republic border is far more passive than when it was part of the Draconis Combine. Mercenaries can expect lower pay than they once enjoyed, but also a greater likelihood of surviving major engagements.

HOUSE KURITA

The Death to Mercenaries edict remains in effect. Despite some slight easing in relations toward mercenaries known to comport themselves with honor, a response to Theodore Kurita's public statements, Coordinator Takashi Kurita has refused to end the policy.

Mercenaries should avoid Combine territory at all costs; any who are captured can expect summary execution at best. There will be no offer or acceptance of ransoms, nor repatriation of prisoners. A few minor exceptions have been reported, notably when a corporation hires a mercenary command to secure its assets. In these cases, the employer takes great pains to repaint the command's units and place the corporate logo on them to prevent any potential difficulties with local DCMS units.

Further, some planetary governments have hired small commands to defend their worlds. These commands have survived only because the Combine views the worlds as strategically unimportant and has focused their own troops elsewhere.

district maintains its own Class Five arena, the premier venues for BattleMech duels in the Inner Sphere. Lesser arenas dot the world, but every MechWarrior strives to feature in the widely broadcast fights scheduled in these foremost arenas. Fortunes are made and lost in the arenas, both by those fighting and those betting--and loss of life is also common in both groups. Still, the warriors fight to become Champion, seeking the wealth and universal fame that accompany the title.

The Game World has long been a choice location to hire mercenaries. However, unlike Galatea or Outreach, many of those available for hire on Solaris VII are individual warriors rather than full mercenary commands. They possess greater independence and are more likely to breach contracts than their brethren of greater experience. That does not mean that the quality of those available for hire on Solaris is lacking. On the contrary, the skills required to succeed in the arenas places those with winning records in high demand. Employers must realize that they might be getting a prima donna, rather than a down-and-dirty warrior.

LESSER HIRING HALLS

In addition to the major hiring halls of Galatea, Outreach, and Solaris VII, there are a number of lesser hiring halls which attract the less savory members of the profession. Whether they are wanted criminals in the nations where the other hiring halls are located and must seek work on the edge of civilization, or simply hit hard times and failed to complete their last few contracts, the quality of troops available for hire on these worlds is very much lacking compared to those found in the major hiring halls.

Antallos

Antallos was a prosperous trading outpost during the Star League. Located in the Periphery, the world suffered terribly after the League fell and its barren surface is now largely uninhabitable, with just a handful of unaligned city states dotting the surface. Port Krin is the largest city and is the primary destination for off-world visitors. The economy is based entirely on slavery, drug trafficking, piracy, and a thriving black market weapons industry. Only renegade mercenaries seek work on Antallos, though there is no true hiring hall to speak of, and these warriors are as likely to attempt to conquer a city-state as to find some semblance of gainful employment. The truly desperate might enter the local arenas and try to cement their reputation in the brutal games found there.

Astrokaszy

Astrokaszy is a sparsely populated world boasting only small settlements, primarily found near precious oases. The society, such as it is, centers around the caliphs running the city-states and the tribal leaders of various nomadic bands. Astrokaszy is truly a world where might makes right. Infighting among the descendants of the mercenary band that settled the world in 2892 has eliminated almost all technology. A few minor factories are capable of building simple weapons or ammunition, but little other remnant technology exists. The closest thing to civilization is the Shervanis Caliphate, which boasts a small spaceport and a minor HPG. Still, any mercenaries seeking work on Astrokaszy must guard themselves and their equipment carefully, as the locals are likely to steal whatever they can and kill those opposing them. No legitimate mercenaries would seek work on Astrokaszy.

Herotitus

Herotitus is a pleasure world in the Periphery between the Magistracy of Canopus, the Taurian Concordat, and the Capellan Confederation. The planet's former agrarian culture was supplanted at the end of the 30th century by the New Hedon group, which subsumed the world and turned it into a place where anything goes. The world's status as a free port and its pleasure industry draws numerous mercenaries, both those seeking work and those wishing to spend what they've recently earned. The capital, New Hedon, and its main suburb Myrmos are the primary hiring centers on Herotitus. Unlike some other Periphery worlds, Herotitus has witnessed a population boom in recent years, primarily due to the world's open nature. Many legitimate employers and mercenaries can be found on Herotitus at any time.

Noisiel

Noisiel is a Lyran world which only recently became a hiring hall thanks to the Noisiel Summer Games, a series of 'Mech-only contests that began in 3047. Though far less popular than Solaris contests, the Summer Games attract numerous talented MechWarriors, along with the gambling that accompanies such competitions wherever they take place. Mercenaries have also flocked to the world, some to show their mettle in the games and others to seek work from the wealthy patrons betting on them.

Westerhand

This Capellan world briefly hosted quarterly BattleMech games during the reign of Chancellor Maximilian Liao, until the Fourth Succession War and Maximilian's descent into madness ended House Liao's support of the games. Westerhand's attempt to compete with Solaris failed miserably; games are still held in various minor arenas outside Victory City, but the contestants are those whose skills were insufficient to gain entry to the Game World. A number of lesser mercenaries, mostly those unable to afford passage to Outreach, can be found on Westerhand. Their desperation for work leads them to the games as well, hoping to gain the slightest measure of recognition and more gainful employment.

HOUSE LIAO

The Capellan Confederation's small House military has always been augmented by large numbers of mercenaries. However, soldiers of fortune in the Confederation's oppressive society are often viewed with suspicion by the various castes due to the individualism that mercenaries bring with them. Mercenaries are constantly monitored by the Maskirovka for any breach of Capellan law.

Because of the government's dictatorial bent, mercenaries will find themselves largely unable to secure command independence. Support rights are also usually not given, due to the nation's inability to provide them. Mercenaries lacking their own transportation are welcomed and provided this service, mainly because the depleted House military can afford to spare the occasional DropShip and JumpShip. Pay is usually fair, though lower than in the past due to the greater number of mercenaries being hired. The House often limits salvage rights so that any recovered equipment can be used to replenish House forces first.

THE BUSINESS OF WAR

CONTRACTS

The contract is an agreement between a mercenary command and its employer, regardless of whether the employer is a Successor State, a Periphery power, a corporation, a planetary government, or even another mercenary command. The Mercenary Review Board ensures that contract negotiations are conducted fairly, though the neutral oversight body will not coddle an ignorant negotiator who agrees to poor terms or fails to understand the consequences of a clause. For many mercenaries, the contract is a binding, honorable agreement, and they will do their utmost to meet even unfavorable terms in order to satisfy their honor. Some commands, however, simply consider it a business agreement, on which they might be willing to renege on if battlefield conditions sour and desertion becomes the better option for their long-term survival. Contracts are typically framed around completing a particular mission or set of missions over a specified time period. These missions can range from simple garrison duty, where the command must defend a specific location against all aggressors, to planetary assault as part of a large invasion effort. Regardless of the mission parameters, the employer generally holds the command to a particularly high standard and expects them to complete the contract to its exact specification. Those commands which play fast and loose with contract terms are likely to find themselves unemployed—and possibly labeled renegades or outright criminals.

NECESSITIES

Surviving as a mercenary command is difficult. While a House military often has quartermasters and logistics chains to handle tasks such as obtaining the proper type and amount of supplies, a mercenary unit often has limited personnel and those responsibilities fall upon the warriors themselves. Foremost among these concerns are consumable supplies, including items such as food, water, paint, fuel, armor, and ammunition. Any command that skimps on the proper supplies is likely to run short during a campaign, and either suffer defeat or be forced to procure supplies through a broker and incur significant debt.

Down-and-out mercenaries may also end up absorbed into House militaries, or locked into long-term and often unfavorable contracts, through the "company store" tactic. Employers accomplish this by selling needed supplies to the mercenaries at rates greater than the compensation offered by their contract, thus obligating the command to add to their contract term to repay the employer. In addition to supplies, the command must concern itself with paying the salaries of its warriors and maintaining their equipment. This often requires hiring or contracting with technicians for repair work, adding to the payroll burden. Many mercenaries make do without proper technical support, and their equipment usually takes the field in poor condition as a result. Transportation is another major concern, as few mercenary commands possess DropShips, and only a handful have JumpShips. This either puts them at the mercy of their employer for transportation, which can result in their abandonment in hostile territory, or requires them to find their own ride, a costly proposition. Most commands place a priority on obtaining their own transportation assets, even with the massive maintenance and crew requirements that accompany them.

HOUSE MARIK

The Free Worlds League is a collection of loosely allied nation-states which often have their own policies toward mercenaries. Overall, it is accurate to say that the Free Worlds League is somewhat distrusting of mercenaries, due in no small part to House units often being bought off with empty promises or outright bribery. If their own troops are so dishonorable, how far should mercenaries be trusted?

Despite these reservations, the League offers fair terms and good pay when hiring mercenaries. However, the initial contract is often non-negotiable, and mercenaries can expect a firm hand from their liaison. For this, mercenaries can thank the Wolf's Dragoons' initial support of Anton Marik's rebellion against the League's rightful leader, Captain-General Janos Marik. Despite later revelations that Anton kidnapped, held hostage, and later murdered many Dragoons officers and dependents, the League closely monitors its employed mercenaries to prevent similar actions.

SURVIVAL

While a few famous merc commands might last centuries, they are truly the exceptions—it's often been said that new commands rarely survive their first contract. This short lifetime is due to many factors specific to each individual command, but a few patterns exist. Foremost is an overestimation of the command's ability, either by themselves or by the employer. If they are thrust into a situation beyond their capabilities, they can easily be destroyed by superior numbers or tactics. Another common cause of premature demise is simply poor business acumen. A novice commander might fail to understand the nuances of a contract, and easily violate one or more terms for something as simple as not handing over a portion of salvage collected from the field. All too often, however, failure to complete a mission is all it takes to doom a new command. If they are defeated in combat, for example, and fall short of the agreed-upon terms, they might find themselves labeled as incompetents or cowards. The reputation of a command is often as important as its equipment and numbers. Once a unit's reputation has been stained, it is incredibly difficult to be made clean again. Mercenaries seeking to overcome negative perceptions usually find themselves saddled with poor contracts and dangerous missions, and have no choice but to throw themselves into the crucible, hoping to be hardened rather than destroyed. The latter is by far the more common result.

OVERSIGHT

The Mercenary Review Board was created by ComStar founder Jerome Blake in 2789, and plays a central role in mercenary life. The Board serves as a neutral party in mercenary matters, representing neither the employer nor the employee. In theory, the MRB simply ensures fair business practices on both sides. In reality, the MRB also provides ComStar with intimate knowledge of the dealings between mercenaries and their employers, including which units are being hired by which Houses, where the mercenaries are being deployed, and what the contract stipulates. Many mercenaries chafe under the Board's authority, leading some to pursue their own negotiations without ComStar oversight. Such commands are then at the mercy of the employer to uphold the terms of any contract, since the mercenaries have no recourse if their employer chooses to abandon or sacrifice the unit or renege on any agreements. With MRB oversight, both the employer and the mercenary command are held to a higher standard; any breach of contract or criminal behavior by either side is made public and damages the reputation of the offending party, providing a powerful check on any lapse of ethics.

MERCENARY COMBAT COMMANDS

The Combat Command entries below include a short history and *Alpha Strike* information for some of the Inner Sphere's most famous or interesting mercenary Combat Commands in existence circa 3049. These briefs will help players assemble the correct Force to represent their favorite mercenaries on the tabletop.

In *Alpha Strike*, a player fields Units, defined as any playing piece with a Point Value in the Master Unit List (www.masterunitlist.info), whether that playing piece represents a single 'Mech or an entire Point of Elementals. Units are the building blocks for Formations. The term Formation may refer to the next-highest echelon of organization, such as a lance, Star, or Level II; or it may refer to a larger grouping of those Formations, such as a company, battalion, Cluster, Galaxy, or regiment. Any organization of Units, whatever the size, is considered a Formation.

The *Combat Manual* series presents the militaries of the Inner Sphere and Clans as lists of Combat Commands, which are further broken into Sub-Commands possessing various Experience Ratings, Force compositions, and special command abilities. For example, Wolf's Dragoons, a mercenary Combat Command, includes the Black Widow Company, a Sub-Command. Smaller Combat Commands might only possess one Sub-Command.

COMBAT COMMAND BRIEFS

Each brief includes the Combat Command's name and a summary of their history.

Their **Common Allies** and **Common Enemies** list which factions the Combat Command may or may not work alongside in a player's Force.

Alpha Strike game information for each Sub-Command follows this history.

Experience Rating: The average Skill of each Unit; see *Experience Rating / Skill Rating Equivalency Table* (p. 86)

Force Composition: The Formations which constitute the Sub-Command. Note that the weight description is an average for the constituent Formations; the average Size for all the Units comprising the Formation must round down or round up to the equivalent Size for that weight. For example, a medium 'Mech regiment must field Units whose average Size does not exceed 2.49. Additional restrictions to the types of Formations the Sub-Command is allowed to field may also apply, as detailed in each brief.

Special Command Abilities: The special benefits which apply to the Sub-Command; see *Special Command Abilities* (p. 44, *Alpha Strike Companion*). Brand-new abilities making their debut in *Combat Manual: Mercenaries* are listed in italics, and are detailed on p. 91.

Force Building Rules: Special advantages or prohibitions which apply during Force creation, intended to convey the flavor of each unique mercenary Sub-Command.

Special Rules: Any additional rules text which applies to the Sub-Command.

Finally, certain Combat Commands include Unique Characters which may be fielded as part of the Force.

Note that several Standard Lances are capitalized in the rules below, such as Command Lance, or Battle Lance. Their capitalization is intended to remind players that these Formations possess special abilities under *Ground Formation Types* (p. 150, *Alpha Strike Companion*), and also that they are available for purchase as ready-to-play Lance Packs.

BLUE STAR IRREGULARS

THE ARES CONVENTIONS

The Ares Conventions were signed by the rulers of the Inner Sphere on 13 June 2412. The Conventions' six articles stipulate moral conduct in wartime, with numerous appendices and addenda specifying details affecting the six articles. The Star League rescinded the Conventions in 2579 to eliminate restrictions in the coming Reunification War, and they were never restored to legal status. Later, the horrors of the first two Succession Wars eventually led the Houses to follow the Conventions in spirit. However, a number of mercenary commands held the Conventions sacred and obeyed them throughout the decline of civilization and loss of technology. This is especially true among commands descended from SLDF forces, which strive to preserve the honor and traditions of their ancestors.

Article I: Nuclear weapons shall not be used within 75,000km of any planetary surface.

Article II: Orbital bombardment is only allowed against military targets far from civilian population centers.

Article III: Surrender must be accepted by any unit that offers the universal standard.

Article IV: Safe passage shall be granted to any person, vehicle, or vessel bearing the universal standard of surrender.

Article V: Battles shall not be waged in urban areas, unless a military objective is within and efforts are made to limit collateral damage.

Article VI: The use, development, and production of biological and chemical weapons is forbidden.

The Amaris Civil War removed a murderous tyrant from the Star League throne. In defeating a monster, a number of heroes were born. The particular privations of the war forced many honorable soldiers to deteriorate into war criminals, making those who held to the Star League Defense Force's high ideals appear even more noble by comparison. After the war, General Aleksandr Kerensky chose to recognize these paragons of military virtue by creating a new award, the Blue Star Medal (later called the Blue Star of Kerensky), and presenting a total of thirty-seven of them to the most deserving warriors in the SLDF. When Kerensky later declared his Exodus, all thirty-seven Blue Star holders chose to remain behind.

The start of the First Succession War prompted Colonel Jeremiah Brighton, a Blue Star recipient, to contact the other remaining thirty-one living recipients and ask them to join him in preserving and upholding their honor and traditions. All thirty-one heeded his call and brought their SLDF comrades along, forming three regiments.

For nearly three centuries, the Irregulars have remained intact and devoted to House Davion and the Federated Suns, the Successor State they feel is most representative of Star League ideals. Their goal is to play a part in reforming the Star League, and they believe the Federated Commonwealth unification is the first step along that path. When a Blue Star holder retires or is killed, the medal is passed down within the unit, based on a vote among the remaining active holders; all thirty-two medals remain with the Irregulars. Only Blue Star holders can command a regiment, though no restriction is placed on lesser commands.

The Irregulars' long association with the Armed Forces of the Federated Suns is evident in the composition of all three regiments. Each 'Mech regiment and battalion has an independent command lance. A fighter wing, armor regiment, and infantry battalion are part of each regimental team.

Common Allies	Davion (Late Succession Wars, Early Clan Invasion)
Common Enemies	Liao (Late Succession Wars), Clan Jade Falcon (Early Clan Invasion)
Special Command Abilities	Banking the Initiative, Enemy Specialization (Clan Jade Falcon), *Esprit de Corps*

1894TH LIGHT HORSE

The Light Horse battalions are each made up of a heavy company, a medium company, and a mixed light/medium company. Rasalgethi has been their homeworld for more than a decade. Colonel Alexander Duff-Gordon commands both the Light Horse and the Irregulars as a whole. The 1894th Cavalry, an armor regiment, has a company of Demolishers in every battalion. The 1894th Tactical Recon Group, the Light Horse's infantry battalion, specializes in advanced scouting.

Experience Rating	Veteran
Force Composition	1 medium 'Mech regiment, 1 heavy aerospace fighter wing, 1 vehicle regiment, 1 infantry regiment, 1 artillery company
Special Command Abilities	*Rapid Strike*

AVATARS OF PAINFUL DEATH

The Avatars of Painful Death are a bruising force known for closing with their enemies and smashing them to pieces. First Battalion's assault 'Mechs are a fearsome sight as they advance under the cover of Second Battalion's LRM-equipped 'Mechs. Third Battalion's scout company routinely infiltrates enemy lines to attack supply dumps and sabotage communication lines. The Death Bringers are the Avatars' armor regiment, made of two battalions of fast hovercraft and one of heavy and assault tanks. The Blue Avatars fly exclusively heavy aerospace fighters, specializing in ground attacks. The Avatars Infantry battalion specializes in anti-'Mech tactics.

Experience Rating	Veteran
Force Composition	1 medium 'Mech regiment, 1 heavy aerospace fighter wing, 1 vehicle regiment, 1 infantry regiment, 1 artillery company; Third ('Mech) Battalion is light 'Mechs (Size 1) only
Special Command Abilities	*Tactical Experts (Physical)*

TWENTY-FIRST RIM WORLDS

The Twenty-first has a reputation for long-range combat, with many MechWarriors regarded as virtual snipers. The Neutron Stars wing specializes in bombing. The Twenty-first Armor regiment's First and Second Battalions consist entirely of tracked vehicles, while Third Battalion has one VTOL company and two medium hovertank companies. Stefan's Nightmare, an infantry battalion, is a fearsome special operations infantry force.

Experience Rating	Regular
Force Composition	1 medium 'Mech regiment, 1 heavy aerospace fighter wing, 1 vehicle regiment, 1 infantry regiment, 1 artillery company
Special Command Abilities	Sharp Shooters, Ground Attack Specialization

Major Dante Ferguson

Major Dante "Dead-Eye" Ferguson is the youngest Blue Star Medal awardee in the Irregulars. Nineteen years old at the height of the Fourth Succession War, he racked up four kills against Vincent's Commandos on Liao as part of the 1894th. He also captured a Commando battalion commander and two company commanders. He now leads Second Battalion in the Twenty-first, dubbed Dante's Deadshots. His nickname derives from his uncanny accuracy with his Gauss rifle. His *Highlander* was his ancestor's, an original SLDF model which was part of the Irregulars' founding. The technological recovery of recent years has returned it to its original configuration for the first time since the Second Succession War.

MAJOR DANTE FERGUSON — **PV:** 50 (70)

Unit Type	Skill	TP	SZ	MV	TMM	S/M/L	OV	A/S	Specials
***Highlander* HGN-732**	2	BM	4	6j	1	3/4/3	1	9/7	CASE, IF2
Special Pilot Abilities: Prior to the beginning of play, assign either Sharpshooter or Sniper to Major Dante Ferguson									

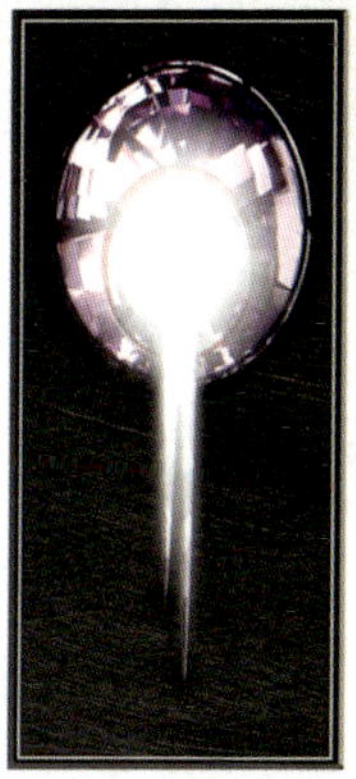

COMSTAR

In 2782 Jerome Blake was entrusted with the largest reconstruction effort in mankind's history. To rebuild the hyperpulse generator interstellar communications network severely damaged during the war between the SLDF and the Usurper Stefan Amaris.

Jerome Blake realized the future of humanity depended upon interstellar communications. To that end, in 2786 he cajoled the Great Houses to recognize the creation of ComStar, a neutral, independent entity to maintain the HPG communication network and ensure its HPG stations would remain free from attack by any Great House. Meanwhile a new economy in the C-bill emerged, quickly adopted as common currency across the Inner Sphere.

Following the death of Blake, Conrad Toyama took control of ComStar. A zealot, Toyama used ROM first to "cleanse" ComStar, then forged a psuedoreligious Order with technology—especially the HPG network—the idol of worship.

Today ComStar presents a face of peace and the protection of technology. It smoothly runs the Mercenary Review Board—taking only a modest cut—while sending missions of mercy and technological preservation around the Inner Sphere.

BRION'S LEGION

COM GUARDS ORGANIZATION

The militaries of the Successor States developed a standard organizational scheme during the Succession Wars, and the lance-company-battalion-regiment system is ubiquitous throughout the Inner Sphere. The Com Guards, however, utilize a unique organizational structure for their combat forces. Foremost is the integration of combined arms at very small force sizes, making the Com Guards a flexible and well-balanced, if inexperienced, military force.

Level I: A single 'Mech, fighter, vehicle, or platoon of infantry (36 troops), operated (commanded) by an Acolyte

Level II: Six Level I units (sometimes called a Demi-Company), commanded by an Adept

Level III: Six Level II units (equivalent to an Inner Sphere battalion), commanded by an Adept or Demi-Precentor

Level IV: Six Level III units (sometimes called a Division), commanded by a Precentor

Level V: Six Level IV units (sometimes called an Army), commanded by a Precentor

Level VI: Six Level V units, commanded by the Precentor Martial

Brion's Legion's history is a study in both poor unit discipline and overcoming adversity through dedication. The Legion's commander, Colonel Pythonius Brion, was killed by the Deneb Light Cavalry during an attack on the Federated Suns planet David. The rest of the Legion broke and fled, leaving their comrades in the Ninth Dieron Regulars to face the Davion defenders alone.

The Legion fled to the local HPG and requested sanctuary, having breached their contract and shown themselves as poor soldiers at best, or cowards at worst. Precentor Martial Anastasius Focht offered Brion's son Octavius a contract with ComStar. He agreed, and the Legion was brought back to regimental strength from ComStar's cache of Star League BattleMechs.

Today, the Legion is part of the Terran Defense Force under Colonel Octavius Brion. Two decades of training with ComStar have made him an elite MechWarrior and an expert in both Com Guard and standard Inner Sphere tactics.

Common Allies	Kurita (Late Succession Wars), ComStar (Early Clan Invasion)
Common Enemies	Davion (Late Succession Wars)
Special Command Abilities	Sharpshooters
Special Rules	If Colonel Brion's *King Crab* (see below) is destroyed, Brion's Legion gains the Special Command Abilities *Berserkers* and *Esprit de Corps*

BRION'S LEGION

Before 3033, the Legion organized itself as a typical Inner Sphere regiment. Their relatively poor state of training, however, left them with no particular combat specialties. They were known for "getting the job done," though never with notable skill or panache. The regiment included a command lance, though individual battalions did not.

After 3033, the Legion's tactics exhibited a noteworthy change. Outwardly, the regiment is still organized along typical Inner Sphere lines. However, thanks to their time with the Com Guards, they have developed a flexible tactical doctrine. At will, the Legion can switch from the standard lance-company-battalion organization to the Com Guard Level I-Level II-Level III organization. This is done by battalion, each reorganizing along pre-determined lines. The Legion prefers long-range combat, a benefit of training with Star League technology for so long.

Experience Rating	Regular
Force Composition	1 Medium 'Mech regiment
Force Building Rules	Post-3033, Brion's Legion may field either Level II or lance formations

Colonel Octavius Brion

Colonel Brion's efforts to redeem his family name after the debacle on David have forged him into an elite MechWarrior. His constant training and intense study of tactics earned him great respect from his troops. He is often able to outmaneuver even the most skilled opponents in simulations and on training missions, and his studies also enhanced his ability to predict where any enemy might place prepared positions or mines.

COLONEL OCTAVIUS BRION									**PV:** 46 (64)
Unit Type	**Skill**	**TP**	**SZ**	**MV**	**TMM**	**S/M/L**	**OV**	**A/S**	**Specials**
***King Crab* KGC-0000**	2	BM	4	6	1	3/3/1	2	10/8	AC2/2/-, CASE, IF1
Special Pilot Abilities: Combat Intuition, Eagle Eyes									

21ST CENTAURI LANCERS

The Twenty-first Centauri Lancers are one of the most respected mercenary commands in the Inner Sphere. Formed in 2875 by members of the St. Ives Armored Cavalry who deserted over unpaid wages, they have served every Successor State with distinction save House Liao, against whom they hold their ancestors' grudge. The Lancers are currently under contract to the Free Worlds League and are deployed to Nestor, where they routinely engage Lyran raiders and return the favor by raiding into the Commonwealth. Colonel Evelena Haskell is the most recent in a long line of Haskells to command the Lancers. She is a fearsome opponent on the field, but she treats even her enemies with honor. Those facing the Lancers can expect fair treatment of prisoners and fair ransoms to repatriate those who surrender. However, any treacherous behavior is swiftly repaid with unfettered rage and remorseless fury—including any mistreatment by their employers.

Common Allies	Marik
Common Enemies	Steiner (Late Succession Wars), Liao (Late Succession Wars)
Special Command Abilities	*Esprit de Corps*, Night Specialization, Environmental Specialization (High Gravity), Environmental Specialization (Low Gravity), Environmental Specialization (Clear), Ground Attack Specialization

LANCERS COMMAND

Late in the Third Succession War, the Lancers discovered a hidden Star League cache containing fully-intact Star League Defense Force 'Mechs and tanks. Haskell kept the prize secret, since the Lancers had full salvage rights in their contract. No one outside the command knows what they possess.

Experience Rating	Elite
Force Composition	1 heavy 'Mech Company
Force Building Rules	The Lancers Command may add access to the *BattleMaster* BLR-1Gb, *Marauder* MAD-2R, *Stalker* STK-3Fb, and *Thunderbolt* TDR-5Sb for 2 FPs each. At least one-third of the Lancers Command must consist of *Grasshoppers*, and may ignore the Rare Units rule for a *Grasshopper*.

17TH ARMORED RECON COMPANY

The Seventeenth is permanently attached to Lancers Command on a platoon-per-lance basis. Colonel Haskell has replaced one lance with Star League-era tanks from the SLDF cache.

Experience Rating	Elite
Force Composition	1 vehicle company, completely comprised of Recon Lances
Force Building Rules	The Recon Company may field a lance of Gabriel tanks for 0 FP.

21ST CENTAURI LANCERS

While the Lancers are a heavy 'Mech regiment, they have at least one Assault Lance and one Light Lance in each battalion. The Twenty-first Centauri Air Lancers are an elite fighter wing specializing in ground attacks.

Experience Rating	Elite
Force Composition	1 heavy 'Mech regiment, 1 heavy aerospace fighter wing
Force Building Rules	The Lancers possess an inordinate number of *Grasshoppers*. Each company must include at least one such 'Mech and may ignore the Rare Units rule for a *Grasshopper*.

21ST CENTAURI ARMORED LANCERS

The Armored Lancers operate as independent companies to concentrate force where needed. The Third Armored Command is Major Borogrove Whitley's command company, and possesses an Elite rating. The other four companies are all of Veteran skill. The Twenty-third Recon is entirely hovercraft; the Fifth Fire Support is equipped with ACs, and PPCs; Eleventh Fire Support's tanks are all equipped with LRMs; and the Second Assault Company consists entirely of heavy and assault tanks.

Experience Rating	Veteran
Force Composition	5 vehicle companies

21ST CENTAURI SECURITY LANCERS

A reinforced battalion of four companies, three companies are defensive specialists guarding the Lancers' base, while the fourth company combines scout operations with artillery support. The Fourth Company is made up of two platoons of Jump Laser scout infantry plus a platoon of artillery (Long Tom).

Experience Rating	Veteran
Force Composition	1 reinforced infantry battalion

Captain Steve Hoyer

Captain Hoyer commands the Second Assault Company of the Twenty-first Centauri Armored Lancers, and his tank crew is the best in the regiment. Their Demolisher outperforms in hindering terrain and excels at long range destruction.

CAPTAIN STEVE HOYER									PV: 32 (44)
Unit Type	**Skill**	**TP**	**SZ**	**MV**	**TMM**	**S/M/L**	**OV**	**A/S**	**Specials**
Demolisher	2	CV	4	6t	1	2/4/4	0	5/4	LRM2/3/3, IF3, TUR(2/4/4, LRM2/3/3, IF3), EE
Special Pilot Abilities: Cross-Country, Sandblaster									

CRANSTON SNORD'S IRREGULARS

Cranston Snord was originally a member of Wolf's Dragoons who was dispatched from the Dragoons in 3006 under the cover of being discharged for dereliction of duty. In truth, Snord was tasked by Colonel Jaime Wolf to locate and secure various Star League caches throughout the Inner Sphere which had never been plundered by the Successor States.

Snord founded the Irregulars around the remnants of McFinney's Manglers, which Snord won from McFinney in a poker game. After paying debts and repairing the sad 'Mechs and fighters of the Manglers, a number of other Dragoons departed the parent unit to join Snord. These included some individuals sent to ensure Snord kept the secret of the Dragoons' origin, and Snord's daughter, Rhonda.

Snord started a mercenary revolt against Janos Marik on Rochelle in 3007, after Marik tried to confiscate the 'Mechs of all mercenaries present on the planet in order to rebuild his own forces. The Irregulars maintain a special hatred for Marik and the Free Worlds League, even though the death of McFinney in the escape from Rochelle ensured Snord's control over the unit. The command finally took the name Cranston Snord's Irregulars after hiring on with Katrina Steiner. Steiner provided a permanent base on Clinton, and the Irregulars served the Lyran Commonwealth loyally, the feud with Janos Marik fueling the first few decades of that service. Much of the Irregulars' time was spent tracking down not just Star League caches, but numerous historical artifacts and ancient artworks thought long-lost to humanity.

Snord was disabled by a severe heart attack in 3034. Rhonda succeeded him as commanding officer; though she has refused to remove her father's name from the command, her command company bears her own name. Cranston focuses on handling the command's finances and continuing his archaeological endeavors.

Rhonda, for her part, enhanced the command's mystique through clever deception. Thanks to three decades of secret digs, the Irregulars had accumulated a great deal of lostech. Rhonda deployed these fully-functional Star League-era BattleMechs without comment during the War of 3039, leading many to conclude the Irregulars had gone as far as raiding Terra to obtain the rare 'Mechs from the Com Guards. Since the War of 3039, the Irregulars make annual trips to Outreach to train with Wolf's Dragoons, abandoning all pretense of Snord's original "falling-out."

The Irregulars have always been a combined arms command. The command company is 'Mech-only, while the second company includes the command's aerospace fighters, and the third company includes conventional units.

Common Allies	Steiner (Late Succession Wars, Early Clan Invasion)
Common Enemies	Marik (Late Succession Wars)
Force Building Rules	After 3038, Snord's Irregulars may access the Star League (Star League Era) faction list for 1 FP per selection.
Command Abilities	Banking the Initiative, Communications Disruption, Off Map Movement

RHONDA'S IRREGULARS

The command company of the Irregulars is the only all-'Mech company in the battalion.

Experience Rating	Elite
Force Composition	1 'Mech company

Rhonda Snord

Rhonda Snord inherited some of her father's curiosity and desire to unearth humanity's past. Like Cranston, she was a freeborn member of Wolf's Dragoons. Instead of taking command immediately after Cranston's heart attack, she chose to ease into the post, sharing command duties with Shorty Sneede for several years while the command expanded to a full battalion. She assumed full command prior to the War of 3039, when she unveiled the command's Star League-era units. Decades spent in and around the rough terrain of dig sites gives her an uncanny maneuvering ability in such environs.

H'CHU'S DIGGERS

Captain Deb H'Chu's command lance consists entirely of light and medium 'Mechs, serving to plug or exploit gaps as needed. The Fire Lance actually boasts five 'Mechs and sometimes maneuvers like a Clan unit. Four anti-'Mech infantry platoons replace a third lance: one jump platoon, one foot platoon, and two motorized platoons.

Experience Rating	Veteran
Force Composition	2 'Mech lances, 1 mixed reinforced infantry company.

SHORTY'S SCAVENGERS

Captain Samuel "Shorty" Sneede commands the combined arms second company of the Irregulars. Each lance is a different Unit type, providing battlefield flexibility to enhance the command company's capabilities. The Scavengers usually serve in a cavalry role for the Irregulars.

Experience Rating	Veteran
Force Composition	1 'Mech lance, 1 vehicle lance, 2 aerospace fighter lances

RHONDA SNORD — **PV:** 30 (42) | 56 (78)

Unit Type	Skill	TP	SZ	MV	TMM	S/M/L	OV	A/S	Specials
***Shadow Hawk* SHD-2H** (pre-3038)	2	BM	2	10/6j	2	2/2/1	0	5/5	IF0*
***Highlander* HGN-732b** (post-3038)	2	BM	4	6j	1	5/6/4	0	9/7	CASE, IF2

Special Pilot Abilities: Heavy Lifter, Maneuvering Ace, Terrain Master (Mountaineer)

CRESCENT HAWKS

The Crescent Hawks were founded by Jeremiah Youngblood at the behest of Archon Katrina Steiner as an off-the-books covert operations lance. Youngblood's *Phoenix Hawk LAM* became something of a boogeyman for the Draconis Combine. More than once, Steiner sent Youngblood to worlds of no importance, simply to have him "buzz" the local leadership and start a minor panic. This was always accompanied by a legitimate raid-in-strength on another world, after Youngblood's diversion successfully focused Combine attention on him.

Jeremiah was assisting instruction at the Pacifica Training School when the Combine invaded prior to the Fourth Succession War. Jeremiah was captured and spirited away to Dieron. His cadet son, Jason, mounted a guerilla campaign and reunited the Crescent Hawks, staving off the invaders long enough for reinforcements to arrive. Jason Youngblood then mounted a rescue operation to recover his father, aided by the Kell Hounds, long time allies of the Hawks.

While still attached to the Kell Hounds, as his father before him, Jason's Hawks remained an independent command free to pursue its own contracts and missions. During that time, the Hawks continued serving the Lyran Commonwealth through covert operations and expanded to a full company. The Hawks saw more action in the War of 3039 and afterward than the rest of the Kell Hounds combined, though these actions were often of limited import. First Prince Hanse Davion sent the Hawks to several FedSuns worlds that had fallen to the Draconis Combine, hoping the covert operators could wrest control back from the invaders.

Most of the original membership has retired since the War of 3039, though their children have taken up their mantles. The Hawks remain under the overall command of the Kell Hounds, though they have not been recalled for several years. Such requests are typically for training purposes, usually in the use of recovered technology.

During the battle of Luthien, Jason's *Phoenix Hawk LAM* suffered irreperable damage. He began piloting a Star League-era *Phoenix Hawk* that the Hawks recovered from a Star League cache.

Common Allies	Steiner, Davion (Late Succession Wars, Early Clan Invasion)
Common Enemies	Kurita (Late Succession Wars), Clan Jade Falcon, Clan Wolf (Early Clan Invasion)
Special Command Abilities	Off-Map Movement, Overrun Combat, Tactical Specialization (Attack)

CRESCENT HAWKS

The Crescent Hawks are a mobile command. They specialize in hit-and-run combat, never engaging enemies in straight-up fights if they can avoid it. Instead, they focus on specific objectives, such as destroying supply caches or isolating enemy command lances.

Experience Rating	Elite
Force Composition	1 'Mech company; all Units must have jump Move or a minimum Move of 10"

Captain Jason Youngblood

Jason Youngblood's first combat command was on Chara III after the Combine invasion, when he forged a guerrilla command from the wreckage of the academy where he had been studying and rallied the scattered members of his father's command. He never abandons comrades in need and always strives to find a way to salvage victory from the jaws of defeat. His years of experience piloting a Land-Air 'Mech give him exceptional maneuverability, even when not in a LAM's cockpit.

CAPTAIN JASON YOUNGBLOOD — **PV:** 28 (40) | 30 (42)

Unit Type	Skill	TP	SZ	MV	TMM	S/M/L	OV	A/S	Specials
***Phoenix Hawk LAM* PHX-HK2** (Late Succession War)	2	BM	2	10j	2	2/2/0	0	4/4	FUEL4, LAM (30g/5a)
***Phoenix Hawk* PHX-2** (Early Clan Invasion)	2	BM	2	12j	2	2/2/0	1	5/4	ECM, ENE

Special Pilot Abilities: Prior to the beginning of play, assign two SPAs to Captain Jason Youngblood from among the following: Combat Intuition, Demoralizer, Speed Demon (affects jump Move)

Hudsenn's Red Devils began serving the Magistracy of Canopus in 3007, until a serious defeat in the Andurien-Canopian invasion of the Capellan Confederation killed commanding officer Colonel Dirk Hudsenn. This led to a major dispute among the ranks of the Red Devils; since Hudsenn's son Derek was not the ranking officer, Major Braderick Morgenstern assumed command of the Red Devils. His command style was harsh and unforgiving. After alienating a great number of Red Devils MechWarriors, Captain Derek Hudsenn and his company eventually split from the Red Devils in 3045 and formed Derek's Devils.

The Devils were immediately hired by the Magistracy, mainly in recognition of his father's long and honorable service. Morgenstern's renamed Slashers left for Taurian service, eventually being ground down to nothing thanks to a lack of employer support services. Meanwhile, the Devils endeared themselves to the people of Dunianshire after catching raiders before they could escape with captives they intended to sell into slavery. Hudsenn himself killed the pirate leader and weathered tremendous incoming fire from the pirate DropShip to disable it on the ground as its engines lit up. The Devils handle threats from Luxen to Dainmar Majoris from their Dunianshire base. Their infantry is well-known for kneecapping and capturing 'Mechs, a practice that has added a second company to the Devils and allowed Hudsenn to assume the rank of major.

Common Allies	None
Common Enemies	None
Special Command Abilities	Brawlers, Force the Initiative

DEREK'S DEVILS

The Devils are two companies of differing character. First Company contains primarily heavy and assault 'Mechs and is made up of former Red Devils MechWarriors. Second Company, by contrast, is an eclectic mix of light, medium, and heavy 'Mechs salvaged from enemy raiders. Hudsenn groups them together in as sensible a fashion as possible, but their differing speeds and armaments prevent Second Company from specializing in any particular tactics.

Experience Rating	Regular
Force Composition	2 'Mech companies. At least 50 percent of First Company must comprise heavy and assault (Size 3 and 4) 'Mechs. First Company Assault Lances may receive the Street Fighter SPA instead of the Demoralizer or Multi-Tasker Bonus Ability. Second Company must have at least 1 light, medium, and heavy (Size 1, 2, and 3) 'Mech in each lance, with no assault (Size 4) 'Mechs in any lance.

VOID DEVILS

The Devils' aerospace squadron is entirely made up of light fighters. Captain Michelle Simpson ensures the fighters never carry bombs, preferring to strafe the enemy.

Experience Rating	Regular
Force Composition	1 aerospace fighter squadron, all Units must be light (Size 1).

PIT FIENDS

The Pit Fiends are leg attack specialists who are reckless in their assaults on enemy 'Mechs. Despite this, their losses are minimal thanks to intensive training in their dangerous methods.

Experience Rating	Veteran
Force Composition	1 infantry battalion

Major Derek Hudsenn

Derek Hudsenn's preference for melee combat is well known among pirates operating in and around Canopian space. His armor routinely requires extensive replacement after wading through enemy fire to engage in physical combat.

MAJOR DEREK HUDSENN									PV: 39 (55)
Unit Type	**Skill**	**TP**	**SZ**	**MV**	**TMM**	**S/M/L**	**OV**	**A/S**	**Specials**
***Awesome* AWS-8Q**	2	BM	4	6	1	3/3/3	0	8/6	ENE
Special Pilot Abilities: Combat Intuition, Melee Specialist									

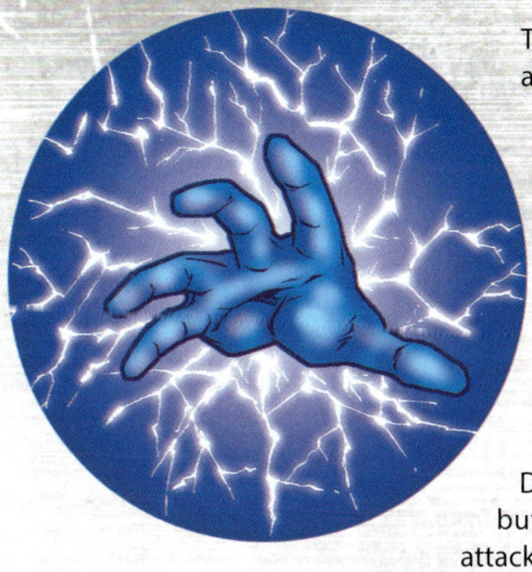

The Dioscuri has served the Federated Suns for more than a century. Their preferred style of fast, mobile combat notably saved their own Castor regiment on Thestria in the War of 3039. The Dioscuri's stand there against the Sixteenth Galedon Regulars after weeks of putting down riots cemented their combat reputation. When the First Proserpina Hussars arrived to help push the invaders off Thestria, Castor regiment was saved when the two Draconis Combine Mustered Soldiery commanders clashed. Though Colonel Timothy Nels and the rest of Castor were prepared for a glorious last stand, the Hussars' commander offered to let the Dioscuri leave Thestria unopposed. Nels gladly accepted, but the Sixteenth's commander did not. The Sixteenth attacked alone, and Castor regiment wiped them out before withdrawing as agreed.

Following the war, the Dioscuri deployed to the former Federated Suns' Periphery border. The proximity to the Pirates Haven Cluster and Tortuga Dominions keeps the two regiments busy. Fortunately, their style of combat is ideally suited to engaging and hunting pirates. The command also rotates a company to Filtvelt to help train cadets at that world's academy.

Common Allies	Davion (Late Succession Wars, Early Clan Invasion)
Common Enemies	Kurita (Late Succession Wars)

CASTOR

The first regiment of Dioscuri 'Mechs is mostly medium 'Mechs, with a single heavy/assault lance per battalion. This lance usually serves to demolish any enemies left behind by the rapid advance of the faster 'Mechs or those attempting to flank the recklessly charging Castor units.

Experience Rating	Regular
Force Composition	1 'Mech regiment; at least half of the regiment's 'Mechs must be medium (Size 2).
Special Command Abilities	Off-Map Movement, Zone of Control

POLLUX

The Dioscuri's second regiment of BattleMechs is very nearly a carbon copy of the first. However, while their compositions are similar, Pollux specializes in defensive operations. First Battalion hides one company and presents the other two as bait. Second Battalion charges in, while Third Battalion tries to sneak forces in behind the enemy.

Experience Rating	Regular
Force Composition	1 'Mech regiment; at least half of the regiment's 'Mechs must be medium (Size 2).
Special Command Abilities	Overrun Combat, Tactical Specialization (Defense), *Tactical Experts (Hidden Units),* Off-Map Movement.

THE BROTHERHOOD

The Dioscuri's infantry support is a well-balanced force. First Battalion's motorized infantry often deploys with one of the 'Mech regiments. Second Battalion is a security force specializing in defense, especially of the Dioscuri's primary base of operations. Third Battalion is composed of two scout units, each with a platoon of VTOLs rounding out the companies; Third Company is artillery support to fire on targets located by the scouts. The Brotherhood is currently deployed with Pollux on Great Gorge.

Experience Rating	Regular
Force Composition	1 infantry regiment

COMSTAR AS AN EMPLOYER

ComStar has long employed mercenaries. However, while commands hired by Successor States can expect significant combat missions during their contract term, ComStar often hires mercenaries for exploration and security duties instead.

In the Periphery, HPGs are precious and many require dedicated defense forces. Also, because the Com Guards are deployed so heavily in the Federated Commonwealth as a check on Hanse Davion's perceived aggression and the threat his policies pose toward ComStar's technological dominance, there is a need for external forces to protect their more remote installations. Mercenaries bearing the ComStar insignia in addition to their own are a common sight on Periphery worlds.

ComStar's Explorer Corps missions often include mercenaries as part of the complement. Rediscovery of lost colonies is fraught with potential danger, and the Com Guards are already stretched thin. Thus, mercenaries enjoy high wages and generous terms in exchange for long-term deployments into the Deep Periphery.

DISMAL DISINHERITED

The Dismal Disinherited lack the reputation of commands such as Wolf's Dragoons, the Kell Hounds, or the Eridanl Light Horse. Nonetheless, the Disinherited's legacy stretches back to the Star League. After the First Succession War ended, a number of Capellan MechWarriors descended from SLDF veterans elected to become mercenaries and leave the Confederation. They were hounded by Confederation troops until they reached Oriente in the Free Worlds League. Captain-General Charles Marik granted them asylum and hired them to a long-term contract. The command chose its name after the desperate flight from former homes and comrades.

The Disinherited served the League well into the Second Succession War, fighting along the Confederation-League border almost exclusively. Their conduct was always beyond reproach, and they carried themselves with honor, skill, and courage lacking among many warriors at the time. By recruiting from among family members, the Disinherited maintained sufficient numbers to remain a viable combat force after suffering horrendous casualties in the war. MechWarriors departing Free Worlds League Military service also swelled the ranks of the Disinherited.

The command later left the League for the Lyran Commonwealth and another long-term contract. The battle for Dromini VI was one of the opening salvos of the Kurita invasion of the Lyran Commonwealth in the Third Succession War, as the Combine sent three regiments of Rasalhague Regulars to secure the world. Dromini VI's defenders included the First and Second Dismal Disinherited; the latter was newly-formed and totaled only eight companies at the time. The First was patrolling the edge of a ruined city when it encountered the heavy and assault 'Mechs of the Ninth Rasalhague Regulars. The speedy Disinherited 'Mechs swarmed and overwhelmed the Combine invaders, while the slower Second Disinherited moved in and destroyed the pinned-down DCMS 'Mechs. However, the world was lost when other DCMS troops overran a Lyran supply depot and cut the Disinherited's communications. The command retreated from the world in good order soon after.

Just after the turn of the 31st century, the command began a long contract with the Federated Suns, which they renewed when the nation became the Federated Commonwealth. The Disinherited saw less action during the Fourth Succession War and War of 3039 compared to the Second and Third Succession Wars. However, the Second Disinherited suffered heavy casualties on Huan at the hands of the Thirty-second Galedon Regulars during the War of 3039. The Disinherited have since served garrison duty on the former Federated Suns' Periphery border, allowing them to recover their losses.

The Disinherited regiments maintain the specialties they developed over decades. However, the Fourth Succession War gave the command a close-up view of the successful application of combined arms by their AFFS comrades. They have added to their conventional forces ever since, though these troops serve primarily as supporting elements instead of being integrated directly with the Disinherited 'Mech regiments. The First and Second regiments each carry a vehicle battalion, a mechanized infantry battalion, and an artillery battalion. Each regiment also has an aerospace wing of heavy fighters.

Common Allies	Davion (Late Succession Wars, Early Clan Invasion)
Common Enemies	Kurita (Late Succession Wars)
Special Command Abilities	Overrun Combat, Zone of Control

FIRST DISMAL DISINHERITED

The First earned its nickname, the Plague of Locusts, after the battle of Domini VI. The First Armored Cavalry's vehicle battalion consisted of all fast tanks and hovercraft.

Experience Rating	Veteran
Force Composition	1 light 'Mech regiment, 1 medium aerospace fighter wing, 1 light vehicle battalion, 1 mechanized infantry battalion, 1 artillery battalion. The 'Mech and vehicle forces prefer fast Formations such as Striker, Pursuit and Recon Lances; at least half the lances in their force must consist of those three Formation types.
Special Command Abilities	Forcing the Initiative

SECOND DISMAL DISINHERITED

The Second Disinherited is also known as the Crypt Kickers, and rely on their complement of heavy and assault 'Mechs to center the command in battle; as a result, the Second always takes the heaviest casualties in major engagements. The Second Armored Regiment's vehicle battalion consists entirely of heavy and assault tanks, matching the 'Mech regiment's specialty for hard-hitting, direct attacks.

Experience Rating	Regular
Force Composition	1 heavy 'Mech regiment, 1 heavy aerospace fighter wing, 1 assault vehicle battalion, 1 mechanized infantry battalion, 1 artillery battalion. The 'Mech and vehicle forces prefer tougher Formations such as Assault, Battle and Fire Lances; at least half of the lances in their Force must consist of those three Formation types.

THIRD DISMAL DISINHERITED

The Third Disinherited was once known as the Hostile LAMs, but centuries of conflicts gradually destroyed their rare and delicate Land-Air-'Mechs; the last two are now nonfunctional museum pieces. The Third instead became the Hostile Hellraisers, relying entirely on jump-capable 'Mechs for maximum maneuverability and shock tactics. The Third Armored Regiment is a reinforced regiment with two battalions of heavy tanks, one of fast hovercraft, and one of artillery. The Third Attack Wing specializes in close air support of ground units.

Experience Rating	Green
Force Composition	1 medium 'Mech regiment, 1 heavy aerospace fighter wing, 2 heavy vehicle battalions, 1 medium vehicle battalion and, 1 artillery battalion. At least half of the Force's 'Mechs must have a jump Move rating.
Force Building Rules	Battle and Striker Lances may assign two Units per Lance the Jumping Jack SPA instead of the standard Battle or Striker Lance Bonus Abilities (Lucky or Speed Demon).

THE BATTLE FOR DROMINI VI

Edge of The Ruins
Dromini VI
Lyran Commonwealth
1 July 2866

A company of First Dismal Disinherited 'Mechs is patrolling the edge of a ruined city when they encounter an advancing assault company of the Ninth Rasalhague Regulars. The First calls for support from the Second Dismal Disinherited, but they must slow the advancing DCMS troops until the Second can arrive.

GAME SETUP

Recommended Terrain: Urban Ruins, Open Terrain

If using terrain, the game table should be divided equally between open terrain on one half and urban ruins on the other.

If using hex maps, arrange two maps with their short edges touching; one should be open terrain while the other should be urban ruins.

The Defender chooses one short edge of the playing surface as their home edge; the Attacker's home edge is the opposite edge.

ATTACKER

Ninth Rasalhague Regulars (Veteran) Assault Company

The Attacker consists of one company of heavy and assault (Size 3 and 4) 'Mechs of the Ninth Rasalhague Regulars seeking a Lyran supply depot. The Attacker enters from their home edge on Turn 1. The Attacker's objective is to exit via the Defender's home edge.

DEFENDER

First (Veteran) and Second Dismal Disinherited (Regular)

The Defender consists of one patrolling company of the First Dismal Disinherited that enters the table on Turn 1. A lance of Second Dismal Disinherited enters the table via their home edge on Turn 6. The Defender must prevent the Attacker's units from exiting via the Defender's home edge.

MECHWARRIOR FAMILIES

When Kerensky departed on his Exodus, the former SLDF MechWarriors who stayed behind retained ownership of their BattleMechs. Because of the longevity of these kings of the battlefield, the BattleMechs often outlived their MechWarriors, leading to the rise of MechWarrior families. Mercenary commands and House militaries both benefited from the long-term service of these families, as MechWarrior aptitude was hereditary in many cases.

When a MechWarrior died, his 'Mech passed to an heir. Knowing this, parents began training their children in BattleMech operation at very young ages. Those who showed the most promise received intense training in their teen years, including simulator training, mock battles, and live-fire drills. The best of these teenagers were admitted to prestigious MechWarrior academies.

Many families, including members of the ruling Houses of the Inner Sphere, have spent generations serving a particular command or House. Many mercenary commands have passed down 'Mechs—along with ownership and leadership of the unit itself—through a family lineage over the centuries.

Often, these MechWarrior families were rewarded for their service with landholds and noble titles, especially when their members displayed gallantry or exceptional valor. These financial rewards, or other employer bonuses, enabled the family to keep their 'Mechs operational. This ability perpetuated the family business as their number of 'Mech-equipped troops slowly increased with successive generations, ensuring a steady supply of well-trained troops for the Succession Wars.

15TH DRACON

The Fifteenth Dracon is one of the longest-serving mercenary commands in existence. Like the Fourth Tau Ceti Rangers, the Fifteenth was a former Star League Defense Force regiment which chose to remain in the Inner Sphere when Kerensky's Exodus took place. Both regiments were hired by Capellan Confederation Chancellor Barbara Liao, and the Fifteenth Dracon served the Confederation for three wars, earning repeated contract extensions thanks to their excellent record of self-sacrifice in the name of the Confederation. The meat grinder of the Succession Wars reduced the Fifteenth from a regiment to two understrength battalions by the end of the Third Succession War.

In a tradition still practiced today, the warriors in the Fifteenth donate a portion of their pay to the local community where they are based to provide for civil improvements such as roads and schools. Such actions from a mercenary command were considered atypical to the point that they were initially flagged for investigation by the Maskirovka as potentially subversive activity. However, the mercenaries' open and honest goodwill soon alleviated these concerns as the Fifteenth left a trail of lightened spirits and improved communities in their wake. Because of their dedication to all civilians, the Fifteenth refuse to fight in a city under any conditions, whether or attacking or defending. Instead, if their enemy appears to be heading for an urban area, the Fifteenth will execute a pincer move to cut off that avenue of approach and ensure any combat occurs away from homes and businesses.

The Fifteenth was briefly loaned to the Draconis Combine late in the Third Succession War, and showed the DCMS that mercenaries were not without honor. The Dracons captured Beta Mensae V from the Federated Suns during this time. Their performance led Coordinator Takashi Kurita to consider seriously hiring mercenaries for such actions, and influenced his later decision to hire Wolf's Dragoons and found the Ryuken. Despite his subsequent Death to Mercenaries decree, the Coordinator continues to deliver a brand-new BattleMech to the Fifteenth every year on the anniversary of their conquest.

The Fifteenth sat out the Fourth Succession War, as they were held in reserve to meet follow-up waves of the Federated Suns invasion which never manifested thanks to ComStar's intervention to stop Hanse Davion. After the war ended, the Fifteenth was transferred to the Confederation's Periphery border to garrison Gunthar. There they stopped the Third Canopian Fusiliers cold during the Andurien-Canopian Invasion, and entered into two-year stalemate with the Canopians that was broken only when the Capellans began to recapture other worlds lost early in the invasion. As the Fusiliers tried to retreat, the Fifteenth's charge captured two DropShips and salvaged numerous 'Mechs.

The salvage from Gunthar allowed the Fifteenth to rebuild to a reinforced regiment. First Battalion was destroyed by the Second FedCom RCT in the War of 3039 after failing to prevent severe damage to the factories on Ares. First Battalion was subsequently rebuilt, and the Fifteenth is currently a reinforced regiment of four battalions. Each battalion is deployed separately and has developed its own tactical specialties.

Common Allies	Kurita (Late Succession Wars), Liao (Late Succession Wars, Early Clan Invasion)
Common Enemies	Davion (Late Succession Wars), Marik (Late Succession Wars)
Special Command Abilities	Overrun Combat, *Tactical Adjustments*
Special Rules	The Fifteenth Dracon treasures its Star League origins, and carefully preserves the 'Mechs it can keep operational as a link to their history. Late Succession Wars: The Fifteenth Dracon has access to the following downgraded Star League-era 'Mechs for 1 FP each: *Flashman* FLS-7K, *Crockett* CRK-5003-0. Early Clan Invasion: In addition to the downgraded models available during the Late Succession Wars, the Fifteenth Dracon has access to the following Star League-era 'Mechs for 2 FPs each: *Flashman* FLS-8K, *Crockett* CRK-5003-1.

Colonel Jean Rosenburg

Jean Rosenburg is the commanding officer of the Fifteenth Dracon and also commands First Battalion in combat. Her 'Mech was procured from the Draconis Combine on the anniversary of the Dracon's capture of Beta Mensae V. This tradition ensures one brand new BattleMech enters the Fifteenth's TO&E (Table of Organization and Equipment) every year.

COLONEL JEAN ROSENBURG — **PV:** 44 (53) | 38 (46) | 30 (36)

Unit Type	Skill	TP	SZ	MV	TMM	S/M/L	OV	A/S	Specials
***Crockett* CRK-5003-0** (pre-3039)	3	BM	4	6j	1	3/3/0	2	9/7	
***Hatamoto-Chi* HTM-26T** (3039-3050)	3	BM	4	8	1	2/3/2	1	8/6	
***Grand Dragon* DRG-5K** (3050+)	3	BM	3	12	2	2/3/2	0	5/3	CASE, IF1, REAR1/1/-
Special Pilot Abilities: Sniper.									
Special Rules: Rosenberg conveys the Stand-Aside Special Pilot Ability to the two MechWarriors nearest her at the start of any turn for the duration of that turn. This ability is usually used to prevent the enemy from moving the battle into an urban area.									

FIRST BATTALION

First Battalion specializes in envelopment tactics. This is most useful when the opposing force is attempting to enter a city. First Company comprises fast heavy 'Mechs, while Second Company consists of fast medium 'Mechs and Third Company is light 'Mechs. First Company anchors the Fifteenth's position as Second and Third Company swing right and left of the enemy and link up to surround the enemy.

Experience Rating	Regular
Force Composition	1 medium 'Mech battalion

SECOND BATTALION

Second Battalion is a bruising assault force. When the entire Fifteenth is deployed, Second is always the center of the command. They are most adept at concentrating force against numerically inferior enemies.

Experience Rating	Regular
Force Composition	1 heavy 'Mech battalion; all Units must be heavy or assault (Size 3 or 4)

THIRD BATTALION

Third Battalion is well-balanced. Each company has a heavy/assault lance, a medium/heavy striker lance, and a light/medium scout lance. Third also has a separate command lance of assault 'Mechs operated by elite MechWarriors. The Third Battalion was destroyed in the Third Succession War, and not rebuilt until the 3030s.

Experience Rating	Green
Force Composition	1 'Mech battalion. Each company must include a Battle or Assault Lance, a Striker Lance and a Recon Lance. The battalion has a separate command lance (not necessarily the Command Lance Formation) consisting solely of assault (Size 4) 'Mechs.
Force Building Rules	Third Battalion's Command Lance assault (Size 4) 'Mechs are of Star League vintage specifications and Elite skill. The following units can be used for the Third's Command Lance at a cost of 0 FP: *Crockett* CRK-5003-1, *Highlander* HGN-732, *Thug* THG-11E, *King Crab* KGC-000. This lance may be built as a Command Lance Formation even if the usual requirements to field that Formation are not met.

FOURTH BATTALION

Fourth Battalion is a combination recon and close-in assault force. Every 'Mech has been optimized by the Fourth's expert technical corps and routinely exceeds its known performance limits. Second and Third Company perform recon while First Company closes with the enemy and engages at close range. The Fourth Battalion was formed in the late 3030s in time to participate in the War of 3039.

Experience Rating	Green
Force Composition	1 'Mech battalion; the Fourth Battalion favors Recon and Assault Lances; at least half the Force should include these Formations

THE BATTLE FOR ARES

Bergan Industries
Ausapolis, Ares
Capellan Confederation
20 August 3039

The Second FedCom RCT has arrived on Ares to carry out a punitive action after McCarron's Armored Cavalry used the world as a staging base for its incursion of the Federated Suns. First Battalion of the Fifteenth Dracon met the Second near the Bergan Industries factory, seeking to slow the invaders long enough for relief to arrive.

GAME SETUP

Recommended Terrain: Light Urban, Open Terrain

If using hex maps, arrange two maps with the edge of the Bergan Industries factory on one end of the map, which is the Defender's home edge. The Attacker's home edge is the opposite edge.

If using terrain, place terrain pieces representing the edge of the Bergan Industries factory on one end of the tabletop, which serves as the Defender's home edge. The Attacker's home edge is the opposite edge.

Victory Conditions: As per Hold The Line (ASC, p. 165).

ATTACKER

Second Federated Commonwealth RCT (Regular)

The Attacker consists of one company of medium and heavy (Size 2 and 3) 'Mechs of the Second FedCom RCT and one company of hovertanks. The Attacker enters from their home edge on Turn 1. The Attacker's objective is to exit via the Defender's home edge.

DEFENDER

Fifteenth Dracon (Regular),

Bergan Industries Corporate Security (Regular)

The Defender consists of one company of the Fifteenth Dracon's First Battalion (one lance from each company). The Fifteenth is placed on the map more than 4", or more than two hexes away, from the edge of the factory area before Turn 1. The Corporate Security consists of one lance of Locusts and one lance of Stingers from the Bergan plant. They deploy to the map before Turn 1, and must be placed within 2" or one hex of the factory; these units may be placed as Hidden Units. The Defender must prevent the Attacker's units from exiting via Defender's home edge.

ERIDANI LIGHT HORSE

THE COMPANY STORE

Occasionally, an employer seeks to lock a mercenary command into a longer term of service than originally agreed upon in the contract. This is done using the ancient "Company Store" method, in which an employer paid its workers too little to afford food and other necessities until the next payday. Doing so forced the workers into debt to acquire basic needs, and prevented them from leaving the job until the debt was paid.

This same practice is now seen in the modern mercenary trade. In this case, the employer supplies required repair parts and consumables—possibly at inflated prices—in such a way that the command's income from the contract is insufficient to cover the expense. Refusing to pay for the needed items may force the command to enter combat in a poor state of repair at the risk of its warriors' lives. Such treatment is forbidden by ComStar's Mercenary Review Board, but can be difficult to prove.

The tactic is most successful when applied to small, underfunded mercenary commands; larger mercenary commands are known to sell off portions of their TO&E to avoid incurring such debt. A mercenary command under threat of the Company Store often has low morale, and will mutiny or go renegade rather than lose its independence. Thus, even employers desperate to force mercenaries into permanent service tend to avoid gouging them, knowing it may drive that command into the arms of the employer's enemies.

The Eridani Light Horse is one of the oldest and most respected mercenary commands in existence. The SLDF founded the unit in 2702 as the Third Regimental Combat Team, including four regiments: two striker regiments, and two light horse regiments. The Nineteenth Striker Regiment was destroyed by the forces of Amaris the Usurper. The remaining three regiments joined General Kerensky in defeating Amaris, avenging their dead comrades across numerous long and bloody battles.

The Light Horse elected to remain behind when the Exodus took place, feeling duty-bound to uphold the honor and traditions of the SLDF. They served as the de facto defense force of several Draconis Combine worlds in the Rasalhague Military District when the First Succession War broke out, and remained there until news of the Kentares Massacre reached them. The Light Horse could not associate themselves with a nation capable of such an atrocity, and departed for the Free Worlds League. They remained in League service until the Third Succession War, when a dispute between the Horse's commanding officer and the troops led most of the latter to mutiny and leave for the Periphery.

Threat of starvation on their new home forced the dissenting Light Horse troopers back to the mercenary life. They served the Lyran Commonwealth for more than a century before signing with the Federated Suns in 3000. Their service to the Suns exceeded expectations, including holding off a Wolf's Dragoons assault on Hoff. The Light Horse fit well into the AFFS. Their officers began teaching tactics and history at the New Avalon Institute of Science (NAIS) and other academies, a practice that continues to the present day.

The command was primarily a support and garrison force during the Fourth Succession War, but the War of 3039 was more eventful. Fellanin II was almost the death of the Seventy-first Light Horse, which seized the world and was mopping up when DCMS reinforcements arrived. The command's other two regiments had already departed to continue the invasion, leaving only the Seventy-first to face the Second Arkab Legion. Outnumbered, the Seventy-first held out for nearly ten days until their defenses collapsed and the Seventy-first was forced to retreat. Most of the regiment was destroyed before they could leave the planet. The Seventy-first was eventually reactivated after a decade of rebuilding.

The Light Horse continues to maintain their SLDF traditions. They always comport themselves with dignity and honor, in and out of combat. Other mercenaries consider the Light Horse snobbish or elitist, when the Light Horse troops simply hold themselves to a higher standard. This includes always honoring the Ares Conventions, even if their enemies do not. The Light Horse's long service to the Federated Suns, and now the Federated Commonwealth, placed them in increasingly greater debt to House Davion, especially after the heavy losses of the War of 3039. The command was considered by outsiders to be bound by the "company store," but the First Prince was convinced to respect the command's honorable and dedicated service and waive the debt rather than coerce them into permanent AFFS membership. Forgiveness of their debt greatly improved relations that had soured after the War of 3039, ensuring even greater loyalty from the Light Horse to the Federated Commonwealth.

Each regiment and battalion has its own command lance. Limited infantry assets support the command, though the Twenty-first Striker has an infantry battalion that often splits into companies and deploys with the other 'Mech regiments as needed.

Common Allies	Davion (Late Succession Wars, Early Clan Invasion)
Common Enemies	Liao (Late Succession Wars), Kurita (Late Succession Wars)
Special Command Abilities	Banking the Initiative, Forcing the Initiative

LIGHT HORSE COMMAND

General Ariana Winston leads the command from a dedicated, independent command company. The company normally attaches itself to the Twenty-first Striker, her former regiment. The company is made up entirely of assault 'Mechs. The company includes jump infantry as well as heavy and assault tanks for headquarters security. The fighter wing often splits into squadrons to support the individual regiments.

Experience Rating	Elite
Force Composition	1 'Mech company, 1 vehicle company, 1 infantry company, 1 aerospace fighter wing; all 'Mechs are assault (Size 4) 'Mechs
Special Rules	Light Horse Command may deploy with any of the three Eridani Light Horse Regiments. If the full 'Mech company of the Light Horse Command is fielded with at least a 'Mech company of any other Light Horse Regiment, the entire Force gains +2 to its Initiative rolls. This ability counts as one of the Force's Command Abilities.

TWENTY-FIRST STRIKER

The Twenty-first contains the Third, Fifth, and Seventh Striker Battalions, plus the First Armored Infantry Battalion. The Third and Fifth use mixed light and medium 'Mechs, while the Seventh comprises medium and heavy 'Mechs. The First Armored is a company of fast wheeled tanks and hovertanks, plus three companies of jump infantry.

Experience Rating	Veteran
Force Composition	1 medium 'Mech regiment, 1 infantry battalion, 1 light vehicle company
Special Command Abilities	Environment Specialization (Hot), Environmental Specialization (Woods), Sharp Shooters

SEVENTY-FIRST LIGHT HORSE

The Seventy-first, or "White Horse Regiment," includes the Eleventh and Seventeenth Recon Battalions, plus the Eighty-second Heavy Cavalry Battalion. The Eleventh and Seventeenth field entirely light and fast medium 'Mechs, specializing in recon and hit-and-run attacks. The Eighty-second includes two heavy 'Mech companies, a heavy and assault 'Mech company, and a company of fast wheeled tanks.

Experience Rating	Veteran
Force Composition	1 medium 'Mech regiment, 1 light vehicle company
Special Command Abilities	Off-Map Movement, Overrun Combat

151ST LIGHT HORSE "DARK HORSE REGIMENT"

The 151st, or "Dark Horse Regiment," contains the Sixth and Eighth Recon Battalions and the Fiftieth Heavy Cavalry Battalion. The Sixth uses light and medium 'Mechs, the Eighth fields medium and heavy 'Mechs, and the Fiftieth consists of heavy and assault 'Mechs.

Experience Rating	Elite
Force Composition	1 medium 'Mech regiment
Special Command Abilities	Off-Map Movement, Overrun Combat, Enemy Specialization (Mercenary)
Special Rules	If using the Battlefield Intelligence and Hidden Unit rules, units in the Dark Horse Regiment with the RCN special ability confer a BI rating of 3 instead of 2.

Captain "Dashing John" MacAllister

Commander of Eridani Light Horse's Forty-first Support Company, the Ass Extractors, "Dashing John" models himself after the cavalry officers of ancient Terran history. During the War of 3039, the Seventy-first Light Horse was left alone on Fellanin II due to a bureaucratic mistake. With the White Horse Regiment pinned down in Fort Jinjiro by the Second Arkab Legion and the remnants of the Fourth Proserpina Hussars, Colonel Alfieri ordered his battered unit to retreat off-world.

Harried all the way back to their LZ, MacAllister fought a desperate rearguard action, setting up numerous ambushes and luring the Kuritans into his artillery's kill zones. The Ass Extractors accounted for more than two companies of Kuritan 'Mechs, allowing the majority of the Eighty-second Cavalry Battalion to safely reach the DropShips. Though blown out of his Thunderbolt, the *"Toujours L'Audace,"* MacAllister was repatriated in early 3040.

CAPTAIN "DASHING JOHN" MACALLISTER									PV: 37 (51)
Unit Type	**Skill**	**TP**	**SZ**	**MV**	**TMM**	**S/M/L**	**OV**	**A/S**	**Specials**
***Thunderbolt "Toujours L'Audace"* TDR-5SE**	2	BM	3	8j	1	4/5/2	0	7/5	ECM
Special Pilot Abilities: Jumping Jack, Speed Demon.									

THE FILTHY LUCRE

The Filthy Lucre served the Lyran Commonwealth for more than two centuries. The mercenaries' families all put down roots in Commonwealth space, and most of their MechWarriors were graduates of Lyran military academies, including the Nagelring. The Federated Commonwealth alliance was greeted with great enthusiasm by the Lucre MechWarriors, especially after they sat out most of the Fourth Succession War and the War of 3039. However, an attempt by an ambitious Lyran officer to co-opt the Lucre into the Armed Forces of the Federated Commonwealth through a Company Store ploy soured relations with the Lucre in a surprisingly short time, and their exit from Lyran service at the dawn of 3050 stunned Commonwealth High Command. They are currently settling into service with the Free Worlds League. Colonel Karl Timson's request not to face his former Lyran comrades was granted, and the Lucre is stationed on Goodna, a world on the Capellan Confederation border.

Common Allies	Steiner (Late Succession Wars, Early Clan invasion), Marik (Early Clan invasion)
Common Enemies	Marik (Late Succession Wars)

THE FILTHY LUCRE

Colonel Karl Timson commands the first battalion, namesake of the regiment. He is a Nagelring graduate and carries himself with dignity and honor. He is making the best of the current situation, but knows most of the regiment dislikes working for their long-time enemies in the League. The regiment continues to wear their Lyran-style uniforms, which causes friction with the local militia forces. The Filthy Lucre Battalion excels in forest combat; Third Company also specializes in night combat.

Experience Rating	Elite
Force Composition	1 heavy 'Mech battalion
Special Command Abilities	Environmental Specialization (Woods), Environment Specialization (Night), Zone of Control

BLOOD MONEY

Major Myron Carpathia blames himself for the departure of the Lucre from Lyran service. He has no forgiveness for the corrupt officer who accused him of cowardice and dereliction of duty, but he would have preferred simply to transfer to a different operations area away from the kommandant who soured the relationship. The Blood Money Battalion excels in urban combat.

Experience Rating	Regular
Force Composition	1 medium 'Mech battalion
Special Command Abilities	Environmental Specialization (Urban), *Tactical Experts (Hidden Units)*

WEREGILT

Major Jedidiah Compton commands Weregilt Battalion with viciousness unmatched by the regiment's other officers. He drills his MechWarriors constantly, especially in close combat. Enemies facing Weregilt are advised to engage them from long range and save themselves the savagery of melee combat.

Experience Rating	Elite
Force Composition	1 heavy 'Mech battalion
Special Command Abilities	Berserkers, Brawlers, Force the Initiative

Captain Jason Sanderson

Captain Sanderson was the last MechWarrior hired by the Lucre before departing the Commonwealth. Sanderson was a Solaris fighter who tired of the arena life and wanted to do some "real fighting." He commands Third Company of Weregilt Battalion and is struggling to acclimate himself to cooperative combat. He brought his upgraded TDR-7M *Thunderbolt* to the Lucre; its extended range laser makes it one of the deadliest long-range weapons in the command. Sanderson has been known to revert to arena form and challenge enemy MechWarriors to individual combat. None have yet refused him, but none have defeated him.

CAPTAIN JASON SANDERSON — **PV:** 39 (55)

Unit Type	Skill	TP	SZ	MV	TMM	S/M/L	OV	A/S	Specials
***Thunderbolt* TDR-7M** (Early Clan Invasion)	2	BM	3	8	1	4/4/2	0	7/5	CASE, IF1

Special Pilot Abilities: Blood Stalker, Antagonizer (Special: Only affects the Blood Stalker "Chosen Enemy").

Much attention is paid to mercenary commands descended from the SLDF. Much less is said about commands descended from those who opposed the SLDF in the war against Amaris. Fuchida's Fusiliers are one such command. The group that would become the Fusiliers was originally known as the Tartan Brigade, a Rim Worlds Republic House unit that fought well for the Usurper in the Amaris Civil War despite being outnumbered and outclassed by the SLDF. The shattered remnants of the Brigade renamed themselves Fuchida's Fusiliers and became mercenaries soon after the Usurper was defeated.

The Fusiliers never stayed in one place or with one employer for long. Throughout the Succession Wars, they served every House at least once, most often the Free Worlds League. The Fusiliers signed on with the Federated Suns after the Fourth Succession War, hoping for combat, and when the War of 3039 broke out, they thought their time had come. However, their liaison was a political appointee who brought along a private volunteer force to aid in the invasion of Royal. The liaison also assumed command of the invasion and repeatedly ordered the Fusiliers into the hardest combat, ensuring the mercenaries suffered the most casualties. The liaison then diverted the salvage from the Fusiliers' own battles to his private troops, angering the command.

Relations soured between the Fusiliers and the peoples of the Draconis March as the command sought redress after the war concluded, resulting in the Fusiliers transfer out of the Draconis March. After several postings over a period of eight years, the Fusiliers were reassigned to their pre-war homeworld of Udibi in the Draconis March. The locals' feelings toward the command have not softened, and High Command is rapidly considering reassigning the Fusiliers to the Lyran portion of the Federated Commonwealth. Major Twylla Sumeral commands the Fusiliers. She splits her time between administration, seeking a different posting for her unit, and trying to keep the peace between her warriors and the people of Udibi.

Common Allies	None
Common Enemies	None
Special Command Abilities	Forcing the Initiative, Overrun Combat, *Esprit de Corps*

FUCHIDA'S FUSILIERS

The Fusiliers have a well-earned reputation for bloodthirsty, reckless behavior in combat. They often make tactically unsound decisions by attacking in the face of superior numbers, accompanied by a characteristic Scottish battle-cry blaring from their external speakers. They are renowned for remaining in combat long past the time when withdrawal would be wise. However, this very steadfastness in the face of the enemy endears the command to employers, since they know the Fusiliers will always stick in the fight. The Fusiliers employ a battle-cry maneuver, where every unit blares a recording from their external speakers while charging the enemy.

Experience Rating	Regular
Force Composition	1 heavy 'Mech battalion, 1 heavy aerospace wing

Lieutenant Benson Pillbox

Lieutenant Benson Pillbox is a typical Fusilier in many respects. He wears a kilt at all times and paints his 'Mech in the same tartan the unit has used for centuries. He joins the charges ordered by his commander, but longs to use his *Hatchetman's* namesake weapon in close combat. When the enemy runs before he can close in, he feels empty inside. He has taken to "calling" his preferred target in battle, threatening anyone who engages "his" target. His single-minded pursuit of those he hunts has already become legend in the command.

LIEUTENANT BENSON PILLBOX — **PV:** 21 (25) | 35 (42)

Unit Type	Skill	TP	SZ	MV	TMM	S/M/L	OV	A/S	Specials
***Hatchetman* HCT-3F** (Late Succession Wars)	3	BM	2	8j	1	2/2/0	0	3/5	AC1/1/-, MEL
***Axman* AXM-1N** (Late Succession Wars)	3	BM	3	8j	1	4/4/0	1	6/3	AC2/2/-, CASE, MEL

Special Pilot Abilities: Prior to the beginning of play, assign two SPAs to Lieutenant Benson Pillbox from among the following: Blood Stalker, Fist Fire, Melee Specialist

THE WAR OF 3039

After the Federated Suns crushed the Capellan Confederation in the Fourth Succession War, most observers assumed Hanse Davion would be satisfied and allow peace to persist. Those who felt otherwise thought he would finish off the Capellans before turning his attentions elsewhere. Few considered it likely that he would attack the Draconis Combine.

Among those who were not surprised was *Gunji no Kanrei* Theodore Kurita. Theodore had planned for just such a move by the Fox. When Lyran Commonwealth and Federated Suns forces swarmed the Combine border, they did not overwhelm and annihilate the defenders as they had in the Fourth Succession War. Instead, they met barely any resistance at all—until, after a few minor victories, the DCMS counterattacked.

These counterattacks landed not just on invaded Combine worlds but also on Federated Suns worlds. The entire Suns strategy was torn asunder when their own worlds were suddenly flying the Combine flag. Many defeated Davion forces reported facing Star League 'Mechs with equipment not seen in generations. Worse, the troops using these units were totally unknown DCMS Formations called Ghost Regiments.

Instead of completing a grand conquest and crippling another age-old enemy, Hanse Davion was forced to consolidate minor gains in exchange for terrible losses. A faulty calculus of worlds won and lost allowed Davion to claim a nearly-pyrrhic victory, but all knew that the Fox had been defeated handily.

The Glory Warriors were formed from the remnants of five small mercenary commands shattered in the Fourth Succession War. The survivors washed ashore on Galatea and found commonality in their misfortune. Their first decade of existence was filled with short-term, low-pay contracts in the Periphery.

The Warriors verged on bankruptcy when Earthwerks hired them to provide corporate security on Victoria. While escorting a convoy from their employer's factory to the spaceport, raiders appeared. The unidentified force's *Union*-class DropShip sought to land at the spaceport and disgorge its contents to capture the shipment. Captain Kent Clark charged his command lance ahead of the convoy and targeted the DropShip as it descended. They damaged its engines and it crashed from a height of about 30 meters.

The DropShip was severely damaged, but not so badly that the Warriors could not investigate the interior. Inside they found the remains of the crew and the raiders. Unlike the human operators, much of the combat equipment within was intact. Their salvage clause allowed the Warriors to pay their debts and add a third 'Mech company.

The command spent the next decade serving garrison contracts. After the War of 3039, the new Free Rasalhague Republic sought experienced mercenaries for garrison and cadre contracts. The Warriors signed a long-term contract and have spent the past eight years repelling pirates and training planetary militias and Rasalhague House troops. Their current posting on the Periphery border world Skallevoll keeps them busy with frequent pirate raids. The Skallevoll People's Militia is a burgeoning force composed of an armored regiment and three mechanized infantry regiments. The mechanized regiments rotate being attached to the Warriors for intense training.

A recent dispute among Major Clark's company commanders led to the departure of Second and Third Companies' officers. This has impacted the command's overall quality, as the newly-hired commanders have not yet integrated with their troops.

Common Allies	None
Common Enemies	None

GLORY WARRIORS

The Warriors are a mobile force whose heaviest units are 60 tons. They specialize in disengaging numerically superior opponents to fight again later by "hiding in plain sight".

Experience Rating	Green
Force Composition	1 Medium 'Mech battalion. The Warriors may not field assault (Size 4) 'Mechs. They may not field more than one heavy (Size 3) 'Mech per three 'Mech lances in their Force; that heavy 'Mech must have a minimum Move of 10".
Special Rules	Any turn when the Glory Warriors are outnumbered by two to one or more (whether by PV or number of Units), any Warrior 'Mech that ends a turn 10" or more from an enemy may become a Hidden Unit, if the terrain permits hiding a 'Mech per the Hidden Units rules. If at the beginning of any turn the odds shift to two-to-one or more in the Warriors' favor, the ability is lost and any hidden Glory Warriors become visible. The ability may be regained on any turn the Glory Warriors are outnumbered by two to one or more. This ability counts as one of the Force's Command Abilities.

Major Kent Clark

Major Kent Clark is a stealthy MechWarrior. Both in and out of the cockpit, he stalks about in the shadows to test those in his command. His efforts have worked, as his command's ability to hide rivals that of the Killer Bees, but without the camouflage. In combat, he prefers to sneak up on the enemy and attack from the rear. His *Quickdraw* was salvaged from a very well-equipped raider force lacking markings of any kind. The MechWarrior killed himself rather than be captured once he was surrounded.

MAJOR KENT CLARK									**PV:** 30 (36) | 32 (38)
Unit Type	**Skill**	**TP**	**SZ**	**MV**	**TMM**	**S/M/L**	**OV**	**A/S**	**Specials**
***Quickdraw* QKD-4G** (Late Succession Wars)	3	BM	3	10j	2	2/3/1	0	4/5	IF1, REAR1/1/-
***Quickdraw* QKD-5K** (Early Clan Invasion)	3	BM	3	10j	2	3/3/0	0	5/5	REAR1/1/-
Special Pilot Abilities: Dodge, Lucky (2)									

SECOND SKALLEVOLL PEOPLE'S MECHANIZED REGIMENT

The Second is currently attached to the Warriors, training in anti-'Mech tactics.

Experience Rating	Green
Force Composition	1 Mechanized Infantry regiment. The first company of each battalion consists entirely of anti-'Mech jump infantry. Each second company constitutes a mixture of tanks and mechanized infantry platoons. The third company of each battalion is composed entirely of hovertanks.

GRAVE WALKERS

The Grave Walkers might be the oldest mercenary command still in existence. The exact date of their creation is lost to history, but their origins predate the Star League and even the BattleMech. Through the centuries, the Grave Walkers have served all five Successor Houses, along with many proto-states absorbed by the Houses centuries ago. The command lacks the fame and legendry of the Eridani Light Horse and some others, but their reputation for professionalism and their obvious skill have few rivals.

The War of 3039 highlighted the Grave Walkers' skills—and the incompetence of old-school Lyran commanders. When the Federated Commonwealth invaded Vega, the Walkers were part of the force that initially secured the world. When the DCMS counterattacked, an assassination attempt placed the forces on-world under command of Hauptman-General Kathleen Heany. Her dated tactical doctrine was outmatched by the Second Dieron Regulars, who were using *Kanrei* Theodore Kurita's new manner of fighting. Disaster followed disaster, and the Walkers were forced to abandon the planet. General Heany accused the Walkers of breach of contract and cowardice, but the MRB exonerated them and other mercenaries who suffered due to her incompetence.

Common Allies	Steiner (Late Succession Wars, Early Clan Invasion)
Common Enemies	Kurita (Late Succession Wars), Clan Jade Falcon (Early Clan Invasion)

FIRST GRAVE WALKERS

Experience Rating	Regular
Force Composition	1 heavy 'Mech regiment
Special Command Abilities	Off-Map Movement, Tactical Specialization (Attack), Environment Specialization (Night), Forcing the Initiative.

The First Grave Walkers uses a uniform organization for lances and the companies to which they belong. First Battalion is filled with fast 'Mechs designed for recon and raiding. Second Battalion is unusual in that every 'Mech exclusively uses energy weapons. The lack of ammo-dependent weaponry allows the Second to operate for extended periods without resupply; it specializes in guerilla fighting behind enemy lines. Third Battalion is a direct assault force which uses heavy and assault 'Mechs to overwhelm enemy positions.

SECOND GRAVE WALKERS

Experience Rating	Regular
Force Composition	1 heavy 'Mech regiment
Special Command Abilities	Environmental Specialization (Woods), Sharp Shooters, Off-Map Movement

The Second Grave Walkers regiment consists of three battalions built along similar lines to each other. First Company of each battalion is a reinforced cavalry Formation of heavy and assault 'Mechs mounting long-range weaponry; the fourth lance is the battalion Command Lance. Second Company of each battalion is a flanking Formation made up of medium and fast heavy 'Mechs, with a single lance of light 'Mechs to lead the encirclement. Third Company of each battalion is a recon-in-force reinforced company with an integrated platoon of fast hovertanks in addition to the speedy light and medium 'Mechs in each lance. Each battalion also possesses its own specialty, making each company especially skilled in two particular brands of combat.

Captain Lenore Staley

Captain Lenore Staley leads Third Company, Second Battalion of the First Grave Walkers. Her *Awesome* is in immaculate condition at the start of every operation, but extended periods behind enemy lines leaves it in tatters by the end. Her lance is filled with other assault 'Mechs, and serves as the anvil to the faster 'Mechs in her company's other two lances. She is especially skilled at long-range combat. As a lieutenant in the War of 3039, her company was caught behind enemy lines on Vega. Her refusal to give ground to the enemy allowed her comrades to escape and eventually allowed her to stop the enemy's assault cold.

CAPTAIN LENORE STALEY									PV: 39 (47)
Unit Type	**Skill**	**TP**	**SZ**	**MV**	**TMM**	**S/M/L**	**OV**	**A/S**	**Specials**
***Awesome* AWS-8Q**	3	BM	4	6	1	3/3/3	0	8/6	ENE
Special Pilot Abilities: Iron Will, Range Master (Long)									

FREE RASALHAGUE REPUBLIC

The Free Rasalhague Republic also came into being thanks to the Fourth Succession War, though less directly. Rasalhague Military District worlds seized in the fighting were harshly treated by Tamar Pact. ComStar and Theodore Kurita conspired to recognize independence of the Rasalhague district to create a buffer state between the Combine and the Lyran Commonwealth, while also fomenting rebellion on former Rasalhague worlds. The new nation largely built its military from former DCMS troops, but recognized the need for mercenaries. The Republic shares some of the Combine's distrust of mercenaries, but is fair in its dealings, if stingy with transportation and reluctant to give up command rights. Most mercenaries can expect to be deployed to the Republic's Periphery border for pirate hunting, while the interior is defended by trustworthy House troops only.

GRAY DEATH LEGION

The Gray Death Legion is one of the Inner Sphere's most famous mercenary commands. They are renowned for pulling off "battlefield miracles," as their tenacity and ingenuity allow them to accomplish the seemingly impossible. The War of 3039 provided one such miracle.

The Legion landed on the Combine world of Altais, and half the command quickly secured the city of Willas and its spaceport. The other half of the Legion was ordered to seize the spaceport at New Ross, but part of the detachment mis-dropped. Those who assembled met the First Ghost Regiment, and Major Davis McCall was hard-put to hold out against the overwhelming DCMS numbers. Colonel Grayson Carlyle and the rest of the Legion were 150 km away, leaving McCall on his own. Instead of trying to hold his ground, McCall attacked. The brutal melee swung in the First's favor, until Carlyle surprised even his own troops by appearing at the spaceport and smashing the stunned Ghosts. The tide quickly turned and the Combine troops retreated, leaving the world in Federated Commonwealth hands.

Following the War of 3039, the Legion remained in Federated Commonwealth employ and was stationed on Sudeten. They have enjoyed the long-term garrison contract, broken up by occasional forays into the Periphery hunting pirates.

Common Allies	Steiner (Late Succession Wars, Early Clan Invasion)
Common Enemies	Kurita, Marik (Late Succession Wars), Clan Jade Falcon (Early Clan Invasion)
Special Command Abilities	*Esprit de Corps*, Communications Disruption, *Hit and Run*

HEADQUARTERS COMPANY

The Headquarters Company includes Colonel Carlyle's Command Lance, though it may operate independently or with any other Legion Formation.

Experience Rating	Elite
Force Composition	1 reinforced 'Mech company

GRAY DEATH LEGION

The Legion are experts at unconventional tactics, and seem to perform best when outnumbered.

Experience Rating	Elite
Force Composition	1 'Mech company with Command Lance, Fire Lance and Recon Lance (pre-3029); 2 medium 'Mech battalions (post-3029)

ARMORED SCOUTS

The Armored Scouts are also known as the Death Cats. The company specializes in recon and hit-and-run tactics.

Experience Rating	Veteran
Force Composition	1 light vehicle company
Special Rules	When at least one Lance of the Armored Scouts are present in a Force, any opposing Hidden Units are revealed at the end of Turn 1.
Special Command Abilities	Off-Map Movement

DEATH EAGLES

The Legion's aerospace detachment uses only medium and heavy fighters.

Experience Rating	Elite
Force Composition	2 aerospace fighter squadrons; all Units must be medium or heavy.

GRAY DEATH INFANTRY

The Legion's infantry are among the best in the Inner Sphere, mercenary or House. Their skill in fighting BattleMechs is legendary. The first company of each battalion comprises expert scouts. The second company of each battalion is made up of jump laser infantry platoons, while the third battalion consists of SRM infantry equipped with Inferno rounds.

Experience Rating	Elite
Force Composition	1 infantry regiment

NOTE: The following Gray Death Legion Unique Pilots can be found later in this book: Charles Bear (p. 98) and Lori Kalmar-Carlyle (p. 104).

HELM MEMORY CORE

The eve of the Fourth Succession War found the Gray Death Legion fighting for their lives against conspirators connected to ComStar and the Free Worlds League, after the Legion's new base on Helm was destroyed and their landhold seized. While hiding in the mountains, Colonel Carlyle discovered the Star League Nagayan Mountain Facility, the prize sought by the Legion's new enemies. ComStar Precentor Rachan sought to continue his order's policy of eliminating advanced technology outside its control by destroying the library core located at the facility before it could be analyzed.

The facility was a treasure trove of priceless lostech. BattleMechs not seen since the First Succession War, mounting Star League-quality weapons, were secured by the Legion and their unexpected ally Duke Hassid Ricol—the Kuritan lord originally responsible for the destruction of Carlyle's Commandos and the Legion's founding.

In addition to the weapons, the Legion found the library core. Fortunately, Carlyle prioritized copying the core, as the Marik troops activated the facility's self-destruct when they blasted their way in.

Carlyle gave a copy of the core to Ricol in appreciation for his aid and also gave it away to various traders and other powers. The information contained in the core ignited a technological renaissance across the Inner Sphere. Lost technologies could once more be manufactured thanks to the specifications and schematics in the core, while agricultural techniques and medical treatments of the time took great leaps forward.

GRIM DETERMINATION

Grim Determination enjoyed a long and successful association with the Federated Suns which has continued with the Federated Commonwealth. More often than not, the command embodies its very name, digging in and refusing to give ground through sheer grit and gumption. The Determination frequently suffers significant casualties as a result of these obstinate tactics. Because of this, the command long ago added a fourth battalion to the regiment. The additional firepower of an extra battalion is often held in reserve for the moment when the Determination is on the verge of breaking. Fourth Battalion then swings into action and pounds the unsuspecting enemy with fresh opposition. Similarly, the fighter wing carries a full fourth squadron instead of a Command Lance. Usually, each squadron flies combat air patrol over a single battalion to ensure enemy fighters do not savage the Determination's ground forces. The command also carries a battle-hardened tank battalion which floats to hot spots in battle rather than attaching itself permanently to any of the 'Mech battalions.

Grim Determination's skills were on display in 3046 when the Twelfth Atrean Dragoons landed on Sarna for what they thought would be a protracted campaign. The Dragoons expected the mercenaries to remain in defensive positions, but instead of hiding behind the fortifications of the Tengo Aerospace factory, the mercenaries arrayed themselves on the windswept plains between the raiders and the Tengo facility. The Dragoons first attempted a flanking maneuver with their tank battalion. The mercenaries wiped out the armor elements and remained arrayed on the plain, inviting the Dragoons in. Eventually, the Dragoons obliged. The heavy 'Mechs swarmed the mercenaries, who calmly returned fire. The first charge was rebuffed, as was the second, and the third. The three Dragoons battalions all showed damage, but their commander refused to relent. He ordered a final charge of his entire remaining force. Again, the mercenaries stood their ground as the two sides clashed in the flatlands. When the battle ended, it was the Dragoons retreating from the field and from Sarna. More than a battalion of 'Mechs joined their tanks on the renamed Salvage Plains.

Common Allies	Davion
Common Enemies	Liao (Late Succession Wars), Marik (Late Succession Wars)
Special Command Abilities	*Esprit de Corps*, Tactical Specialization (Defense), Environmental Specialization (Winter), Environmental Specialization (Night), Zone of Control

GRIM DETERMINATION

Grim Determination prefers defensive actions to offensive engagements, allowing them to become familiar with the terrain and plan surprises for their enemy, if needed. Each battalion includes a Command Lance. First Battalion uses primarily heavy and assault 'Mechs, Second consists of heavy 'Mechs, Third fields medium and heavy 'Mechs, and Fourth comprises assault 'Mechs. The aerospace wing can perform ground attacks, but the fighters generally remain on patrol to deal with enemy aerospace assets approaching the battlefield. The tank battalion includes one company each of hovercraft, LRM-carrying tanks, and assault tanks.

Experience Rating	Regular
Force Composition	1 reinforced 'Mech regiment, 1 reinforced heavy aerospace fighter wing, 1 vehicle battalion. At least half of the Force's 'Mechs and aerospace fighters must be heavy or assault (Size 3 or 4).

PLAIN DETERMINATION

Tengo Plains
Backtail, Sarna
Federated Commonwealth
9 March 3046

The Twelfth Atrean Dragoons arrived on Sarna to raid the Tengo Aerospace factory for DropShips and fighters. They knew the Grim Determination mercenary command defended the world, but they believed their faster 'Mechs would be able to evade the mercenaries and allow them to secure some of the factory's products. Grim Determination prepared the field, stationed themselves on the windswept Tengo Plains, and waited for the Dragoons to show themselves.

GAME SETUP

Recommended Terrain: Flatlands, Open Terrain

If using hex maps, arrange two maps with their long edges touching.

The Defender chooses a home edge. The Attacker's home edge is the opposite edge. Swirling, high winds limit jumping Units to half their jumping Move (rounding down). Defender places 2d6 Rough terrain patches and places Rough barriers along home edge, leaving only two 2", or two one hex, openings. These barriers prevent hovercraft passing through, but function as Rough terrain for 'Mechs. A 'Mech can jump the barrier, but only if standing adjacent to it.

Victory Conditions: As per Hold The Line (*ASC*, p. 165).

ATTACKER

Twelfth Atrean Dragoons (Veteran)

The Attacker consists of one company of medium and heavy 'Mechs of First Battalion, Twelfth Atrean Dragoons and one company of hovertanks. The Attacker's 'Mechs enter from home edge on Turn 1, while the hovertanks enter on turn 4 via either of the non-home edges, at least 20" or 10 hexes from the Defender's home edge. The Attacker's objective is to exit via the Defender's home edge, where the factory is located.

DEFENDER

Grim Determination (Regular)

The Defender consists of one company of the Grim Determination's First Battalion. The Defender's 'Mechs are placed on the map at least 16" or eight hexes from the home edge before Turn 1. The Defender must prevent the Attacker's units from exiting via the Defender's home edge. The Defender's Units are not subject to Forced Withdrawal.

HANSEN'S ROUGHRIDERS

Hansen's Roughriders have a convoluted history. The oldest portion of the command descends from a House Davion line regiment. These MechWarriors feared being targeted in a purge of dissident troops after the assassination of First Prince Peter Davion. Rather than be tainted by false guilt from First Prince Andrew Davion's paranoia, the Roughriders fled Davion space in 2961. Colonel Ludwig Hansen led these rogue troops to the Free Worlds League, where Hansen had some distant relatives. These warriors merged themselves into the Twelfth Atrean Dragoons, commanded by Major-General Gerhardt Hansen.

The Roughriders remained loyal to the League for more than six decades. However, the civil war that broke out forced the Roughriders to fight against their own comrades. Colonel Gerhardt Hansen, Ludwig's grandson and namesake of the relative who had welcomed them to the League, led troops of the First and Twelfth Atrean Dragoons, who were similarly sickened by the internecine fighting, out of the League. They headed for Steiner space, where their reputation as fierce but honorable warriors earned them their first contract as mercenaries in 3018.

It was not long before the Roughriders proved their reputation was well-deserved. When Wolf's Dragoons, in service to the Free Worlds League, assaulted Hesperus II in 3019, it was Hansen's Roughriders that stopped a breakthrough by the famed Black Widow Company. The Roughriders suffered horrendous casualties at the hands of the elite enemy, but they did not break. Their resolve and determination allowed them to stand strong, while weight of numbers cemented the successful defense.

The Roughriders gained renown for their deployment of the Patton tank. The prototypes were given to the Roughriders for field testing. They were putting the tank through its paces on Solaris VII, including some pit fights, when Marik forces raided the world. The Roughriders joined the defense, using the tank to sow confusion among the enemy troops. The new tank played a crucial part in the defense. This performance guaranteed the tank's acceptance by the LCAF, and mass production was soon implemented.

The Roughriders were instrumental in the Fourth Succession War in reconquering three worlds lost to the Draconis Combine in recent years. The Roughriders made peace with the Federated Suns after the Fourth Succession War, primarily due to the Federated Commonwealth merger and were stationed in Davion space for a time.

The command attained a nadir in the War of 3039. The Roughriders were savaged on Pike IV by the counterattacking Fifth Sword of Light. This performance showed the inability to command on the part of Major Wolfgang Hansen, Colonel Gerhardt Hansen's son and designated successor. Rather than retire, Gerhardt remained in command. Another five years passed before Gerhardt finally retired, entrusting the command to his son.

Colonel Wolfgang Hansen has embraced the combined-arms mentality of the Federated Suns. During the years away from the Davion nation, the Roughriders had fallen into the common mindset of relying on their 'Mechs, with other unit types as support elements only. Hansen is working to change that mode of thinking, especially given the Roughriders Armor Support's fierce combat reputation.

Common Allies	Marik (Late Succession Wars), Steiner (Late Succession Wars), Davion (Late Succession Wars/Early Clan Invasion)
Common Enemies	Kurita (Late Succession Wars), Liao (Late Succession Wars)
Force Building Rules	Patton Tank (Standard) and Rommel Tank (Standard) are available for 0 FPs.
Special Command Abilities	Brawlers, Environmental Specialization (Urban), Zone of Control, *Tactical Experts (Siege)*
Special Rules	When in urban terrain, Roughriders units cannot be targeted by Point Blank Shots from Hidden Units.

HANSEN'S ROUGHRIDERS

Hansen's Roughriders lacks independent command lances. Instead, each company and battalion commander simply commands a lance in the first lance or company, respectively, of his or her subcommand. The Roughriders are well-known for their urban combat expertise. Even in such environs, though, they take special pains to avoid collateral damage. Their skill in city-fighting is so acute that they seem to possess extra-sensory perception, avoiding ambushes regardless of how well-concealed the enemy might be.

Experience Rating	Veteran
Force Composition	1 heavy 'Mech regiment

ROUGHRIDERS AIR SUPPORT

Roughriders Air Support uses light and medium fighters almost exclusively. However, each squadron has a pair of "heavy hitters" as the third fighter lance. These heavy fighters always trail the faster, lead elements. As the lighter fighters divert attention from the enemy, the heavy hitters arrive, laden with bombs, to lay waste to the enemy. The Roughriders fighters have spent so many years directly supporting ground forces that they are almost unknown for aerial combat operations.

Experience Rating	Regular
Force Composition	1 heavy aerospace fighter wing

ROUGHRIDERS ARMOR SUPPORT

Lieutenant-Colonel Barabbas Thomas commands the tank regiment of the Roughriders. This regiment is feared by conventional and BattleMech forces alike. Roughriders Armor Support has long operated independently of the rest of the command. Thus, they have developed their own tactical specialties. As reward for their dedicated service, and especially their efforts in field-testing new tanks for the Commonwealth, Roughriders Armor Support makes up losses with Patton and Rommel tanks gratis, per Archon Katrina. This policy remains in effect under Archon Melissa.

Experience Rating	Veteran
Force Composition	1 heavy vehicle regiment, at least 50 percent of Armor Support force must consist of Patton or Rommel tanks.
Force Building Rules	May use Demi-Company formations for 1 FP each
Special Command Abilities	*Camouflage*

ROUGHRIDERS INFANTRY SUPPORT

The Roughriders infantry force is primarily dedicated to defensive operations. They safeguard the command's bases and secure the families and other civilians.

Experience Rating	Regular
Force Composition	1 infantry regiment

Colonel Wolfgang Hansen

Wolfgang Hansen is driven to overcome his disappointing command performance in the War of 3039. Intense study of tactics and strategy finally convinced his father to trust him with command, but some of his warriors are less than convinced. He inherited his father's directness, though, and openly calls out subordinates who exhibit disrespect or other morale-busting behavior. This has endeared him to some, but alienated others. The end result, though, is a force of warriors who either hold him in the highest esteem or seek to prove him wrong. Both types end up fighting their hardest for the command. Despite commanding the Roughriders, Hansen prefers closing with the enemy and engaging in melee combat. His father was never able to break him of this habit, though it does seem to intimidate enemies who see the lumbering *Cyclops* charging into close quarters with them.

COLONEL WOLFGANG HANSEN — **PV:** 39 (55)

Unit Type	Skill	TP	SZ	MV	TMM	S/M/L	OV	A/S	Specials
Cyclops CP-10-HQ	2	BM	4	8	1	2/3/1	0	5/7	IF1, CCM

Special Pilot Abilities: Dodge, Street Fighter

Leftenant Amelia Holliday

Holliday loves nothing more than shredding opposing 'Mechs with heavy autocannon fire. Her willingness to rush into combat has earned her command of a lance of new Rommel tanks in a regiment notorious for its toughness.

LEFTENANT AMELIA HOLLIDAY — **PV:** 27 (37)

Unit Type	Skill	TP	SZ	MV	TMM	S/M/L	OV	A/S	Specials
Rommel Tank	2	CV	3	8	1	3/3/0	0	6/4	AC2/2/-, TUR(3/3/-, AC2/2/-)

Special Pilot Abilities: Sandblaster, Speed Demon

DEATH IN THE ARROYO

Dry Riverbed
Hesperus II
Lyran Commonwealth
31 May 3021

Wolf's Dragoons have assaulted Hesperus II, seeking to control the valuable Defiance Industries factory. The attack has stalled due to massive defenses. But Captain Natasha Kerensky of the Black Widow Company has discovered a weakness in the defense. She sends her forces into a dry riverbed, circumventing most of the defenders. Only Hansen's Roughriders stand in her way...

GAME SETUP

Recommended Terrain: Open Terrain, Desert Terrain

If using hex maps, arrange at least two maps with their long edges touching.

Defender chooses one edge as home edge. Attacker's home edge is the opposite edge.

Victory Conditions: As per Hold The Line (*ASC*, p. 165).

ATTACKER

Wolf's Dragoons: Black Widow Company, Gamma Regiment, Delta Regiment

Attacker consists of elements of Wolf's Dragoons (see pp. 74-77). The Black Widow Company enters via home edge on Turn 1. A single lance of reinforcements, from either Gamma Regiment or Delta Regiment, may enter via home edge once per turn starting on Turn 5, provided at least half the total Dragoons force to that point (counting reinforcements) remains operational. Attacker must destroy at least half the Defenders force (to that point, including reinforcements) before exiting units off the Defender's home edge.

DEFENDER

Hansen's Roughriders, Roughriders Armor Support

Defender consists of Hansen's Roughriders. At the start of battle, the Roughriders deploy an equal number of BattleMechs as the attacker. The Roughriders also begin with the same number of vehicles from Roughriders Armor Support. Beginning on Turn 6, reinforcements arrive in the form of one lance of 'Mechs, alternating turns with a lance of tanks. Defender must prevent Attacker from exiting unit's via Defender's home edge until Turn 10.

ILLICIAN LANCERS

The Illician Lancers are one of the most storied mercenary commands of all time. The Lancers were first formed in 2572 by the Illician Order based in Sicily, Terra. The command grew to more than a 'Mech division (more than nine regiments) as members of the Order resigned their posts and assembled among their new comrades. Even before the Star League fell, the Lancers worked for every Star League member state. When Stefan the Usurper murdered the Cameron family on Terra and ignited the Amaris Civil War, the Lancers continued fighting alongside the SLDF. Two Lancers regiments, the First and Seventh Rangers, were annihilated in the final battle for Terra. The Illician Order was also a casualty of that war, as the surviving Lancers discovered the Order's base had been levelled some time earlier.

The Succession Wars were as unkind to the Lancers as to any other military command; the Lancers' numbers were cut in half during the first two wars. In the Third Succession War, the Lancers suffered under Capellan employ. The Confederation's attempt to force the Lancers into the Company Store was averted only when the mercenaries sold most of their JumpShips to pay off its debt. The Lancers then signed on to serve House Davion. They have been in service to the Federated Suns, and later the Federated Commonwealth, ever since. The Lancers have been stationed along the Capellan border for nearly forty years; they have grown familiar with the territory on many of the worlds on both sides of the border—and their enemies across it.

Each of the Lancers' four regiments includes a full fighter wing. Various sizes and types of infantry and vehicle formations are also part of each regiment. Because of the command's long association with the Federated Suns, the Lancers are adept at combined arms fighting. The command has its own academy for training both the dependents of its own warriors and promising recruits from the local populations. The Lancers have a unique system of command: a commanding general is elected to a six-year term by a Council of Elders. The same Elders select every colonel in the command, assigning them either to combat commands, administration, or logistics as their talents warrant. The officers may be re-elected any number of times, provided they still possess the necessary skills.

Common Allies	Davion
Common Enemies	Kurita (Late Succession Wars), Liao (Late Succession Wars)
Special Command Abilities	*Esprit de Corps*

LANCERS COMMAND

The Lancers command company is under the direct command of General Brenda Bradley. The command company is often attached to the Fifty-ninth Strike in combat, with General Bradley assuming command of the regiment from Colonel Stockton. The command company comprises entirely assault 'Mechs, some still meeting original Star League specifications. The company's attached fighters and vehicles match that weight class and technology level.

Experience Rating	Elite
Force Composition	1 'Mech company, 1 aerospace fighter squadron, 1 vehicle company
Force Building Rules	All 'Mechs must be assault class (Size 4); Lancers Command may add access to the following 'Mechs for 3 FPs each: *Thug* THG-11E, *King Crab* KGC-000, *Highlander* HGN-732.
Special Rules	Lancers Command may deploy with any of the four Illician Lancers Regiments. If the full 'Mech company of the Lancers Command is fielded with a minimum of a 'Mech company of any other Lancers Regiment, the entire Force gains +1 to its Initiative rolls.

KINGS OF THE BATTLEFIELD

BattleMechs have long been recognized as the kings of the battlefield. Their combination of firepower, armor, and maneuverability in all terrain types makes them the optimum battlefield asset.

BattleMechs are constructed of the most advanced materials known to man. Their chassis is a skeleton of extremely strong and tough composite materials, including foamed aluminum cores, titanium-steel alloys, and ceramic fibers which often require zero-G processing for proper fabrication.

The engine and gyro are the most important components, and are attached to the chassis before other parts are installed. The fusion engine powers the 'Mech's systems, from weapons and sensors to the motive system itself. The gyro stabilizes the 'Mech, while actuators make up the joints and motor controllers power the 'Mechs limbs and allow it to move. These include the myomer bundles, artificial muscles driven by the electric power supplied by the engine.

The MechWarrior operates the 'Mech from the cockpit. A neurohelmet links the MechWarrior to the gyro and ensures the 'Mech stays upright. Neurohelmets sometimes also contain advanced electronics which relate information about the location and orientation of the 'Mech's limbs.

59TH STRIKE REGIMENT

The Fifty-ninth Strike Regiment is a mobile command drilled in closing fast with the enemy and engaging at close range. As the fastest 'Mechs distract the enemy, the slower, better-armed 'Mechs move up to finish them off. The heaviest 'Mech in the regiment is 75 tons. First Battalion concentrates its companies around a particular weapons range: LRMs are common in First Company, PPCs in Second Company, and autocannons in Third Company. Second Battalion uses entirely light and medium 'Mechs with exceptional maneuverability. Third Battalion is a mix of medium and heavy 'Mechs, especially bruisers like *Hunchbacks* and *Thunderbolts*.

Experience Rating	Veteran
Force Composition	1 medium 'Mech regiment, 1 heavy aerospace fighter wing, 1 infantry battalion, 1 vehicle battalion. The Force may not field assault (Size 4) 'Mechs.
Special Command Abilities	Forcing the Initiative, Tactical Specialization (Attack)
Force Building Rules	The Fifty-ninth Strike Regiment can replace any Special Pilot Abilities they receive from their Lance Type with the Weapon Specialist SPA.

4TH ILLICIAN RANGERS

The Fourth Rangers are the heaviest regiment in the Illician Lancers; all 'Mechs are heavies and assaults. This also makes them the slowest of the Lancers regiments. Second Battalion hoards the fastest assaults and heavies, serving as the cavalry unit for the regiment. As Second Battalion moves into the enemy, weak points for exploitation are relayed to the other battalions. The fighter wing and vehicle regiment are similarly high-tonnage. The latter includes a full company of artillery. The infantry company is a mechanized force loaded with heavy field guns and SRMs. While they often capture downed 'Mechs for salvage, they are capable of destroying targets on their own.

Experience Rating	Regular
Force Composition	1 'Mech regiment, 1 aerospace fighter wing, 1 mechanized infantry company, 1 vehicle regiment; all 'Mechs and aerospace fighters must be heavy or assault (Size 3 or 4)
Special Command Abilities	Sharp Shooters
Force Building Rules	Fourth Illician Rangers' Assault Lances add the Speed Demon SPA to the list of SPAs that may be chosen for their Bonus Ability.

9TH ILLICIAN RANGERS

The Ninth Rangers field two battalions of fast, light and medium 'Mechs. The privations of the Succession Wars, however, have cost Third Battalion most of its heavy 'Mechs. Thus, First and Second Battalions maintain their flanking attack and hit-and-run specialties, while Third has developed into a frontal assault command. The jump infantry battalion specializes in incendiary operations, being especially adept with Inferno missiles. The vehicle company consists entirely of fast hovercraft attached to Third Battalion to prevent flanking by faster enemies.

Experience Rating	Green
Force Composition	1 medium 'Mech regiment, 1 medium aerospace wing, 1 infantry battalion, 1 vehicle company
Special Command Abilities	Off-Map Movement, Overrun Combat

21ST ILLICIAN RANGERS

The Twenty-first has long specialized in air-mobile operations. They are renowned for never missing their drop zones when making combat drops from any height. Their fighters are especially adept at ground attacks. The infantry regiment is a complement of jump infantry troops skilled at space and air insertions, and possess an exceptional ability to operate behind enemy lines.

Experience Rating	Regular
Force Composition	1 medium 'Mech regiment, 1 heavy aerospace fighter wing, 1 infantry regiment
Special Command Abilities	Ground Attack Specialists, *Combat Drop Specialists*.

KINGS OF THE BATTLEFIELD [CONTINUED]

'Mechs are layered in armor and bristle with weaponry. BattleMech armor is incredibly strong and tough; it is ablative in nature and can absorb tremendous energy before breaking, thus sparing the internal components from damage. Like the internal structure, 'Mech armor is an advanced composite combining strength, thermal conductivity, and toughness.

The weaponry installed on BattleMechs is among the most powerful ever developed. Lasers and particle cannons rely on the engine for power, while ammunition bins feed missile launchers and autocannons. Some 'Mechs rely on anti-personnel weaponry, such as flamers and machine guns, though these are less effective against other BattleMechs.

Some 'Mechs also mount jump jets. Jump jets divert power from the fusion engine to superheat the nearby atmosphere and allow the 'Mech to rocket short distances. This increases the already-impressive maneuverability of the 'Mech and allows it to clear obstacles, flank enemies, or penetrate fortifications.

Combining these advances of science and technology into one machine, it is no wonder BattleMechs are the kings of the battlefield.

KELL HOUNDS

The Kell Hounds were founded only a few decades ago, but the fame the command achieved in very short time made the Hounds an Inner Sphere phenomenon. Brothers Morgan and Patrick Kell founded the Hounds in 3010 with an inheritance from their cousin, Duke Arthur Luvon, the late husband of Archon Katrina Steiner. The brothers first hired the best technicians on Galatea, which in turn attracted the best MechWarriors to their banner. They carefully selected only the most skilled and most experienced MechWarriors who applied.

The Kell Hounds' first major action was with the AFFS on Mallory's World, where a determined invasion by the Draconis Combine claimed the life of First Prince Ian Davion. The timely arrival of the Kell Hounds after his death prevented the Kurita forces from making off with the First Prince's body as a war trophy. The Hounds continued to defend Mallory's World, but the planet's fate was decided when unit commander Colonel Morgan Kell met the Second Sword of Light's commander, Yorinaga Kurita, in single combat. Kell surprised the entire Inner Sphere by shaming Kurita so thoroughly that the samurai ordered all Combine forces off the world.

Morgan then broke up the Hounds and entered a monastery, leaving a battalion under Patrick's command. Eleven years later, Yorinaga Kurita achieved a measure of revenge by killing Patrick Kell. His brother's death led Morgan to return to duty and recall the troops he had dispersed after Mallory's World. Kell met Yorinaga Kurita again on Nusakan during the Fourth Succession War, and again defeated him; Kurita committed *seppuku* in a public ceremony soon after.

The Kell Hounds have since distinguished themselves time and again as an elite command of the highest order. When Archon Katrina Steiner died, she left another inheritance to Kell, who honored her request to add a second regiment to the Hounds.

Common Allies	Steiner (Late Succession Wars, Early Clan Invasion)
Common Enemies	Kurita (Late Succession Wars), Clan Jade Falcon (Early Clan Invasion), Clan Smoke Jaguar (Early Clan Invasion)
Special Command Abilities	*Esprit de Corps*

KELL HOUNDS COMMAND LANCE

The Hounds' Command Lance always remains independent of any contract, but the Hounds reserve the right to attach it to any contracted unit at will. Morgan Kell leads the lance, though he personally enters combat much less frequently in the past few years. Even though they rate the rank, the regimental commanders refuse to accept the rank of colonel while Morgan Kell remains in command.

Experience Rating	Elite
Force Composition	1 'Mech lance
Force Building Rules	The Command Lance's members may choose any 'Mechs they wish from any of their availability lists for 0 FP.

FIRST KELL HOUNDS

The First Kell Hounds is commanded by Lieutenant Colonel Dan Allard, Morgan Kell's son-in-law and heir-apparent for command of the Kell Hounds. Each battalion includes a Command Lance. Third Battalion is under a separate contract to the Free Rasalhague Republic and is stationed on Outpost for pirate hunting duties. First and Second Battalions remain under contract to the Federated Commonwealth. The third company of each battalion specializes in particular terrain or tactics: the 113th in urban fighting, the 123rd in amphibious operations, and the 133rd in jungle operations. The jump infantry battalion is known as the Pit Bulls.

Experience Rating	Elite
Force Composition	1 medium 'Mech regiment, 1 heavy aerospace fighter wing, 1 infantry battalion
Special Command Abilities	Off-Map Movement, Environmental Specialization (Urban), Environmental Specialization (Water), Environmental Specialization (Woods), *Tactical Adjustments*
Force Building Rules	The commanders of each lance, company, and battalion, as well all members of the battalion Command Lances, may choose any 'Mech from their availability lists for 0 FP.

SECOND KELL HOUNDS

The Second Kell Hounds is well-trained in night combat. Each battalion includes a command lance. The third company of each battalion specializes in a particular terrain or tactic: the 213th in low- or zero-g conditions, the 223rd in long-range operations, and the 233rd in extreme weather and terrain. The Bad Dogs infantry battalion is a jump infantry Formation.

Experience Rating	Elite
Force Composition	1 medium 'Mech regiment, 1 heavy aerospace fighter wing, 1 infantry battalion
Special Command Abilities	Environmental Specialization (Night), Environmental Specialization (Low Gravity), Environmental Specialization (Wind), Sharp Shooters
Force Building Rules	The commanders of each lance, company, and battalion may choose any 'Mech on their availability lists for 0 FP.

Phelan Kell

Phelan Kell is the son of Morgan Kell. He is a Nagelring washout, due to his attitude rather than any failure of skill. Phelan is a MechWarrior savant, having inherited his father's exceptional skill in the cockpit. Phelan is captured by Clan Wolf in one of the first battles of the Clan Invasion in 3049.

PHELAN KELL — **PV:** 22 (34)

Unit Type	Skill	TP	SZ	MV	TMM	S/M/L	OV	A/S	Specials
***Wolfhound* WLF-1**	1	BM	1	12	2	2/2/0	1	4/3	ENE, REAR1/1/-

Special Pilot Abilities: Human TRO, Lucky (2), Tactical Genius; Phelan Kell is not available to field as part of a Kell Hounds Formation post-3049

HARD PLACE ON THE ROCK

Sisyphus' Lament
The Rock system
Periphery
13 August 3049

A recon lance from Third Battalion, First Kell Hounds is tracking a group of Kenny Ryan's pirate band which escaped the rest of the Hounds company dispatched to The Rock system to deal with the raiders. They are closing in on Ryan when an unidentified force arrives in the system and attacks both groups.

GAME SETUP

Recommended Terrain: Rolling Hills, Moonscape

If using hex maps, arrange two maps with their long edges touching.

The Defender chooses a home edge. The Attacker's home edge is the opposite edge.

ATTACKER

Clan Wolf Golden Keshik

The Attacker consists of one Star of OmniMechs from the Golden Keshik of Clan Wolf's Alpha Galaxy. The Attacker is led by Vlad (Elite, *Mad Cat*), along with two *Man O' Wars* and two *Ryokens*, all of Veteran skill. The Attacker's 'Mechs enter from their home edge on Turn 1. The Attacker's objective is to disable all of the Defender's 'Mechs, as the Attacker wants to question or make bondsmen of any downed MechWarriors. Each Attacker will offer a single combat duel to one or more of the Defender 'Mechs; if accepted, only that Attacker may fire on that Defender. Any Defender who violates such a duel frees the Attackers to target whomever they wish. The attacker's efforts to limit damage reduce the damage from their weapon attacks by half (round up).

DEFENDER

Scout Lance, Third Battalion, First Kell Hounds; Pirate Lance (Regular Skill Rating)

The Defender consists of one Command Lance of pirate 'Mechs and a recon lance of the First Kell Hounds. The pirate lance is commanded by Kenny Ryan (Veteran, *Griffin*) and consists of a *Locust*, *Panther* and a *Rifleman*. Reduce the armor of all pirate 'Mechs by half (round up) to represent damage inflicted by the Hounds in pursuit. The Scout Lance is commanded by Lieutenant Jackson Tang (Veteran, *Blackjack*) and includes Phelan Kell (see above). The Defender's units are placed on the map before Turn 1; they must be placed within 6" or three hexes of the Attacker's home edge. The Defender's units must escape the unknown attackers by exiting via their home edge. Phelan Kell must attempt to defeat the obviously technologically-superior enemy 'Mechs.

THE RETURN OF KERENSKY

In the centuries since the Exodus, the militaries and mercenaries of the Inner Sphere wondered if and when Kerensky's forces would return. Amid the catastrophes of the Succession Wars, no one was sure if the departed SLDF would have suffered a similar decline and loss of technology that so greatly affected the Inner Sphere nations. If they returned, would they be benefactors or conquerors? The sheer number of troops that departed might be enough to demolish any two or more House militaries. Could the Successor States stand up to the enormous military force that departed the Inner Sphere so long ago?

Those questions were largely academic, as few thought the departed troops would ever return after being gone so long. But in late 3049, communication ceased from numerous systems in the Coreward Periphery. Soon after, invaders of unknown origin appeared on the edge of the Draconis Combine, Free Rasalhague Republic, and Lyran portion of the Federated Commonwealth. These invaders possessed technology that far outclassed even the recovered weapons and components of the best Inner Sphere military units. Some even speculated that the invaders might be aliens, due to the ease with which they initially sliced through Inner Sphere defenders.

The invaders progressed almost without challenge, wiping away House units and mercenary commands of the highest caliber with ease. Eventually, the invaders revealed their origins to ComStar: they are the heirs to Kerensky, they call themselves the Clans, and their goal is to re-establish the Star League in their new image, eradicating the long decay that set in after the Exodus. The Clans possess a strange sort of honor that guides their conduct in battle, but they are also military dictatorships bent on subjugating all others to their will.

The Federated Commonwealth, Free Rasalhague Republic, and Draconis Combine are mobilizing their forces to stop this new threat. But unless a sheer weight of numbers plays in their favor, it is unknown if anything can truly stop the Clans.

KILLER BEES

The Killer Bees were founded in 3025 by Cal-Boeing test pilots. These daring warriors wanted some real action for a change, and hired on with the Lyran Commonwealth before moving to the Magistracy of Canopus. They took part in the Andurien-Canopian Invasion of the Capellan Confederation, but withdrew from their contract when ordered to stop the counterattacking McCarron's Armored Cavalry. The move would have adversely affected the command's reputation, except the Bees publicized the details of their orders and shamed their erstwhile Canopian employers for trying to use them as cannon fodder.

The Bees handled a number of near-Periphery contracts for several years before returning to Lyran service in time for the War of 3039, during which they distinguished themselves by raiding the Draconis Combine. One particular raid into the Alshain Military District resulted in the Bees' infantry capturing a Combine *Invader*-class JumpShip. The seizure was a coup for such a small mercenary command, but the maintenance expenses nearly bankrupted the Bees. They were able to stay afloat through various means, such as ferrying DropShips to their destinations for nominal fees, while some of their pilots performed in air shows to raise necessary funds. The efforts paid off, as the JumpShip is crucial to keeping the command independent and free from the risk of being left behind on a hostile world.

In 3048, the Bees left Lyran service for Irian BattleMechs Ltd. in the Free Worlds League. In addition to security duties, the Bees have field-tested several of Irian's newest products, including BattleMechs constructed with recovered technology.

The Bees are renowned throughout the Inner Sphere for their excellent camouflage skills. While they appear in parade reviews in gaudy yellow with black stripes, in the field they are far more difficult to spot. The command is a mixed reinforced battalion of 'Mechs, tanks, fighters, VTOLs, and infantry. Their unit coordination is excellent thanks to their recent past association with Federated Commonwealth RCTs.

Common Allies	Steiner (Late Succession Wars), Marik (Early Clan Invasion)
Common Enemies	None
Special Command Abilities	*Camouflage, Tactical Experts (Engineers)*

STINGER COMPANY

Stinger Company is a mixture of light and medium scouts. They rely primarily on speed to achieve surprise and flank their enemies. Their 'Mechs are much harder to target thanks to the company's legendary camouflage skills.

Experience Rating	Regular
Force Composition	1 reinforced 'Mech company; all Units must be light or medium (Size 1 or 2)

YELLOWJACKET SQUADRON

Yellowjacket Squadron is a fast, hit-and-run group whose pilots rely primarily on speed to achieve surprise and flank their enemies. The light fighters in the squadron possess very little armor, and Yellowjacket pilots will leave a battle rather than risk being shot down.

Experience Rating	Regular
Force Composition	1 aerospace fighter squadron; all units must be Light (Size 1)

SWARM COMPANY

Swarm Company is an all-VTOL formation adept at concentrating their firepower.

Experience Rating	Veteran
Force Composition	1 VTOL company
Force Building Rules	New Formation Type: **Swarm Lance** **Requirements:** No Unit may be greater than Size 2. All Units must be VTOLs. **Bonus Ability: Coordinated Fire.** The Lance may make a standard weapon attack against a target within Short Range and Line of Sight of all members of the Lance as if it were a single Unit. The targeted player then chooses any one of the attacking units from which to calculate the to-hit modifiers. A single to-hit roll is made, with the Swarm Lance hitting or missing the target as one. If they hit the Unit using coordinated fire, the attacking player may add 1 damage point to one of the attacks; the rest do their standard damage.

BUMBLEBEE COMPANY

The Bumblebees are a laser rifle company with four squads of seven troopers each. The infantry rarely enters combat, instead guarding the Bees' base of operations. One notable exception was the capture of the JumpShip *Mobile Nest*, when the troopers exceeded their own estimates of their abilities in boarding the JumpShip, capturing most of the crew, and safely co-opting the vessel for their own command.

Experience Rating	Veteran
Force Composition	1 infantry company

LANGENDORF LANCERS

The Langendorf Lancers began service as the private army of the merchant princes of Calloway VI during the First Succession War. The Lancers were intended to deter the increasingly frequent and violent raids by Capellan forces along the League-Confederation border. However, the troops under headstrong former SLDF General Mortimer Langendorf became increasingly restive. As the war dragged on and losses increased, the princes offered the Lancers to the Free Worlds League, an offer the Captain-General gladly accepted. The princes transferred the command and assets of the Lancers to the League and quickly removed themselves from any association with them. The Lancers have served the League ever since.

Time was unkind to the Lancers. Though the command started with a regiment, the depredations of the Succession Wars whittled their numbers down to a single battalion. It was only after Colonel Gregory Millsey took command that the Lancers began to recover. Discipline cases were dealt with harshly, most being sent packing. Millsey brought in new blood that showed proper respect for authority, and the once-rough and tumble battalion is now a professional mercenary regiment.

The Lancers recently completed a mission for the League on Dixie. They were sent to raid the Lyran supply base there, and also to pick up some passengers "to be determined." On Dixie, they faced the Filthy Lucre mercenary command and were handily defeated. As the Lancers fled back to their JumpShip, they were stunned to receive a communique that the Lucre were the passengers they were waiting for. Tensions ran high as they delivered the Filthy Lucre to their new duty station in the League, but things worsened when the Lucre refused to return the salvage they claimed from the Lancers on Dixie just weeks before. The rivalry between the two commands led the Captain-General to station the Lucre far away on the Confederation border.

To vent the command's frustration, Colonel Millsey carried out an unauthorized raid on Bolan in January 3050. The raid was a great success, mainly due to lack of significant defenders. Bolan was chosen as the Lancers' target as it had the longtime homeworld of the Filthy Lucre. The raid did not motivate the Lucre to respond in any way, only increasing Colonel Millsey's anger at the other mercenary command.

Common Allies	Marik (Late Succession Wars, Early Clan Invasion)
Common Enemies	Steiner (Late Succession Wars, Early Clan Invasion)
Special Command Abilities	Tactical Specialization (Defense), Off-Map Movement

LANGENDORF LANCERS

The Lancers are a fairly typical regiment. Their battalions each contain a recon company, a fast-moving strike company, and an assault company. However, the Lancers are notable for their lack of supporting elements. Their 'Mech-only TO&E has resulted in tactical defeats more than once. Millsey is actively seeking pilots with their own fighters to augment the Lancers' capabilities. The Lancers prefer to fight defensive engagements, which provide security and stability.

Experience Rating	Regular
Force Composition	1 medium 'Mech regiment

Captain Stanwick Reginald Hoffenmeier III

Captain Stanwick Hoffenmeier is a prim and proper gentleman whom most would expect to be anything but effective as a MechWarrior. However, his manners and mannerisms disappear once he buttons himself into the cockpit of his *Griffin*. As the commander of Second Company, Third Battalion, Hoffenmeier stealthily leads his men beyond enemy positions and springs an attack from unexpected directions. His *Griffin* was captured from Federated Commonwealth forces raiding Colfax in November 3049. It is in pristine condition and under his deft control often seems to skulk along like a murderer in a back alley.

CAPTAIN STANWICK REGINALD HOFFENMEIER III									PV: 30 (42) | 31 (43)
Unit Type	**Skill**	**TP**	**SZ**	**MV**	**TMM**	**S/M/L**	**OV**	**A/S**	**Specials**
***Griffin* GRF-1S** (Late Succession Wars)	2	BM	2	10j	2	2/3/0*	1	5/5	IF0*
***Griffin* GRF-1DS** (Early Clan Invasion)	2	BM	2	10j	2	2/3/2	0	5/3	CASE, IF1, LRM1/1/1
Special Pilot Abilities: Dodge, Natural Grace, Hoffenmeier retains a +1 Target Movement Modifier when Standing Still									

LEXINGTON COMBAT GROUP

The Lexington Combat Group is a sizeable mercenary command which descends from the SLDF. As Kerensky planned his Exodus, nine close friends, all high-ranking officers who attended the Lexington Military Academy on Terra, made plans of their own. They recruited hundreds of fellow officers and NCOs from across the breadth of the SLDF. Together, they conspired to store abundant supplies on Bryant for the force they were building. As Kerensky departed, they journeyed to Bryant and organized the Lexington Combat Group.

Three centuries later, the Group has worked for every Successor State, but spent most of the Succession Wars and the entire last hundred years in the employ of the Federated Suns. Occasional strained relations with their employer were always overcome by generous contract terms to retain the Group's services. In the past decade, the Group went into severe debt to upgrade every combat unit with recovered technology. This debt essentially placed the Group in House Davion's Company Store. Instead of reacting with anger, as they willingly sought the debt they accrued, the Group chose to sign a seventy-year contract with the Armed Forces of the Federated Suns.

The Group has long formed a critical component of the Capellan March's defense forces. The three combat brigades are all organized along similar lines, combining 'Mechs, tanks, fighters, and infantry in the unified tactics so embraced throughout the Suns for generations. Each combat group also possesses its own DropShip and JumpShip assets.

The Group uses an involved process for promotions to avoid favoritism of any kind. Three individual councils meet to approve every NCO promotion to gunnery sergeant and higher and officer promotion to major and higher. These councils consist of senior officers, mid-level officers, and NCOs and recruits, respectively.

Common Allies	Davion (Late Succession Wars, Early Clan Invasion)
Common Enemies	Liao (Late Succession Wars)
Special Command Abilities	Forcing the Initiative

LEXINGTON COMBAT GROUP COMMAND

The loss of the Group's commanding general, attached to the Thirty-Second Recon, in the First Succession War threw the command into disarray and led to the conquest of their homeworld of Bryant. Group Command was created to free the commanding general from duties to the Thirty-second and to enable that person to focus on administrative matters and overall strategic concerns. In practice, Group Command is usually attached to the Thirty-second despite this history. Group Command differs from the Thirty-second in that all its 'Mechs are heavy- and assault-class. This makes them ill-suited for the mission profile of the Thirty-second, but ideal to secure a base of operations.

Experience Rating	Elite
Force Composition	1 assault 'Mech company, 1 assault vehicle company, 1 infantry company
Special Command Abilities	Zone of Control
Force Building Rules	Group Command's MechWarriors are all Elite (or better) and may select any available assault or heavy (Size 3 or 4) 'Mech for 0 FP each. The vehicle company comprises all heavy and assault (Size 3 and 4) tanks and each must have the AC special ability of 1 or higher at short range.

32ND RECON COMBAT GROUP

The Thirty-second has specialized in recon, pursuit, and raiding missions since it was the Thirty-second Recon Regiment of the SLDF. Thus almost all its 'Mechs and vehicles are light and fast. Only the third company of each battalion includes heavy 'Mechs, and they are always among the fastest of their weight class. These 'Mechs are often detailed to provide security for the Thirty-second's base and for the artillery battalion.

Experience Rating	Veteran
Force Composition	1 reinforced light 'Mech regiment, 1 aerospace fighter wing, 2 light vehicle battalions, 2 mechanized infantry battalions, 1 artillery battalion, 1 aviation (VTOL) battalion.
Special Command Abilities	*Hit and Run*, Environmental Specialization (Urban).
Force Building Rules	At least half of all the Force's 'Mechs and vehicles must be light (Size 1), and all 'Mechs must have a Move of 10" or more. Thirty-second Recon 'Mech lances may add the Speed Demon Special Pilot Ability to the list of SPAs available for their Bonus Ability.

180TH DRAGOON COMBAT GROUP

Also known as Marie's Golden Hammers, the 180th Dragoon Combat Group is a slow-moving, death-dealing assault force. The unit's missions usually center on breaching and capturing enemy fortifications. Despite the high tonnage of the 180th's 'Mechs, they are renowned for their ability to close distances faster than enemies expect. Enemies are often stunned at the quick reactions and devastating firepower of the Golden Hammers.

Experience Rating	Regular
Force Composition	1 assault 'Mech regiment, 1 heavy aerospace fighter wing, 2 heavy vehicle battalions, 2 mechanized infantry battalions, 1 artillery battalion, 1 aviation battalion; all 'Mechs must be heavy or assault (Size 3 or 4).
Special Command Abilities	*Gun It*, Overrun Combat

241ST BATTLE COMBAT GROUP

The 241st uses mostly heavy 'Mechs, despite being known as Frederic's Gazelles. Unlike the other two combat groups, the 241st is a non-specialized force. They simply move in against the enemy and slug it out until their opponents retreat or stop moving. They are known for carrying out precision combat drops into the midst of heavy fighting without missing a beat. The 191st Tactical Fighter Wing are experts at ground support operations which prevent enemy forces from targeting the incoming DropShips and dropping troops of the 241st.

Experience Rating	Regular
Force Composition	1 heavy 'Mech regiment, 1 heavy aerospace fighter wing, 2 medium vehicle battalions, 2 mechanized infantry battalions, 1 artillery battalion, 1 aviation battalion. At least half of all the Force's 'Mechs must be heavy (Size 3).
Special Command Abilities	Off-Map Movement, Combat Drop Specialists, Ground Attack Specialists
Special Rules	One aerospace fighter, if any are in the force, can be assigned the Ground-Hugger SPA.

Lieutenant James Ismail

Lieutenant James Ismail commands the second lance in Third Company, Second Battalion, 180th Dragoon Combat Group. His modern Marik *Archer* has been refit for close combat; each LRM-20 has been replaced with four SRM-4s and the fire control system was scrapped to move the rear-firing lasers to the front and replace them with pulse versions. Ismail lives for close combat, and loves that training with the 180th has taught him to exceed his *Archer*'s normal speed limitations.

LIEUTENANT JAMES ISMAIL — **PV:** 39 (47) | 44 (53)

Unit Type	Skill	TP	SZ	MV	TMM	S/M/L	OV	A/S	Specials
***Archer* ARC-2R-modified** (Late Succession Wars)	3	BM	3	8	1	4/4/0	4	7/6	CASE, SRM3/3/-
***Archer* ARC-4M-modified** (Early Clan Invasion)	3	BM	3	8	1	6/6/0	2	7/6	CASE, SRM4/4/-

Special Pilot Abilities: Prior to the beginning of play, assign two SPAs to Lieutenant James Ismail from among the following: Slugger, Fist Fire, Zweihander.

ST. IVES COMPACT

The St. Ives Compact was born in the Fourth Succession War when Duchess Candace Liao declared the St. Ives Commonality independent of the Capellan Confederation. The Compact has cleaved closely to the Federated Suns, depending on that nation for defensive assistance. The Compact is similarly generous to mercenaries, guaranteeing fair treatment and generous compensation in pay, salvage, and transportation rights to those willing to defend the Compact from its former countrymen.

LINDON'S COMPANY

Lindon's Battalion—née Company—reinforced a team of special operators in conquering Bergman's Planet during the War of 3039. The Twenty-first Galedon Regulars deployed a recon force to the world, leading to a cat-and-mouse game of minor engagements for a month until the rest of the Twenty-first arrived. Though Lindon's Battalion fought well, they could not overcome the superior number of Combine troops and retreated from Bergman's Planet soon after.

The end of the conflict saw the battalion returned to their pre-war duty station of Kennard on the Outworlds Alliance border. In the relative peace since the War of 3039, the Company was rewarded for their efforts on Bergman's Planet. In less than a decade, the Federated Commonwealth aided the command in bulking up from a battalion to a full regiment. They remain on Kennard, but are agitating for a more combat-rich posting now that they field such numbers.

A recent engagement against pirate raiders on Kennard may have convinced the High Command to grant their request. The unknown pirates landed in company strength, but Lindon's Battalion lay in wait in the terrain they know so well, and slaughtered the pirates as they attacked warehouses in the capital city of Clayton. None of the pirates escaped, and the Regiment added another DropShip to its roster.

Common Allies	Davion (Late Succession Wars)
Common Enemies	Kurita (Late Succession Wars)
Special Command Abilities	Tactical Expert (Hidden Units), Off-Map Movement, Ground Attack Specialists

LINDON'S REGIMENT

The BattleMechs of Lindon's Regiment are organized into three similar battalions. Each battalion has a recon company composed of light and medium 'Mechs which specialize in ambush tactics. The strike company is a mix of two lances of medium 'Mechs and one lance of heavy 'Mechs. The assault company comprises two lances of larger heavy 'Mechs and one lance of assault 'Mechs. Each battalion also includes an independent command lance composed of heavy and assault 'Mechs.

Experience Rating	Veteran
Force Composition	1 medium 'Mech company (pre-3029), 1 medium 'Mech battalion (3029-3042), 1 medium 'Mech regiment (post-3042)

LINDON'S AIR WING

Routine engagements with the Outworlds Alliance's excellent fighters have drilled the Air Wing to the highest skill level. The command sports a full aerospace wing of light and medium fighters which specializes in ground support missions, but is less adept at space combat.

Experience Rating	Elite
Force Composition	1 aerospace fighter wing; all Units must be light or medium (Size 1 or 2)

OTHER NOTABLE MERCENARIES

No single volume could contain descriptions of every known mercenary command. Besides those listed here, there are a great number of well-known mercenaries worthy of mention. Following is a partial listing of these notables.

- Always Faithful
- Ambermarte's Highlanders
- Bad Dream
- Barrett's Fusiliers
- The Blackhearts
- Clifton's Rangers
- Crater Cobras
- Dragon's Breath
- The Fighting Urukhai
- The Green Machine
- Gregg's Long Striders
- Hampton's Hessens
- Harlock's Warriors
- Helmut's Hermits
- Hsien Hotheads
- Kingston Caballeros
- The Knights of St. Cameron
- The Krushers
- Lockhardt's Ironsides
- Lone Star Regiment
- Markson's Marauders
- Martian Cuirassiers
- Miller's Marauders
- Mobile Fire
- Narhal's Raiders
- St. Cyr Heavy Assault Group
- The Stealthy Tigers
- Swann's Cavaliers
- The Thumpers
- Tooth of Ymir
- Vinson's Vigilantes
- Winfield's Regiment

LITTLE RICHARD'S PANZER BRIGADE

Little Richard's Panzer Brigade has a checkered past. The command was originally a Davion House unit called the Panzer Brigade. When the Brigade's commanding officer was caught dealing drugs, the executive officer threw his former commander and his cronies out. The rest of the command joined the XO in mutinying from the Federated Suns, stealing the DropShips the FedSuns had assigned them as "separation pay," and fleeing.

The command spent the rest of the Third Succession War working for Houses Liao, Marik, and Kurita before finally taking a more legitimate contract with the Lyran Commonwealth near the end of the Third War. The planned union of the Steiner and Davion ruling lines drove the command back to the Capellan Confederation, where it has remained ever since.

The Panzer Brigade is well-known for brutal, dishonorable conduct in battle. The command uses subterfuge to overcome superior enemies, while barely respecting the mercenary code of accepting surrender and repatriating those who offer it. Colonel Richard Whitman inherited the outfit from his father before the Fourth War but often falls short when compared to him, giving rise to the nickname "Little" Richard's Panzer Brigade—there was no such embellishment when his father commanded. Even after more than two decades, Whitman feels he has something to prove and plans to do so against the Federated Suns, which he blames for his father's early death.

Common Allies	None
Common Enemies	None
Special Command Abilities	Enemy Specialization (Davion), Communications Disruption, Off-Map Movement, *False Flag*

LITTLE RICHARD'S PANZER BRIGADE

The Panzer Brigade maintained its combined arms approach to warfare after departing the Federated Suns, and the command's various unit types work well together. However, the three 'Mech battalions are usually deployed independently. The Brigade is well-known for its subterfuge in combat, including impersonating other commands and broadcasting false IFF signals. The command also deals harshly with enemies, often giving no quarter. When surrenders are accepted, the opposing warriors can expect to be relieved of all their equipment before being cast out or ransomed back. The 'Mech battalions each have their own Command Lances, which attach themselves to any company they wish. The fighter wing relies primarily on medium fighters, and comprises three squadrons each with a Command Lance which deploy with their corresponding 'Mech battalion (First with First, etc.). The same holds for the vehicle battalions, which have one company each of hovercraft, fast wheeled tanks, and heavy tracked tanks.

Experience Rating	Veteran
Force Composition	1 heavy 'Mech regiment, 1 reinforced medium aerospace fighter wing, 1 vehicle regiment; at least half of all the Brigade's aerospace fighters must be medium (Size 2)

Captain Samantha Whittaker

Captain Samantha Whittaker commands Second Company, First Battalion of the Panzer Brigade. After taking command, she had to kill two of her less cooperative MechWarriors to engender greater discipline. Those she recruited to replace them were more respectful and have become lance commanders. The company now specializes in night combat and city fighting. Her preference is to take out local power plants to plunge a city into darkness, where she and her company will have the advantage in the dark on slick pavement.

CAPTAIN SAMANTHA WHITTAKER — **PV:** 36 (42)

Unit Type	Skill	TP	SZ	MV	TMM	S/M/L	OV	A/S	Specials
***Warhammer* WHM-6D**	3	BM	3	8	1	3/3/2	0	7/6	ENE

Special Pilot Abilities: Iron Will, Terrain Master (Nightwalker)

LONE WOLVES

The Lone Wolves have always been a loose collection of warriors. It's unclear whether the various bands using the name since the mid-2900s were even associated with the group claiming the moniker of the Lone Wolves today. The rotating roster of the Wolves was such that, for decades, there was no identifiable command hierarchy. The group would simply live up to its name, attacking stragglers or strays on the edge of battle to earn their pay.

Things changed after the Wolves took part in the battle for Rochelle in 3007 and a group of MechWarriors joined the Wolves en masse. These MechWarriors began to discipline other members of the Wolves, driving away some of the worst of the lot, while garnering support for a collective command structure. However, this structure was different from any other. Instead of a unified command, these MechWarriors formed The Committee, overseeing the Wolves as a sort of logistics cartel. The Wolves maintain their "come and go as you like" mentality and membership, but members must pay for all their supplies, repairs, and transportation, sourced by the Committee. Individual members can choose at any point not to fight, but their pay stops until they resume combat operations. The Committee decides where and when the Wolves will fight, often picking up and leaving when the situation becomes uncertain. This occurred on Galtor in 3025, when the Wolves abandoned their contract once the DCMS killed the AFFS commander. That campaign was also marked by infighting between disparate elements of the Wolves over salvage, a failure of discipline which allowed Combine troops to escape certain destruction. Such behavior typifies the Wolves' actions in combat, as each member ultimately is in it for him or herself.

The Wolves have never registered with the Mercenary Review Board. Instead, the command gathers intel from multiple sources and divines the site of raids, skirmishes, battles, and even invasions. The Wolves generally appear before the start of hostilities and offer their services to the defending force. If they cannot agree to terms, they instead offer their services to the aggressor. This occurred numerous times during both the Fourth Succession War and the War of 3039. In the former case, the Wolves appeared in small numbers on world after world in the Capellan Confederation, seemingly with insider information as to where the Federated Suns forces would strike. Sadly, the Capellans ignored the obvious warning and lost most of those worlds as a result. That the Wolves always look out for themselves first, though, remains a constant trait; their studious avoidance of the Lyran portion of the Federated Commonwealth prior to the Clan Invasion is one such example.

Common Allies	All Great Houses and Periphery Powers
Common Enemies	None
Special Command Abilities	Environmental Specialization (Urban)

LONE WOLVES

The Lone Wolves generally total to a full regiment, but their Force composition varies drastically from month to month and battle to battle, as members come and go, and choose which battles to participate in. The Lone Wolves are notorious for territoriality and are known for fighting one another even during combat operations against a common enemy, usually over salvage from downed enemy units. The Lone Wolves have a reputation as urban specialists, and exhibit excellent maneuverability and skill in such terrain.

Experience Rating	Veteran
Force Composition	Any Inner Sphere Formation up to a regiment of 'Mechs and a battalion of non-'Mechs
Special Rules	Whenever two or more Lone Wolf Units of the same type combine fire on a target in the same turn that it is crippled or destroyed, roll 2d6. On a 2 or 12, the MechWarriors involved will fight one another over the salvage rights, to the exclusion of the battle raging around them. The two units suffer from the effect of Blood Stalker with each other as the "Chosen Enemy" until one is either destroyed or is forced to withdraw.

MARSHIGAMA'S LEGIONNAIRES

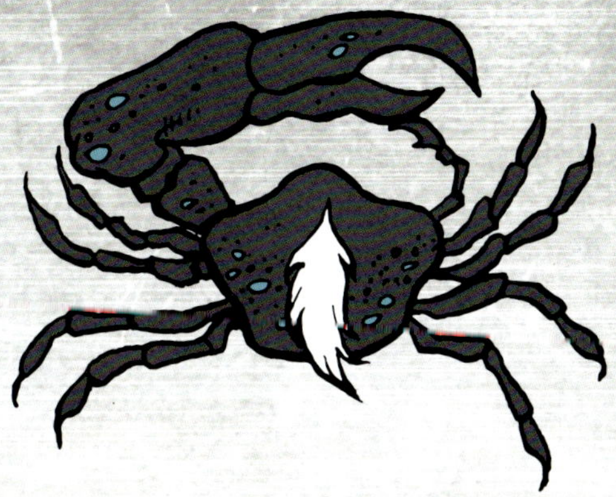

Marshigama's Legionnaires has served the Capellan Confederation for decades. They were never more than a run-of-the-mill outfit until the unit commander's daughter won a beauty contest. Ju-Lei Marshigama won Miss Ningpo in 3017, and inherited command of the Legionnaires soon after. It was then that the command gained some notoriety, as Marshigama cashiered all those who did not "look the part." Her view of the mercenary profession was a unique one, to say the least. She recruited only the most beautiful female MechWarriors, while male MechWarriors were required to have both facial hair and extensive, visible scarring. MechWarrior competence was a secondary concern, and a number of exceptional MechWarriors were turned away for not matching Marshigama's skewed opinion of how a MechWarrior should look. As a result, the Legionnaires attract some of the most vain, self-obsessed, and haughty MechWarriors in the mercenary profession.

The Legionnaires once boasted a considerable number of *Scorpion* and *Goliath* BattleMechs but lost almost all of these Quad 'Mechs during a disastrous mission to New Aragon late in the Third Succession War. The Aragon Borderers, alerted to the raid, sowed extensive command-detonated minefields and channeled the Legionnaires battalion into them. The Quad 'Mechs suffered greatly after the Borderers detonated the mines once the command was fully engulfed in the trap. Only a company of Legionnaires escaped. Since then, Marshigama has prioritized the command's Quads, of which only one of each type remains, as sort of a command mascot.

During the brief war sparked by the Andurien-Canopian invasion, the Legionnaires raided Bethonolog after taking a circuitous route from Borden, where the command saw no action. The Legionnaires spent the time following that conflict expanding back to a battalion for the first time since 3024. Colonel Marshigama still adheres to her unusual requirements, but her persistence and local fame has succeeded in delivering skilled MechWarriors who also match her physical ideal. The arrogance of the Legionnaires sometimes intimidates lesser enemies, the type of opponent the command prefers to fight.

Common Allies	Liao (Late Succession Wars, Early Clan Invasion)
Common Enemies	Davion, Marik (Late Succession Wars, Early Clan Invasion)
Special Command Abilities	Enemy Specialization (Davion), Brawlers, Sharp Shooters
Special Rules	If both Brawlers and Sharp Shooters SCAs are chosen for the Legionnaire Force, they may not be used at the same time. At the beginning of each turn the player must choose one of the two to apply that turn.

JU-LEI'S QUEENS

The command lance of the Legionnaires is entirely made up of former beauty queens such as Colonel Marshigama herself. Their self-centeredness makes them almost combat-ineffective at times, while they focus on their own actions rather than commanding the battalion.

Experience Rating	Veteran
Force Composition	1 'Mech lance; Colonel Marshigama's 'Mech is a *Scorpion*
Special Rules	All MechWarriors in Ju-Lei's Queens receive the Demoralizer Special Pilot Ability

MARSHIGAMA'S LEGIONNAIRES

The Legionnaires are organized along typical Inner Sphere battalion lines.

Experience Rating	Veteran
Force Composition	1 'Mech battalion; at least half of its 'Mechs must be medium (Size 2). Legionnaires XO Major Ti Ephem pilots a *Goliath* and commands the first company, Ephem's Exquisites. All lances must be Recon, Striker, Assault or one of the variants of those Formation types.
Special Rules	Designate one 'Mech per lance as the lance or company commander. Assign her either the Antagonizer or Demoralizer SPA. This replaces any one of the Special Pilot Abilities granted by the Formation's Bonus Ability.

THE PRETTY-BOYS

Colonel Marshigama's newest addition to the Legionnaires is a squadron of aerospace fighters. The pilots must meet the same requirements as MechWarriors, though they need not have facial hair. At present, only male fighter pilots have made the cut.

Experience Rating	Regular
Force Composition	1 aerospace fighter squadron.

The Northwind Highlanders are among the largest, longest-lived, and most respected mercenary commands of all time. The unit was first formed in 2362 by Clan Stuart on Northwind with the raising of the First Kearny Highlanders. The Scottish peoples who settled Northwind contained the last members of the families that served in the original Scottish regiments on Terra, a lineage tracing back centuries. The traditions maintained by those families formed the core of the First Kearny Highlanders' own practices. The regiment's success led to the formation of the Second Kearny Highlanders just one year after the First. Marion's Highlanders was raised in 2369, with Stirling's Fusiliers following in 2377.

The Highlanders achieved fame far and wide throughout human space even before the Star League existed. Once the League formed, the Highlanders were greatly respected by the SLDF, such that the Royal Black Watch which guarded the First Lord himself counted a number of Highlander MechWarriors among its force. When Stefan Amaris virtually wiped out the Black Watch with a nuclear attack, the few survivors hid among the Northwind Highlanders, who have kept that unit's traditions and memory alive, but secret, to the present day.

Even before the Exodus, the Highlander regiments had grown apart from the Northwind Clan elders who oversaw them. As a result, the Highlanders accepted a contract with the Capellan Confederation even while the Star League limped toward its ignominious end. When Northwind was captured by House Davion and two recently-founded Highlander regiments were destroyed, those in Capellan service simply accepted the fact with typical Highlander stoicism, knowing that one day they would return to their homeworld. Throughout the Succession Wars, the Highlanders served House Liao with honor and loyalty, never straying.

A poignant example of the steadfastness to see every mission to its bitter end occurred when the Second Kearny spent forty years hunting down every last member of Gladstone's Gladiators, a mercenary command that breached its contract with the Confederation. In 3008, the First Kearny faced down and actually defeated Zeta Battalion of Wolf's Dragoons, though only after calling in the Second Kearny. MacLeod's Highlanders fought the AFFS on numerous occasions throughout the First and Second Succession Wars, dealing significant defeats to the Deneb Light Cavalry on Acala in 2834, and crushing a battalion of the Second Avalon Hussars on Brighton in 2872. However, after centuries of loyal service, the Highlanders defected from the Confederation in the midst of the Fourth Succession War to take up employment with the Federated Suns, after Hanse Davion offered to restore the Highlanders to their homeworld.

The four active Highlander regiments each possess a separate command company and an aerospace fighter wing. Each battalion also has its own Command Lance. Each regiment has at least one company of combat vehicles instead of BattleMechs, giving the command tactical flexibility and excellent skill at combined arms warfare. Infantry is rare among the Highlanders, with the only such Formation of notable size attached to the First Kearny.

Even during the Succession Wars, the Highlanders were known for the large number of *Highlander* BattleMechs in their ranks. Most of these retained their Star League-era weaponry and components well into the Succession Wars, which contributed greatly to their long history of success in battle. The Highlanders are especially skilled in delivering the famed "Highlander Burial" maneuver.

Common Allies	Liao (Late Succession Wars), Davion (Early Clan Invasion)
Common Enemies	Davion (Late Succession Wars), Kurita (Late Succession Wars)
Special Command Abilities	Tactical Adjustments, *Highlander Burial*
Force Building Rules	The Northwind Highlanders may add access to the *Highlander* HGN-733 for 0 FP during the Late Succession Wars and the HGN-732 for 2 FPs in the Early Clan Invasion era.

FIRST KEARNY HIGHLANDERS

The First Kearny Highlanders are well-known for their utter refusal to leave the field of battle until they have achieved victory. This practice has resulted in horrific casualties, but the First Kearny has never retreated before an enemy. The elite command company admits only the best of the best. The fighter wing is an elite formation of medium fighters combining speed, armor, and weaponry. Third Company, Third Battalion is a tank company, with 'Mechs making up the rest of the regiment. The First Gurkhas are a special operations battalion of excellent quality, trailing only Wolf's Dragoons' Seventh Kommando for renown among mercenary special operators.

Experience Rating	Veteran
Force Composition	1 reinforced heavy 'Mech regiment, 1 medium aerospace fighter wing, 1 vehicle battalion, 1 infantry battalion
Special Command Abilities	*Esprit de Corps*, Forcing the Initiative

SECOND KEARNY HIGHLANDERS

The Second Kearny refuses to work in concert with any other mercenary command except their fellow Highlander regiments. When fighting against other mercenaries, the Second never accepts surrender. The elite command company always leads the regiment into battle. Second Company, Third Battalion is a tank company, with 'Mechs making up the rest of the regiment. The Second's fighter wing consists entirely of heavy fighters.

Experience Rating	Regular
Force Composition	1 medium 'Mech regiment, 1 heavy aerospace fighter wing, 1 vehicle battalion
Special Command Abilities	Enemy Specialization (Mercenary), Overrun Combat, Forcing the Initiative

MACLEOD'S HIGHLANDERS

MacLeod's Highlanders is notorious for its poor discipline; their disdain for authority once reached such a degree that the Capellan Confederation ordered the regiment disbanded. The order remained in effect for 13 years, during which time the Highlanders simply ignored it. The regiment has no specialization, as that would require a level of discipline and coordination between MechWarriors the unit does not possess. Instead, the regiment launches unconventional attacks that often defy tactical wisdom, snatching victory through sheer force of will rather than strategic acumen. Third Company, Third Battalion is a tank company, with 'Mechs making up the rest of the regiment. The members of the elite command company rarely coordinate their actions, instead pursuing personal targets in battle.

Experience Rating	Veteran
Force Composition	1 medium 'Mech regiment, 1 medium aerospace fighter wing, 1 vehicle battalion
Special Command Abilities	*Savages*

STIRLING'S FUSILIERS

Stirling's Fusiliers are nearly as reckless as MacLeod's Highlanders. Instead of the fierce individuality of that regiment, however, Fusilier MechWarriors simply improvise as the situation requires. This usually manifests itself as a headlong charge straight at their enemies—stealth is never an option. The veteran command company coordinates closely with its fighter wing to direct ground attacks. The second companies in both Second and Third Battalions are tank companies.

Experience Rating	Veteran
Force Composition	1 light 'Mech regiment, 1 light aerospace fighter wing, 1 vehicle battalion
Special Command Abilities	Tactical Specialization (Attack), Ground Attack Specialization

Captain Donald MacDonald

Captain Donald MacDonald is a fierce MechWarrior in command of Third Company, Second Battalion, First Kearny. His father was a Highlander who was killed by the Draconis Combine in the return to Northwind. He harbors a hatred for the Combine as a result, and lives for the day he might repay the Fifth Sword of Light. He trains constantly in Highlander Burials and has radically increased his accuracy firing when jumping.

CAPTAIN DONALD MACDONALD — **PV:** 46 (55) | 50 (60)

Unit Type	Skill	TP	SZ	MV	TMM	S/M/L	OV	A/S	Specials
Highlander **HGN-733** (Late Succession Wars)	3	BM	4	6j	1	3/3/2	1	9/7	IF1
Highlander **HGN-732** (Early Clan Invasion)	3	BM	4	6j	1	3/4/3	1	9/7	CASE, IF2
Special Pilot Abilities: Jumping Jack, Melee Master									

MCCARRON'S ARMORED CAVALRY

One of the Inner Sphere's most storied mercenary commands is McCarron's Armored Cavalry. The MAC is the only mercenary command that can actually rival Wolf's Dragoons in sheer size.

In 3022, the Cavalry mounted an ambitious assault on the Federated Suns. McCarron's Long March stunned the Davions by savaging defenses on more than a dozen worlds. They spent the next few years rebuilding before launching an equally audacious extraction raid against Kincaid Defiance Industries on Hesperus II.

The Cavalry was one of the few Capellan mercenary units that did not simply fold during the Fourth Succession War. In the Andurien-Canopian invasion, the Cavalry was seemingly everywhere, launching counterattacks to free worlds and spearheading invasions of Canopian worlds.

The MAC have since rebuilt to six active regiments, with a seventh training regiment on their homeworld, Menke. Because they are an integral component of the Capellan military, the Cavalry will be detailed in *Combat Manual: Liao*.

RAMILIE'S RAIDERS

Ramilie's Raiders has served the Magistracy of Canopus exclusively for almost 30 years, an association that began when the Raiders tired of contract breaches by the Capellan Confederation. They announced the end of their time in the Confederation by raiding a supply depot on the border and fleeing into the Periphery. Despite the dead-or-alive reward offered by the Chancellor, the Canopians welcomed the Raiders with open arms. The command was only a battalion at that time, but its specialization in speed provided an ideal quick reaction force for the Magistracy.

During their time in the Magistracy, the Raiders have doubled in size. Command Battalion remains primarily a fast, mobile battalion of 'Mechs. Assault Battalion, however, lacks any light 'Mechs and its few medium 'Mechs are the best-armed and armored of the class. The fighter complement of the Raiders is especially well-regarded in the Magistracy, where fighters and skilled pilots are precious commodities. Each battalion has a Command Lance, while Colonel Ramilie leads alongside an independent Command Lance.

Their long service to the Magistracy, where most of their current personnel were born, leads most military observers to consider the Raiders a Canopian unit.

Common Allies	None
Common Enemies	None
Special Command Abilities	Off-Map Movement, Banking Initiative, Tactical Specialization (Attack), Enemy Specialization (Mercenary)

COMMAND LANCE

Colonel Newton Ramilie enters battle less often than he once did. However, his Command Lance is composed of excellent MechWarriors who are experts with their 'Mechs.

Experience Rating	Elite
Force Composition	1 medium 'Mech lance

COMMAND BATTALION

Command Battalion is composed entirely of light and fast medium 'Mechs. The battalion is renowned for its incredible flanking maneuvers.

Experience Rating	Elite
Force Composition	1 light 'Mech battalion; all Units must be light or medium (Size 1 or 2)

ASSAULT BATTALION

Assault Battalion is a hard-hitting battalion of mostly heavy and assault 'Mechs. One lance of each company is made up of heavier medium 'Mechs with robust armor and weaponry including *Hunchbacks*, *Wolverines*, and *Griffins*. The Command Lance is a fearsome sight of four *Atlas*es, with Major Nicholas Ramilie, the colonel's son, forgoing the typical Raiders paint scheme for a flat charcoal gray with the death's-head cockpit a skeletal white.

Experience Rating	Veteran
Force Composition	1 heavy 'Mech battalion; at least half of the Units must be heavy or assault (Size 3 or 4).
Force Building Rules	The Assault Battalion may replace any SPA gained from a lance Bonus Ability with Speed Demon or Dodge.

SKY PIRATES

The Sky Pirates are two excellent squadrons of medium fighters. They excel at escort duties, but suffer in atmospheric combat.

Experience Rating	Elite
Force Composition	2 aerospace squadrons

THE PERIPHERY

Most mercenary commands in the Inner Sphere look down on their comrades who serve Periphery powers. However, service in the Periphery can be very rewarding, even compared to employment by a Great House. While wages and technical assistance may be lacking in the Periphery, mercenaries are likely to receive greater respect and autonomy when working for one of the larger Periphery powers.

Taurian Concordat

The Taurians are very generous with mercenary commands. However, if the mercenaries were previously employed by the Federated Suns, they may be regarded as spies or outright invaders. The Taurian citizenry often distrusts mercenaries, since it's rare for such warriors to seek employment outside the Inner Sphere.

Magistracy of Canopus

The Canopians are always eager to hire battle-tested mercenaries, whom they hold responsible only for their own actions and not those of the entire industry. Unlike the Taurian peoples, Canopians are happy to engage with mercenaries. This is largely due to the relatively high wages mercenaries receive, and the various pleasure industries that cater especially to recently-paid soldiers of fortune.

17TH RECON REGIMENT

The Seventeenth Recon Regiment, also known as Camacho's Caballeros, is a professional mercenary unit that is often compared to a traveling circus—a criticism that falters when the commentator observes the Seventeenth in battle.

Composed of Free Worlds League expatriates mostly hailing from the Trinity Worlds, the Seventeenth has spent the bulk of its existence working contracts for the Federated Commonwealth. A recent raid ordered by the Commonwealth against the Capellan world of Larsha humbled the Seventeenth. A lone civilian, armed with a rifle and broom, single-handedly disabled one of the Seventeenth's *Wolverines*. For any other command, this humiliation might be difficult to overcome, but Colonel Carlos Camacho's daughter, Lt. SG Patricia Camacho, instead recruited the brave woman. Lt. JG Cassie Suthorn is still adjusting to life in the Seventeenth, and the command's posting to Borgan's Rift under contract to the Magistracy of Canopus seems certain to test her resolve. The current contract is to hunt down the Red Lion pirate band; Lt. Suthorn has been assigned as a scout for this mission.

Common Allies	Steiner (Late Succession Wars)
Common Enemies	Kurita (Late Succession Wars)
Special Command Abilities	Environmental Specialization (Urban), Environmental Specialization (Night), *Hit and Run*

SEVENTEENTH RECON REGIMENT

The regiment is composed of three battalions plus a single regimental Command Lance.

Experience Rating	Regular
Force Composition	1 light 'Mech regiment; at least half of the Unit's 'Mechs must be light or medium (Size 1 or 2)

SCOUT COMPANY

Scout Company is a special forces infantry unit who are experts at spotting concealed enemies for the 'Mech regiment and greatly reducing the success of enemy ambushes.

Experience Rating	Elite
Force Composition	1 infantry company

THE PERIPHERY [CONTINUED]

Outworlds Alliance

The Outworlds Alliance is unique in the Periphery for refusing to hire mercenaries, though individual planetary governments occasionally engage mercenary services for defensive operations only.

Bandit Kingdoms

The many bandit kingdoms dotting the Periphery are always eager to court mercenaries. However, commands hired by these pirates can expect low pay, unsavory missions, and almost certain betrayal.

SCREAMING EAGLES

The Screaming Eagles descend from the SLDF's 250th BattleMech Division, nicknamed the Stalingrad Division. As part of the Seventh Army's LVIII Corps, the division was deployed to the Capellan Confederation and was part of the force sent to end the Second Periphery Rebellion. After defeating the Periphery rebels, the division joined Kerensky in liberating Terra. However, when the general called for the Exodus, the division split on whether to join those leaving the Inner Sphere. The 555th and 556th Honor Brigades chose to remain behind. They entered service as mercenaries contracted to the Federated Suns, deeming House Davion to be closest to embodying the ideals of House Cameron and the Star League. The brigades chose the name Screaming Eagles as they transitioned to their new lives.

The First and Second Succession Wars were as terrible for the Eagles as for the rest of the Inner Sphere, and the two brigades were shattered during the decades of war. Of their initial six regiments, only two survived, along with one tank regiment, the Seventy-seventh Heavy Armor. The command has never fallen much below this size, at least not for long. As a premiere mercenary command with an excellent reputation, the Eagles always replace losses quickly and with excellent personnel. The command embraced the combined arms tactics of the AFFS and added regiments of fighters and infantry through the years.

Through the first three Succession Wars, the Screaming Eagles remained a stalwart and honorable component of the Federated Suns military. That changed in the Fourth Succession War. As part of the invasion force hitting New Canton, the First Screaming Eagles were harassed repeatedly by the Fourth Confederation Reserve Cavalry. The Eagles were frustrated after failing time and again to pin down the mobile Fourth. When they finally cornered the Fourth on the banks of the Canton River, the Capellans surrendered. Instead of taking the enemy MechWarriors into custody, however, Colonel Opson Mathis had their cockpits welded shut and the 'Mechs pushed into the swollen river. This casual murder of surrendered enemy troops led to Colonel Mathis' dismissal from the Eagles and strained the unit's relationship with House Davion. The Eagles bore up under the stain on their honor, though, and remained in service to the Federated Commonwealth.

The War of 3039 was not much kinder to the Eagles. After missing out on the conquest of Elidere IV due to a misjump, the First Eagles settled in as the world's garrison force. When two of the Combine's surprise Ghost Regiments arrived and engaged them, the Eagles were sorely outmatched. The Ghost Regiments utilized Star League-era 'Mechs whose weapons had greater range and inflicted greater damage than the Eagles' own. The First lost half its force before surrendering and leaving the world in abject defeat.

The poor performance in 3039, compounded with their dishonorable actions in the Fourth Succession War, has left the Eagles in an untenable position. They are frankly not trusted by the AFFC High Command, as evidenced by their posting to the Periphery border. The nearby Filtvelt Academy has not approached them to aid instruction of cadets, while Tortuga Prime sends pirates regularly to raid the Eagles' garrison worlds of Mararn and Sodertalje. Though the raiders rarely escape unscathed or with any loot, the Eagles remain demoralized and unable to remove the stain on their honor. The High Command does not expect to renew the Eagles' contract, and the mercenaries will be forced to seek employment outside the Federated Suns for the first time ever.

The Eagles remain a very effective combined arms command. Besides the two 'Mech regiments, the Eagles have full regiments of fighters, combat vehicles, and infantry. These elements often coordinate their combat actions with one of the 'Mech regiments, but they are equally effective when operating independently.

Common Allies	Davion (Late Succession Wars)
Common Enemies	Liao (Late Succession Wars), Kurita (Late Succession Wars)
Special Command Abilities	Off-Map Movement, Tactical Specialization (Attack)

FIRST SCREAMING EAGLES

The First Screaming Eagles are a medium 'Mech regiment. Each battalion's Command Lance is comprised of heavy 'Mechs, making them the slowest lances in the regiment. Light 'Mechs make up one lance in each company and serve as advanced scouts while the speedy medium 'Mechs of the other two lances follow in their heels. The First relies on the First Wing of the Diving Eagles to bomb enemies into submission before engaging directly, as the they prefer flanking maneuvers and oblique attacks.

Experience Rating	Regular
Force Composition	1 medium 'Mech regiment; at least half of the Force's 'Mechs must be medium (Size 2)
Special Command Abilities	Environmental Specialization (Woods), Environmental Specialization (Rough).

SECOND SCREAMING EAGLES

Each battalion of the Second Eagles has a particular specialty. First Battalion excels at night combat, Second Battalion is an infiltration unit, and Third Battalion specializes in long-range engagements, using pinpoint accuracy to shatter enemies from extreme range. Like the First Eagles, the Second Eagles are a medium 'Mech regiment, though the Second's Command Lances are also of medium weight. Each battalion includes a heavy 'Mech lance which usually joins the Seventy-seventh Heavy Armor's tanks when that regiment is attached to Second.

Experience Rating	Regular
Force Composition	1 medium 'Mech regiment; at least half of the Force's 'Mechs must be medium (Size 2)
Special Command Abilities	Environmental Specialization (Night), Sharp Shooters

DIVING EAGLES

The Diving Eagles are a regiment of three fighter wings, plus a command squadron encompassing the Command Lances of each wing. Each wing relies exclusively on heavy fighters, usually loaded with as many bombs as they can carry. These fighters usually endure punishment from enemy dogfighters thanks to their heavy armor, and once their bombs have been loosed, they engage and seek air superiority.

Experience Rating	Regular
Force Composition	1 heavy aerospace fighter regiment; all Units must be heavy (Size 3).

77TH HEAVY ARMOR

The Seventy-seventh Heavy Armor is the only armor Formation remaining from the Eagles' original SLDF brigades. The tanks are primarily heavy and assault Units, used to maintain the holes opened by the lighter 'Mechs of the First and Second Eagles. The Seventy-seventh's ability to integrate with either 'Mech regiment achieves a combat synergy beyond that of the individual elements.

Experience Rating	Regular
Force Composition	1 heavy vehicle regiment; at least half the Force's vehicles must be heavy or assault (Size 3 or 4)
Special Command Abilities	Overrun Combat

NESTED EAGLES

The Nested Eagles are the infantry regiment of the Screaming Eagles. The regiment is usually tasked with base security. However, when entering combat, the Nested Eagles deploys jump infantry battalions to support other ground units. The infantry shines brightest when operating in urban areas.

Experience Rating	Regular
Force Composition	1 infantry regiment
Special Command Abilities	Environmental Specialization (Urban)

Major Cindy "Sin" Johanson

Major Cindy Johanson is a known carouser when off-duty, but is a fierce opponent in her *Cicada*. Her maneuvering skills allow her to skirt enemy fire lanes and return fire with unerring accuracy. As the executive officer of the Second Screaming Eagles, she wields considerable influence over the regiment. However, disciplinary problems have kept her from being promoted further. She has often considered leaving the Eagles in hopes of joining a command with a better reputation, with whom she might see combat against more than occasional pirates. Her 'Mech is an experimental model, and no one knows precisely how or when she acquired it. When asked, she simply winks and smiles. Its many advanced technologies often result in problems while in the field.

MAJOR CINDY "SIN" JOHANSON — **PV:** 17 (23) | 25 (35)

Unit Type	Skill	TP	SZ	MV	TMM	S/M/L	OV	A/S	Specials
***Cicada* CDA-3C** (Late Succession Wars)	2	BM	2	14	3	2/1/1	0	2/3	
***Cicada* CDA-3F** (Early Clan Invasion)	2	BM	2	16j	3	2/1/1	0	4/2	ENE
Special Pilot Abilities: Lucky, Speed Demon; enemies targeting Johanson suffer a +1 To-Hit Modifier at Long Range									
Quirk: Johanson's CDA-3F has the Prototype Quirk									

SIMONSON'S CUTTHROATS

Simonson's Cutthroats was long known as McGee's Cutthroats, which served the Draconis Combine for most of the Third Succession War. In 2953, the Cutthroats landed on Alexandria in the Lyran Commonwealth, but their efforts to raid Lyran supply depots soon turned for the worse. The Twentieth Arcturan Guards and the Alexandria Militia coordinated their defensive efforts and cut the mercenaries off from their DropShips. Unable to retreat, the Cutthroats called for reinforcements. The arriving DCMS troops led the Commonwealth to send in reinforcements of their own, and a grinding stalemate resulted. The Cutthroats finally withdrew alongside their DCMS allies two years later, ending the largest battle along the Commonwealth-Combine border in the Third War. More than seven regiments took part in the ultimately inconsequential conflict.

The Cutthroats remained a lynchpin of the DCMS into the Fourth Succession War, fighting on even after the Death to Mercenaries decree. However, the Combine citizenry increasingly targeted the mercenaries with protests and vandalism. After the Cutthroats invaded and conquered Groveld III for the Combine, the command's executive officer was assassinated by guerilla troops. The replacement XO was Matthew Simonson, who mutinied along with much of the command due to the anti-mercenary vitriol. Colonel Andrew McGee was eventually defeated, and the remaining and renamed Cutthroats followed now-Colonel Simonson to Galatea after exercising the command's early escape clause from Combine employ. They signed on with the new Federated Commonwealth and have remained there since.

Matthew Simonson's son, Jeri, inherited command several years ago and is grooming his own son Victor to one day lead the Cutthroats.

Common Allies	Kurita (Late Succession Wars)
Common Enemies	Steiner (Late Succession Wars)
Special Command Abilities	*Hit and Run, Tactical Expert (Hidden Units)*, Off-Map Movement

SIMONSON'S CUTTHROATS

The Cutthroats specialize in guerilla-style warfare. Their best successes have come when operating for extended periods behind enemy lines and destroying supply depots, enemy headquarters, and communication stations. As a result, a very large percentage of their 'Mechs rely on energy weapons rather than ammunition-dependent systems. The Cutthroats' stealth tactics and camouflage expertise make them exceptional at moving undetected, even by BattleMech sensors in the right environments. Many defenders report sudden attacks by the Cutthroats from close range despite the presence of friendly BattleMechs on patrol.

Experience Rating	Veteran
Force Composition	1 medium 'Mech regiment; at least half the Force's 'Mechs must have the ENE special ability or not have an ammo-based special ability (AC, SRM, LRM, IF, NARC, TOR, ART)
Force Building Rules	The Cutthroats may replace any SPA granted by a lance's Bonus Ability with the Weapon Specialist SPA.

Captain Victor Simonson

Captain Victor Simonson is the son of the Colonel Jeri Simonson and commands Second Company, First Battalion of the Cutthroats. He has been disciplined for his single-mindedness in combat, often suffering target fixation instead of focusing on the big picture. In addition to the stealth tactics the Cutthroats practice, Victor has been training his company for flanking maneuvers. While mid-speed 'Mechs fill much of the regiment, Victor's company is entirely fast medium and light 'Mechs. They are training in flanking maneuvers and have become fairly adept as a cavalry force.

CAPTAIN VICTOR SIMONSON — PV: 16

Unit Type	Skill	TP	SZ	MV	TMM	S/M/L	OV	A/S	Specials
Spider SDR-5V	4	BM	1	16j	3	1/1/0	0	2/3	ENE

Special Rules: Simonson possesses the Blood Stalker SPA. At the end of each turn, his controlling player rolls 2d6. On an 8+, a new "Chosen Enemy" for Simonson may be designated.

SMITHSON'S CHINESE BANDITS

Smithson's Chinese Bandits formed just prior to the First Succession War when two venerable mercenary commands, Dawson's River Raiders and the Jade Warriors, were chased out of the Capellan Confederation for alleged dereliction of duty. In truth, the commands' Capellan liaison was embezzling their pay, so the two "independent BattleMech specialists" units refused to fight on Aldebaran and Azha, respectively. When the two commands arrived on Galatea within days of one another, and knowing each had been victimized by the same corrupt official, they joined forces. The lighter Raiders and heavier Warriors combined to form two regiments of hard-hitting mercenaries with no love for the Confederation. They named themselves the Chinese Bandits, with Warriors' CO Alan Smithson taking command after winning a game of dice over the Raiders' commander. The command almost immediately signed on with the Free Worlds League, giving them a chance to repay their former Capellan employers.

The command has spent the last two and a half centuries fighting for the Federated Suns, the Lyran Commonwealth or Free Worlds League, primarily the latter. Their contract terms ensure the command receives greater pay for fighting non-Capellans than for fighting their hated enemies. This places them against the Confederation more often than not.

The Bandits supported Captain-General Janos Marik in the Marik Civil War, and briefly faced Wolf's Dragoons on Fuentes. In the Fourth Succession War, the Bandits invaded and captured Milton from the Lyran Commonwealth. Since then, the command has sated itself with occasional raids across the Confederation border from Kyrkbacken and Asuncion.

Common Allies	Marik (Late Succession Wars)
Common Enemies	Liao (Late Succession Wars)
Special Command Abilities	Enemy Specialization (Liao)

FIRST SMITHSON'S CHINESE BANDITS

The Bandits use a traditional organizational scheme for their BattleMechs. The heavier Second Battalion moves in steadily when needed, while the lighter First and Third Battalions hit the enemy on the flanks. Jungle and wooded terrain are the Bandits' preferred environments. The First's heavy fighter wing, the Air Bandits, fights for air superiority in all cases, launching ground attacks once the enemy's fighters have been eliminated. The Ground Bandits, a mixed force of infantry and tanks, excels in urban combat while the 'Mechs remain outside the tight confines of cities.

Experience Rating	Veteran
Force Composition	1 medium 'Mech regiment, 1 heavy aerospace fighter wing, 1 infantry battalion, 1 vehicle battalion; all aerospace fighters must be heavy (Size 3)
Special Command Abilities	Environmental Specialization (Woods), Environmental Specialization (Urban).

MechWarrior Wendall Puritan II

Puritan left the Lyran Commonwealth when he learned his family 'Mech was slated to be scrapped by the Quartermaster Corps. He has struggled with its upkeep after the Fourth Succession War and was unable to procure a replacement for his damaged PPC and has been forced to use a large laser instead. Though he misses the bite of the PPC, he enjoys using the additional tonnage to add more armor.

MECHWARRIOR WENDALL PURITAN II — **PV:** 27 (32) | 32 (38)

Unit Type	Skill	TP	SZ	MV	TMM	S/M/L	OV	A/S	Specials
***Scorpion* SCP-1N Wendall**	3	BM	2	12	2	2/2/0	0	5/5	
***Scorpion* SCP-1N Wendall 2**	3	BM	2	14	3	3/3/0	0	6/3	

Special Pilot Abilities: Hopper, Lucky (3)

SECOND SMITHSON'S CHINESE BANDITS

The Second Bandits use the same organization as the First Bandits, but the Second specializes in combat in harsh terrain. First Battalion are experts in alpine warfare, Second Battalion is best in desert and airless conditions, and Third Battalion is devastating in urban areas. The Sky Bandits use a mix of medium and heavy fighters, specializing in dogfights with enemy fighters. The Rock Bandits train extensively with the Ground Bandits, sharing the same tactical expertise.

Experience Rating	Regular
Force Composition	1 medium 'Mech regiment, 1 heavy aerospace fighter wing, 1 infantry battalion, 1 vehicle battalion
Speical Command Abilities	Anti-Air Specialists, Environmental Specialization (Mountains), Environmental Specialization (Hot), Environmental Specialization (Vacuum), Environmental Specialization (Urban)

Lieutenant Lissa Gompers

After years of excellent service, Lissa Grompers was promoted to command a lance in the Second Bandits. Her *Crusader* was acquired via the black market. Her LRMs are only a means to provide cover as she closes on the enemy; Gompers' uncanny accuracy when charging an opponent has earned her a reputation for deadly efficacy in combat.

LIEUTENANT LISSA GOMPERS — **PV:** 34 (41)

Unit Type	Skill	TP	SZ	MV	TMM	S/M/L	OV	A/S	Specials
***Crusader* CRD-3K**	3	BM	3	8	1	3/3/2	1	6/5	IF1, LRM1/1/1, SRM1/1/1

Special Pilot Abilities: Prior to the beginning of play, assign two SPAs to Lieutenant Lissa Gompers from the following: Cluster Hitter, Luck (2), Speed Demon

12TH STAR GUARDS

The Twelfth Star Guards began as two SLDF regiments that remained behind after the Exodus. The Forty-second Striker and Tenth Heavy Assault Regiments signed on with the Capellan Confederation and were assigned the defense of twelve systems, from which they took the name the Twelve Star Guards. This name evolved into the command's current moniker.

From the original two regiments, the Twelfth actually grew in size during the Succession Wars, swelling to seven regiments at one point in the Second Succession War. During service to the Draconis Combine, one regiment mutinied and fled when the Combine failed to pay them for nearly a year. Another regiment was abandoned by the Combine and destroyed by the Federated Suns, ending the command's association with the Combine forever.

The Twelfth then alternated between the Lyran Commonwealth and Federated Suns, sometimes dealing with payroll issues and other morale-damaging actions. The Guards have remained in the employ of the Federated Commonwealth since the two nations' unification.

The Guards have maintained many of their Star League traditions through the centuries, giving them a certain bearing even in battle that affects their enemies. Many opposing forces report being outmaneuvered with ease despite possessing better tactical deployment. The Guards are excellent when on the attack, but suffer slightly on defense.

Common Allies	Steiner (Late Succession Wars), Davion (Late Succession Wars)
Common Enemies	Kurita (Late Succession Wars)
Special Command Abilities	Tactical Specialization (Attack), *Esprit de Corps*, *Tactical Adjustments*, *Tactical Experts (Engineers)*

GUARD PRIMARY

Guard Primary is the command company of the Twelfth, comprising the four Command Lances of each regiment. Guard Primary rarely assembles as a single combat force, as the four regiments are usually deployed to separate worlds. However, on annual maneuvers, Guard Primary attaches itself to each regiment in turn to observe performance as the four Guards regiments engage in mock battles against one another.

Experience Rating	Elite
Force Composition	1 reinforced 'Mech company. Each lance must be a Command Lance.

FIRST REGIMENT "RIVERS GAMBLERS"

First Regiment is the primary Formation of the command. Guards commanding officer Colonel Charles Carranza usually remains at headquarters to oversee the entire regiment's deployment. When he enters battle, however, his troops are motivated to impress him and perform beyond their usual capabilities. First regiment consists of mostly medium and faster heavy 'Mechs.

Experience Rating	Veteran
Force Composition	1 medium 'Mech regiment, 1 medium fighter wing; at least half of the Force's 'Mechs must be medium or heavy (Size 2 or 3) with a minimum Move of 10"

SECOND REGIMENT "OHELL'S HEAVIES"

Second Regiment holds tightly to its grudge against the Draconis Combine, in honor of those comrades lost due to Combine duplicity. The ferocity they tap into when fighting any Combine units or their allies has greatly impressed the Guards' Federated Commonwealth employers. Second Regiment's First and Second Battalions use assault and heavy 'Mechs, while Third Battalion fields light and medium 'Mechs.

Experience Rating	Regular
Force Composition	1 heavy 'Mech regiment , 1 medium fighter wing
Special Command Abilities	Enemy Specialization (Kurita)

THIRD REGIMENT "PAGET'S WAR PONIES"

Third specializes in long-range combat, a focus that has caused a deterioration in combat acumen at close range. Their preference for engaging at range has improved their skills in hindering terrain. Third Regiment uses a mix of medium, heavy, and assault 'Mechs in each company.

Experience Rating	Veteran
Force Composition	1 heavy 'Mechregiment, 1 medium fighter wing; the Force may not field light (Size 1) 'Mechs
Special Command Abilities	Sharp Shooters, Environmental Specialist (Woods), Environmental Specialist (Rough)

SEVENTH REGIMENT "SCOVY'S IRONMEN"

The Seventh is a combined arms regiment. The current incarnation is still relatively green and is training to improve individual warriors' skills. However, intense training with Federated Commonwealth RCTs has greatly smoothed operations between the regiment's varying Unit types. The regiment has devoted a special focus to combat in wooded terrain. The Seventh uses fast medium and light 'Mechs, fast wheeled and hovertanks, and jump infantry.

Experience Rating	Green
Force Composition	1 light 'Mech regiment, 1 light vehicle battalion, 1 infantry battalion, 1 medium fighter wing; the Force may not field assault (Size 4) 'Mechs
Special Command Abilities	Environmental Specialist (Woods)

Captain Leif Fogerty

Captain Leif Fogerty competed in the Noisiel Summer Games in 3049. While he didn't win the championship, his exceptional performance caught the eye of many mercenary recruiters. Five different commands bid for his services, with Third Regiment of the Twelfth Star Guards winning the competition. Fogerty's reward for advancing to the semi-finals of the games only recently arrived at the Third's Station on Icar, but his *Marauder* is the most advanced 'Mech in the Guards. Fogerty is still growing accustomed to his new situation; he often ignores orders and does what seems best to him, including leaving his comrades open to flanking attacks.

CAPTAIN LEIF FOGERTY — **PV:** 36 (43)

Unit Type	Skill	TP	SZ	MV	TMM	S/M/L	OV	A/S	Specials
Marauder MAD-5S	3	BM	3	8	1	4/4/4	1	6/3	CASE

Special Pilot Abilities: Combat Intuition, Lucky (1)

Special Rules: Captain Leif Fogerty is not available to field as part of a Star Guards Formation in the Late Succession Wars era.

VALLEY OF DESPAIR

Dun Valley
Loric
Lyran Commonwealth
4 June 2978

The Twelfth Star Guards were on annual maneuvers with the Eridani Light Horse on Loric when the Third Regulan Hussars arrived to avenge a Guards raid into Marik space three months earlier. The Eleventh Recon Battalion of the Seventy-first Light Horse Regiment performed a combat drop behind the Hussars' lines. but ran into a Hussars assault battalion. The Eleventh retreated into the Dun Valley and found themselves trapped. First Regiment of the Twelfth Star Guards was nearby, and charged in to break through the Hussars and relieve the Eleventh. The First detailed its First Battalion, which split into companies to seek weak points in the Hussars' line. Other efforts to break through took place in Digger Pass and along the Duren River, while the other Guards distracted the assault battalion.

GAME SETUP

Recommended Terrain: Rolling Hills, Scattered Woods

If using hex maps, arrange two maps with their short edges touching.

The Defender chooses a home edge. The Attacker's home edge is the opposite edge.

ATTACKER

Twelfth Star Guards (Veteran)

The Attacker consists of one company of First Battalion, First Regiment of the Twelfth Star Guards. The Attacker must exit at least one lance via the Defender's home edge before Turn 8.

DEFENDER

Third Regulan Hussars (Veteran)

The Defender consists of one company of Second Battalion, Third Regulan Hussars. Second Battalion is composed entirely of heavy and assault (Size 3 and 4) 'Mechs. The Defender is placed on the map before Turn 1. The Defender's objective is to prevent the Attacker's units from exiting via the Defender's home edge.

4TH TAU CETI RANGERS

The Fourth Tau Ceti Rangers trace their lineage back to the SLDF's Eighty-first Mechanized Infantry Division, which already bore the nickname "4th Tau Ceti Rangers" and stayed behind when the SLDF departed. The division chose to become mercenaries in order to preserve their own legacy and traditions, rather than disband or become House troops. They signed with Chancellor Barbara Liao on the condition of maintaining independent command rights; that agreement has been honored by every Chancellor since, ensuring the Rangers remain in Capellan service.

Fate has been alternately kind and indifferent to the Rangers. The command has reached regimental size and been battered back to a single battalion more than once, most recently in the Fourth Succession War. The Rangers' determined defense of Tikonov failed against overwhelming Davion numbers; later in the war, the reorganized command mauled the First NAIS Cadet Cadre. In a subsequent action, the Rangers' second battalion was defeated by the First Kathil Uhlans, who used the Rangers' surrendered DropShips to infiltrate Sian and attack the Capellan capital directly.

In 3042, the last hereditary Branderberg commander retired, ending a line of leadership which began during the Second Succession War. The Jax family assumed command, with Colonel Jacoby Jax currently leading the Rangers. Their deployment to Sian is a measure of recognition of their long service, but also serves to keep them close after their role in allowing the Kathil Uhlans to land unopposed on Capellan soil.

Common Allies	Liao (Late Succession Wars, Early Clan Invasion)
Common Enemies	Davion (Late Succession Wars), Marik (Late Succession Wars)
Special Command Abilities	*Esprit de Corps*, Environmental Specialization (Urban), Environmental Specialization (Woods), Environmental Specialization (Mountains), *Tactical Experts (Engineers)*, Tactical Specialization (Defense)

4TH TAU CETI RANGERS

Tau Ceti Command is a hard-hitting battalion composed entirely of heavy and assault 'Mechs. Colonel Jax is an inspirational commander who makes his troops perform better simply by his presence. Second Company includes two lances of Star League era 'Mechs, which make good use of their advanced technology to overwhelm opponents, and specializes in urban warfare. Third Company is the alpine combat company, preferring combat in mountainous, wooded terrain.

Experience Rating	Veteran
Force Composition	2 heavy 'Mech battalions (pre-3029); 1 heavy 'Mech battalion (post-3029); at least half of the Force's Units must be heavy or assault (Size 3 or 4)
Force Building Rules	The Fourth Tau Ceti Rangers may select from the following Star League era 'Mechs for 0 FP each: *Flashman* FLS-7K, *Crockett* CRK-5003-0, *Crab* CRB-20. During the Early Clan Invasion, they may add access to the following 'Mechs for 2 FPs each: *Flashman* FLS-8K, *Crockett* CRK-5003-1, *Crab* CRB-27.

HARD AIR

The Rangers' fighter wing is a deadly Formation of heavy aerospace fighters. In space combat, the fighters routinely head directly at incoming enemies, counting on their guns to destroy the enemy before they collide. In atmospheric combat, the fighters often select the heaviest enemy 'Mech and make an example of it. They will form a strafing or bombing line and engage the same target in series; the massed firepower often leaves little more than a crater behind.

Experience Rating	Veteran
Force Composition	1 heavy aerospace fighter wing; the Force may not include any light (Size 1) Units.

Captain Orion Saddleford

Captain Orion Saddleford forms the anvil of the Tau Ceti Rangers. In a unit known for its ability to hold at all costs, Saddleford is the one trusted to center the Rangers' line. Soft-spoken, his calm in the face of even the strongest attack reassures those under his command, even when engaging in constant withdrawals like those the Rangers faced on Tikonov.

Orion's *Crockett* is one of the last remaining Star League-quality models left in the Rangers. The techs have managed to keep its advanced heat sinks working, but had to replace the weaponry with more common components.

CAPTAIN ORION SADDLEFORD									**PV:** 49/59
Unit Type	**Skill**	**TP**	**SZ**	**MV**	**TMM**	**S/M/L**	**OV**	**A/S**	**Specials**
***Crockett* CRK-5003-0 (Saddleford)**	2	BM	4	6j	1	4/5/2	0	9/7	AC1/1/-,SRM1/1
Special Pilot Abilities: Dodge, Iron Will									

WACO RANGERS

The Waco Rangers were a band of down-on-their-luck MechWarriors, including rejects and washouts from House militaries and other mercenary commands until Wayne Waco forged them into a respectable fighting force. Waco's focus changed when his son John was killed in battle with Wolf's Dragoons. Waco swore revenge based on reports that a Dragoon 'Mech deliberately stepped on John after he ejected from his 'Mech; this account was never verified and has always been denied by the Dragoons.

Every Rangers' contract contains a clause requiring that Waco be informed if his employer plans to hire the Dragoons, so Waco can cancel his own contract. Chancellor Maximilian Liao ignored this and hired the Dragoons in 3011, leading Waco to void the contract and raid warehouses on Korion before departing Capellan space. Liao was livid, primarily because his attempt to ignore the contract he agreed to blew up in his face.

Waco spent the next few decades pursuing his one-sided vendetta, catching up with the Dragoons in 3024. Hearing rumors of a battalion of Dragoons on Hyperion, he planned to exterminate them. The two Dragoon regiments he found there drove him off, though the Rangers did destroy a number of Dragoons before fleeing.

Waco is semi-retired, having turned command over to Colonel Wayne Rogers, who dislikes the fact that his officers check with Waco first before obeying his orders. Their current posting to Epsilon in the Duchy of Tamarind-Abbey of the Free Worlds League positions them on the Lyran border of the Federated Commonwealth. The posting has been uneventful, and several MechWarriors have departed the command seeking more action.

Common Allies	None
Common Enemies	None
Special Command Abilities	Enemy Specialization (Mercenary), Ground Attack Specialists, *Berserkers*
Force Building Rules	Waco Rangers may select up to three units from any House availability list, for the Late Succession Wars, per company. These units must each be from a different House availability list, and cost 2 FPs each

RANGER COMMAND

The regimental command company often deploys to combat independently to maintain its warriors' skills.

Experience Rating	Elite
Force Composition	1 'Mech company
Special Command Abilities	If facing any Wolf's Dragoons Force, Ranger Command gains *Esprit de Corps* and duplicates the effects of *Berserkers*, resulting in a -2 To-Hit modifier for all attacks and reducing their Target Movement Modifier by 2 to a minimum of 0.

WACO'S RANGERS

The Rangers have a reputation for instability, earning them the nickname "Wacko's Rangers." However, their prior status as the dregs of the industry vanished long ago as they proved their mettle time and again against tough opposition. They lose as often as they win, but exact a toll on those who defeat them.

Experience Rating	Veteran
Force Composition	1 heavy 'Mech regiment

AIR RANGERS

Major Alfred Pointers has commanded the Air Rangers for the past four years. The Rangers have four spare fighters captured from the Federated Commonwealth three months ago, but have not yet secured skilled pilots to operate them.

Experience Rating	Veteran
Force Composition	2 medium aerospace fighter squadrons

12TH VEGAN RANGERS

TYPICAL RANK STRUCTURE

Most mercenaries use a simplified Star League rank structure. When employed by a House military, a unit's commander reports to an officer at least one rank higher than themselves. When working for a corporation, they likely report to a security chief, regardless of the commander's rank. Ranks typically lead the formation size noted, including a mixed-unit force adding up to the stated size.

Brigadier General: Brigadier generals are only found in multi-regiment mercenary commands as the commanding officer of the entire unit. The admiralty equivalent rank is Rear Admiral for officers commanding a fleet of space vessels.

Colonel: A colonel commands a regiment. The admiralty equivalent is captain, who commands a JumpShip or DropShip.

Lieutenant Colonel: A lieutenant colonel is often a colonel's executive officer, but may command a battalion (or aerospace wing) in a regiment-sized force. The admiralty equivalent is commander, either the executive officer or the senior officer overseeing department heads.

Major: A major commands a battalion (or wing). The admiralty equivalent is lieutenant commander, who leads a large department.

Captain: A captain commands a company (or squadron). The equivalent admiralty rank is lieutenant, who would oversee a small department or large work center, or serve as an aide to the captain.

The legendary origins of the Twelfth Vegan Rangers and the Duke of Verde is a romantic tale of Dumasian revenge set at the waning years of the First Succession War. What is on record, however, is that the Rangers were officially formed during the Second Succession War, when the Duke did not want his personal army to be nationalized by the desperate AFFS and converted his troops into a mercenary command. Income from hiring out the force enriched the duke and Verde, allowing the Rangers to expand to four full regiments. In the centuries since, the Rangers have honorably and ably served both the Suns and the Lyran Commonwealth.

Perhaps the Rangers' greatest claim to fame came during the Galtor Campaign, a planetary assault which saw the return of combat on a scale not seen since the Second Succession War. Margrave Sheridan Douglass of Verde led Alpha Regiment into the campaign. Alpha was seemingly everywhere during the fighting, bailing out flagging AFFS troops and mauling Combine forces one after another. The world remained in Davion hands, thanks primarily to the daring, effort, and self-sacrifice of Alpha Regiment.

The Fourth Succession War found all four Rangers regiments driving into Capellan territory, and conquest of what became the Sarna March benefited greatly from the skilled Rangers. The unit garrisoned a quartet of the new Federated Commonwealth worlds after the war, ensuring that the Capellans would not easily recover their lost territory.

Gamma and Delta Regiments took part in the War of 3039. Both initially succeeded in their first objectives, as the worlds of Nashira and Telos IV fell to them and their Commonwealth allies. However, bureaucratic and logistics failures caused the front-line combat troops to remain in place, putting down riots and guerilla attacks while their security and military police relief forces were seriously delayed. Both regiments soon retreated back to Federated Commonwealth territory when the war swung to the Combine's favor.

Margrave Douglass retired and turned command over to Tom Stancel, the first time in several generations the Rangers were led by someone other than a royal from Verde. By virtue of long service and high respect for the Rangers, Stancel was recognized as a full general by the AFFC, a rare honor for a mercenary command.

The four Rangers regiments operate as completely independent commands, except on extremely rare occasions when a truly large force is required to achieve a single objective. Each regiment has a permanently attached fighter wing and tank battalion in addition to the 'Mech forces.

Common Allies	Davion (Late Succession Wars, Early Clan Invasion)
Common Enemies	Kurita (Late Succession Wars), Liao (Late Succession Wars)
Special Command Abilities	*Esprit de Corps*

THE RANGERS CODE

A Ranger lives simply and honestly without delusions or manias.
A Ranger values loyalty, but never follows others blindly.
A Ranger must serve people, not corporations.
A Ranger must be prepared body, mind and soul to fight for what is right.
Above all, a Ranger must remain free to follow his own destiny.

—*Eleven Against the Stars*, John R. Loran, SVC Publishers, 2343

12TH VEGAN RANGERS

ALPHA REGIMENT

"The Concrete Crushers" is the command regiment of the Rangers. General Stancel leads the Rangers from the front, continuing the legacy of Margrave Douglass and those who came before. Only Stancel can assume command of another Ranger regiment; thus, if more than one Ranger regiment is present in a single battle, Alpha will be among them. First Battalion fields exclusively heavy and assault 'Mechs; Second consists of an even mixture of weight classes; and Third uses primarily light and medium 'Mechs, plus one lance per company of jump-capable heavy and assault 'Mechs. Alpha Armor is entirely made up of heavy and assault tanks, most having been upgraded by the Rangers technical arm.

Experience Rating	Elite
Force Composition	1 assault 'Mech regiment, 1 medium aerospace fighter wing, 1 assault vehicle battalion; all vehicles are heavy or assault (Size 3 or 4)
Special Command Abilities	Off-Map Movement, Environmental Specialization (Urban), Sharp Shooters
Force Building Rules	Alpha Regiment may replace any SPA gained from a lance's Bonus Ability with the Multi-tasker SPA.

BETA REGIMENT

"The Victories" specializes in open-field tactics. First and Second Battalion often deploy together to assault the enemy, while Third Battalion either flanks or supports First and Second as needed. Beta Armor is entirely composed of hovertanks for slashing attacks.

Experience Rating	Veteran
Force Composition	1 assault 'Mech regiment, 1 medium aerospace fighter wing, 1 light vehicle battalion; all vehicles must have a hover Move type
Special Command Abilities	Brawlers, Forcing the Initiative

GAMMA REGIMENT

"The Deadly Dancers" organizes their forces for combined arms actions. Third Battalion specializes in close combat and includes multiple lances of *Hatchetman* (and, in the Early Clan Invasion era, *Axman)* 'Mechs. Each 'Mech battalion has an armor company permanently attached, with the tank company sharing the 'Mech battalion's specialization.

Experience Rating	Veteran
Force Composition	1 heavy 'Mech regiment, 1 medium aerospace fighter wing, 1 vehicle battalion
Special Command Abilities	Environmental Specialization (Woods, Mountains,Night, Rain), Brawlers
Force Building Rules	Beta Regiment may replace any SPA gained from a lance's Bonus Ability with the Melee Specialist or Slugger SPA. They may add access to the *Hatchetman* HCT-3F in the Late Succession Wars era for 0 FP, and the *Axman* AXM-1N in the Early Clan Invasion era for 1 FP.

DELTA REGIMENT

"The Noble Nasties" fell in overall skill after the War of 3039. While the regiment rebuilt, many MechWarriors were transferred to Gamma Regiment; as a result, Delta has the youngest average MechWarrior age in the Rangers. First Battalion specializes in direct assaults, while the Second is expert in fast, mobile warfare. Third Battalion and Delta Armor are unmatched among the Rangers in long-range combat.

Experience Rating	Regular (Veteran prior to 3040)
Force Composition	1 heavy 'Mech regiment, 1 medium aerospace fighter wing, 1 vehicle battalion
Special Command Abilities	*Hit and Run*, Sharp Shooters

TYPICAL RANK STRUCTURE [CONTINUED]

Lieutenant: A lieutenant typically commands a lance. The equivalent admiralty rank is ensign (lieutenant junior grade after the first year), who would command a small work center. Infantry lieutenants command platoons.

Sergeant: A sergeant is often the senior enlisted rank in a command (though many units have master sergeants or sergeants major, who oversee other sergeants and report directly to the commanding officer rather than a junior officer). Armor sergeants command vehicle platoons and infantry sergeants lead squads, but in a lance or squadron they would be MechWarriors or pilots. The admiralty equivalent is chief petty officer (again, possibly including senior chief petty officers and master chief petty officers).

Corporal: Corporals serve as go-betweens for sergeants and privates. A corporal might lead an infantry squad or command a tank crew. The equivalent admiralty rank is petty officer.

Private: Privates are entry-level enlisted personnel. The equivalent admiralty rank is spaceman (or spacer). However, the person's responsibility is often used instead when addressing them (crewman, for example, on a tank).

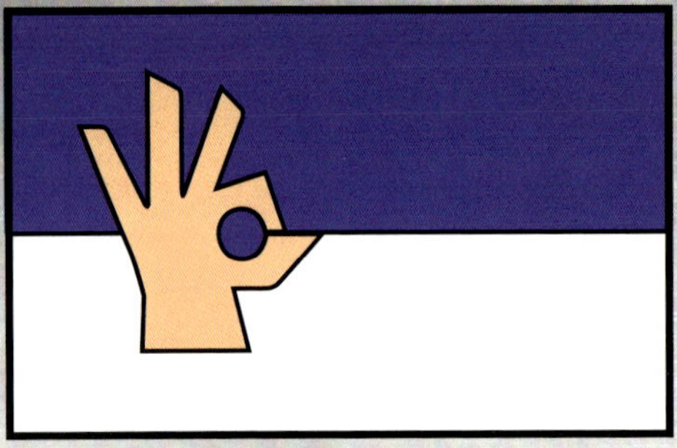

Wilson's Hussars, often referred to as Wilson's Wimps, descends from a prestigious Liao House unit called Lafarge's Hussars, a battalion of the Seventh Andurien Hussars. Lafarge's Hussars were crushed by the Sixth Syrtis Fusiliers during the Third Succession War, and the vagaries of that war of attrition saw the surviving Hussars switch allegiance to the Davion victors. After a decade of below-average service, Major Jennifer Langstrom led the rebuilt battalion into the mercenary life, seeking fortune and glory. Brief service with the Draconis Combine ended poorly, and the Hussars returned to Capellan employ. The Hussars' defense of St. Ives against Federated Suns raiders ended in Major Langstrom's death. Her brother Michael assumed command and plunged the Hussars even further from glory. Michael's command incompetence and cowardice killed most of the Hussars in a DropShip crash on Ingersol. Executive Officer David Wilson assumed command of the shattered Hussars and led the few survivors into disaster after disaster.

Wilson's Hussars were eventually unable to secure any contract in the Inner Sphere. In 3021, Wilson's Hussars were under contract to the bandit king Redjack Ryan and operating out of Butte Hold, when they were crushed by the small-time Garrison Warriors mercenary command on Kimball VI. The near-blasphemous defeat of a company of BattleMechs to a garrison unit of VTOLs aided by planetary militia sent the Hussars even further down the mercenary ranks.

The Hussars were absent from the Fourth Succession War and the War of 3039. They recently resurfaced on Outreach, numbering a mere two lances and desperately seeking any contract no matter how suicidal. Their zeal to prove themselves is almost certain to finally wipe them out, but their drive to succeed despite a complete lack of interest or common sense endears the lovable "Wimps" to the media. Their never-say-die attitude will likely garner them a contract, but only one all other commands turn down.

David Wilson remains in command, but the unit's clear heir is his daughter, Lieutenant Donna Wilson. She grew up among the Hussars and hates their lowly status. She learned to lead the Hussars in the worst possible situations, her courage providing the backbone that has kept the command going. Her *Catapult* curiously mounts advanced heat sinks of a kind not seen before. She will not reveal how or where she acquired them, but the look in her eyes suggests the dark story that lies behind them.

Common Allies	Liao (Late Succession Wars)
Common Enemies	None
Special Command Abilities	*Hit and Run*, Overrun Combat, Zone of Control

WILSON'S HUSSARS

Wilson's Hussars 'Mechs look on the verge of collapse, and in this case looks do *not* deceive. The Hussars MechWarriors perform their own repairs, as the command lacks technical support. Their dilapidated DropShip is the same one that evacuated them from Ingersol over thirty years ago. They have no JumpShip and are completely at any potential employer's mercy.

Experience Rating	Veteran
Force Composition	1 'Mech company. One lance consists of light and medium (Size 1 and 2) 'Mechs; the others field medium and heavy (Size 2 and 3) 'Mechs.
Special Rules	Prior to the start of any scenario or campaign, apply 1 point of damage per 3 armor points to every Hussars Unit. Choose one Unit per Formation, roll 2d6 on the Determining Critical Hits Table (p. 41, *AS*) and apply its effects; a result of 2 or 12 instead requires two further rolls on the table. Further results of 2 or 12 are ignored. In a campaign setting, the Hussars begin with 25 percent less starting resources than other commands their size.

ESCAPE FROM KIMBALL VI

Serval Canyon
Kimball VI
Draconis Combine
31 May 3021

Wilson's Hussars pursued a company of mercenary Warrior VTOLs into Serval Canyon, only to find the planetary militia waiting in ambush.

GAME SETUP

Recommended Terrain: Desert Canyon

If using hex maps, arrange two maps with their short edges touching.

The Defender chooses a short edge as their home edge. The attacker's home edge is the opposite edge.

ATTACKER

Garrison Warriors mercenary command, Kimball VI militia

The Attacker consists of the Garrison Warriors (one Regular company of Warrior H-7 VTOLs) and a battalion of infantry (Regular, SRM infantry). Infantry platoons may begin the battle as Hidden Units. Warrior VTOLs must begin the battle on the table, arrayed along its long edges (half on each side).

DEFENDER

Wilson's Hussars

The Defender consists of Wilson's Hussars (one Regular company of 'Mechs: Recon Lance, Striker Lance, Heavy Lance). The Hussars reduce the armor points on all Units by half to reflect damage absorbed from the Warriors' harassing attacks en route to Serval Canyon. The Defender's Units enter via the Attacker's home edge on Turn 1. The Defender must exit via their home edge before Turn 12.

Wylie's Coyotes possessed origins nearly as mysterious as those of Wolf's Dragoons. In 3009, the Coyotes appeared in Davion space, their battalion of pristine light BattleMechs ferried about in fantastically-well maintained DropShips by the *Geronimo*, their *Star Lord*-class JumpShip. The Coyotes also boasted a complement of technicians far in excess of the number required by a 'Mech battalion. The Federated Suns quickly hired the Coyotes, assuming (correctly, as it turned out) that they were getting as good a deal as they recieved with the Dragoons.

Unlike the Dragoons, though, the Coyotes never left the Suns' employ. Over the next two decades, the Coyotes expanded from a battalion to a full regiment, all without hiring any outside personnel. All their MechWarriors and technicians came from the considerable ranks of their dependents, all of whom received excellent educations and combat/technical training. The Coyotes also never acquired any new BattleMechs on the open market or even through salvage, which they always sold at a discount to House Davion. Instead, periodically, a lance of pristine light 'Mechs would appear among their ranks, piloted by young MechWarriors from within.

The Coyotes were often considered strange by the natives of the world on which they were stationed. Periodically, the entire Coyote force and their dependents would disappear for days at a time. When queried, they would simply offer that they were "communing with nature" out of sight of "outsiders." They were never stationed on any world for more than a year, per their contract terms. During their time in service to the Federated Suns the Coyotes traveled the breadth of the nation, sowing their strange behavior among the locals on several worlds. Mystical communes sprung up on those worlds and remain in operation, living in balance with nature.

The Coyotes specialized from the start in the very tactics espoused by Mercer Ravannion of the DCMS. The Coyotes never engaged in stand-up fights, for which their light 'Mechs were ill-suited. Instead, they swarmed their enemies, always moving at top speed, rarely engaging a single enemy for any protracted period. Instead, they would flash past, firing as they went, and trust those who followed to finish the job. Opposed sweeps would often catch enemies in a pincer, exposing vulnerable rear armor to attack.

The Fourth Succession War began with the Coyotes stationed on Bromhead. Given free rein by the AFFS High Command, the Coyotes attacked Zanzibar in 3029 and crushed Bullard's Armored Cavalry before disappearing for several months afterward. When they returned, they delivered to their command liaison on Bromhead a package of intelligence. This valuable information was crucial in securing the borders of the St. Ives Compact, even before the realm's birth was envisaged. Further, it is believed that this information was shared with the Duchy of Andurien and formed the basis for the Andurien-Canopian Invasion that occurred several years later.

Their unusual time in the Federated Suns ended in 3030. The command simply disappeared one night. Curious liaison officers investigated after unit officers missed regular meetings. When they arrived at the Coyotes' base, they found it all but deserted. The only inhabitants were a few locals who had served the Coyotes as civilian employees, and a number of dependents who had married into the unit, along with their children. Without exception, those left behind possessed ancestry alien to the Coyotes from the time of their arrival. Their departure was less a "disappearance" and more a "calculated withdrawal." They managed to effect their self-removal without anyone noticing, which is remarkable considering the difficulty of launching DropShips undetected. Their status since disappearing is unknown, as they have not been sighted since.

Common Allies	Davion (Late Succession War)
Common Enemies	Kurita (Late Succession War), Liao (Late Succession War)
Special Command Abilities	Off-Map Movement, Overrun Combat, Brawlers

WYLIE'S COYOTES

The Coyotes are a fast, mobile regiment composed entirely of light 'Mechs. Every 'Mech is in perfect condition.

Experience Rating	Veteran
Force Composition	1 'Mech regiment, 1 vehicle company, 1 infantry company; 75 percent of all 'Mechs are light or medium (Size 1 or 2) and all vehicles are light (Size 1) Units. The infantry company consists of three platoons of Jump Infantry with Laser rifles.
Force Building Rules	Wylie's Coyotes may replace any SPA gained from a lance Bonus Ability with Blood Stalker or Speed Demon.
Special Rules	The Coyotes never begin a battle with pre-existing damage or reduced ammunition, regardless of the scenario's specifications, due to their excellent and over-staffed technical corps. In a campaign setting, repair factors (time, cost, etc.) are 20 percent less than standard. The Coyotes may not be fielded as a Force after 3030.

DEATH TO MERCENARIES

Mistreatment by Warlord Grieg Samsonov caused Wolf's Dragoons to allow their contract with the Draconis Combine to expire. Unaware of Samsonov's machinations, Coordinator Takashi Kurita felt dishonored by the Dragoons' decision. The dispute led to a terrible battle on Misery that cost the Dragoons half their forces, but it was Warlord Grieg Samsonov's attempt to murder the Dragoons' families that ensured mutual hatred.

The Federated Suns' Draconis March border became the focal point for the ongoing feud. Wolf deployed his remaining Dragoons across three worlds, per his new contract with the Suns. He challenged Takashi to come and take the worlds from him by confronting the Coordinator at the wedding of Hanse Davion and Melissa Steiner. As the Fourth Succession War broke out across the Inner Sphere, Takashi and Wolf fought their own war on the Suns border.

The Dragoons faced massively superior DCMS numbers, but ground down the Coordinator's samurai with every assault. Nonetheless, the Combine replenished its troops while the Dragoons' own force dwindled; finally, only a rescue out of a holodrama saved the remnants of the Dragoons from four regiments of Galedon Regulars. As the Combine retreated, Coordinator Takashi lashed out in rage and declared, "Death to Mercenaries!" His edict banished mercenaries from DCMS employ for decades, and many of those not fast enough to cross the borders were put to death. After nearly two decades, Theodore Kurita's influence has finally begun to ease this harsh policy.

WOLF'S DRAGOONS

Wolf's Dragoons appeared seemingly from nowhere in 3005, and their five-regiment strength stunned the Inner Sphere. Their 'Mechs were in perfect condition; they included many not seen since the Star League, as well as a number of unique 'Mechs never seen before at all. Rumors sprang up that the Dragoons were a portion of Kerensky's SLDF troops returned at long last, or that they had discovered a huge, hidden SLDF cache somewhere outside the Inner Sphere. The Dragoons spent most of the next 23 years serving each Successor State in turn, moving clockwise from one to the next, starting with the Federated Suns and ending with the Draconis Combine.

The Dragoons ran afoul of Inner Sphere politics in 3014 when Chancellor Maximilian Liao placed them under the command of Duke Anton Marik, thrusting them into the Marik Civil War. After the Dragoons refused Marik's suicidal orders, Anton took a number of Dragoons and their dependents hostage, and eventually executed them. The dead included Colonel Jaime Wolf's brother, wife, and two younger children.

The Dragoons were enraged as never before, and directly assaulted the duke's forces. As the slaughter of the Marik troops was underway, the newly-formed Black Widow Company under the mysterious Captain Natasha Kerensky attacked the duke's palace directly, destroying it and killing Duke Anton. New Delos was laid waste as the Dragoons exterminated every ducal combatant they could find.

After the Dragoons' legendary assault on Hesperus II in 3019, they simply disappeared. They returned a year later fully rebuilt—though the Successor States would have been hard-pressed to restore five regiments in twice the time—and signed on with the Lyran Commonwealth. Rumors of a secret Dragoon storage depot in the Periphery circulated the Inner Sphere.

Finally, the Dragoons took a contract with the Draconis Combine. Again, politics took their toll on the command. After angering Warlord Grieg Samsonov, the Dragoons were ordered to train a new Combine command, the Ryuken, to be the Combine's own version of the Dragoons. Samsonov arranged for a disastrous defeat in the assault on Barlow's End to be laid at Jaime Wolf's feet, ruining the relationship between Wolf and the Coordinator. The Combine captured the Dragoons' space station *Hephaestus*, forcing Jaime Wolf to enact a contingency plan created after Anton's betrayal. Dragoon civilians were evacuated from Combine space while the Dragoons rallied at Misery. The space station was destroyed in orbit over An Ting with all hands, while the Ryuken attacked the Dragoons. After mauling the Ryuken, Wolf led Alpha Regiment from An Ting to Misery.

Misery was a great and a terrible battle. While the Dragoons defeated the Ryuken, they lost half their own forces, as well as some true friends among the enemy force with whom they had trained for years. The events of An Ting and Misery led Jaime Wolf to challenge the Coordinator personally at the Steiner-Davion wedding on Terra. Amid the Fourth Succession War, the Dragoons and the Combine fought their own personal conflict, which cost Kurita any gains he might have made in the larger war, and cost the Dragoons more than 80 percent of their strength.

First Prince Hanse Davion gave Wolf's Dragoons the world of Outreach as reward for their actions. The Dragoons immediately set to rebuilding both their forces and the ruined Star League-era factory they uncovered on Outreach. Over the next fifteen years, the Dragoons fully rebuilt, with each regiment boasting a command company, vehicle battalion, fighter wing, and infantry battalion.

Common Allies	Davion (Early Clan Invasion)
Common Enemies	All Great Houses (Late Succession Wars), Clan Smoke Jaguar (Early Clan Invasion)
Special Command Abilities	*Esprit de Corps*, Communications Disruption
Force Building Rules	Wolf's Dragoons has their own Availability List (see *Availability Lists*, p. 84), and may add access to Units on this list for 1 FP each. Starting in the Early Clan Invasion Era, BattleMech Forces use a Clan-style organization of five-'Mech Formations; Lances must have five Units, each of which are counted for the purposes of Formation Requirements and Bonus Abilities.

ALPHA REGIMENT

Alpha is the prestige regiment of the Dragoons—but their shiny paint and parade ground manners do not diminish their combat skills.

Experience Rating	Elite
Force Composition	1 heavy 'Mech regiment, 2 aerospace lances, 1 vehicle battalion, 1 infantry battalion
Special Command Abilities	Forcing the Initiative, Overrun Combat

BETA REGIMENT

Beta is highly-mobile assault force, known for outmaneuvering and then smashing their enemies.

Experience Rating	Elite
Force Composition	1 heavy 'Mech regiment, 2 aerospace lances, 1 vehicle battalion, 1 infantry battalion
Special Command Abilities	Off-Map Movement

GAMMA REGIMENT

Gamma specializes in night-fighting and other impaired-sight conditions.

Experience Rating	Elite
Force Composition	1 heavy 'Mech regiment, 2 aerospace lances, 1 vehicle battalion, 1 infantry battalion
Special Command Abilities	Environmental Specialization (Night, Rain), Sharp Shooters

DELTA REGIMENT

Delta specializes in combined arms warfare.

Experience Rating	Elite
Force Composition	1 heavy 'Mech regiment, 2 aerospace lances, 1 vehicle battalion, 1 infantry battalion
Special Command Abilities	*Tactical Adjustments*, Brawlers

EPSILON REGIMENT

Epsilon is renowned for making reckless charges directly against enemy positions.

Experience Rating	Elite
Force Composition	1 heavy 'mech regiment, 2 aerospace lances, 1 vehicle battalion, 1 infantry battalion
Special Command Abilities	Off-Map Movement, Brawlers

ZETA BATTALION

Zeta is the assault force of the Dragoons. Composed entirely of assault and upper-end heavy 'Mechs, no opposing commander wants to see Zeta arrayed against them. Zeta Battalion is one of the only two Dragoons independant units (see p. 76), that was not absorbed into an Operational Command, instead retaining its independance along with the Black Widow Battalion.

Experience Rating	Elite
Force Composition	1 'Mech battalion. All units must be heavy or assault (Size 3 or 4), with the exception of one unit per company may be medium (Size 2)
Special Command Abilities	Overrun Combat, Forcing the Initiative, Zone of Control
Force Building Rules	Any SPA received from a lance's Bonus Ability may be replaced with Demoralizer.

INDEPENDANT UNITS [OPERATIONAL COMMANDS]

The Dragoon's independant units are never hired out. Instead, Dragoon commanders deploy units from these commands to augment contracted Dragoons forces as needed. This affords the Dragoons the flexibility to provide a force tailor-make for any combat misson. Near the end of the Late Succession War Era many of these independant units are reorganized into Operational Commands.

FIRE SUPPORT GROUP [SUPPORT COMMAND]

The FSG provides the Dragoons with pinpoint artillery targeting and supressive fire. The FSG formed the core of the Support Command.

Experience Rating	Elite (Late Succession Wars), Veteran (Early Clan Invasion)
Force Composition	1 heavy 'Mech company, 1 light aerospace lance, 1 artillery company, 2 light vehicle lances, 1 infantry platoon (Late Succession Wars); 1 'Mech regiment, 1 vehicle regiment, 1 artillery battalion, 1 reinforced Elemental Cluster (Early Clan Invasion)

SUPPORT BATTALION

The "Rogues" have never operated as a unit, having been always lent out piecemeal to other forces. The Support Battalion was eventually absorbed into the Support Command (see above).

Experience Rating	Elite (Late Succession Wars)
Force Composition	2 reinforced vehicle companies, 1 VTOL company, 1 infantry company, 1 aerospace squadron (Late Succession Wars)
Force Building Rules	The vehicle companies may create five-unit lances for 2 FP each or Demi-Companies for 4 FP each (without the 2 per company restriction).

ORBITAL/AEROSPACE OPERATIONS GROUP [AEROSPACE COMMAND]

In addition to being the backbone of the Dragoon's aerospace fighter support, all of Wolf's Dragoons' DropShip, JumpShip and (later) WarShip assets fall under the aegis of the Aerospace Command.

Experience Rating	Elite (Late Succession Wars), Veteran (Early Clan Invasion)
Force Composition	1 aerospace wing (Late Succession Wars); 5 aerospace regiments (Early Clan Invasion)

SPECIAL RECON GROUP [SPECIAL OPERATIONS COMMAND]

The SRG was built for speed, stealth and versatility, and has peformed diverse missions for the Dragoons and their employers over the years. Along with WolfNet and the Seventh Kommando, the SRG eventually formed the Special Operations Command.

Experience Rating	Elite
Force Composition	1 light reinforced 'Mech company, 1 VTOL lance, 1 light vehicle lance, 1 infantry platoon

SEVENTH KOMMANDO

Seventh Kommando is the combat arm of WolfNet, the Dragoons intelligence apparatus. They never appear on the battlefield, but their efforts are felt far and wide.

Experience Rating	Elite
Force Composition	1 infantry battalion; no Unit may possess less than a Veteran rating

SEVENTH KOMMANDO

Seventh Kommando never appears on the battlefield, but are among the most devastating operators in the Inner Sphere. This collection of infiltrators, saboteurs, and assassins is the rival of the finest special operations troops of any House, including the Rabid Foxes of the Federated Suns and the DEST Commandos of the Draconis Combine.

Typically operating behind enemy lines or in advance of ground operations, Seventh Kommando smooths the way for the 'Mechs. Collecting valuable intel, destroying supply dumps, attacking rear-echelon bases, and eliminating enemy commanders are their stock in trade. This highly-mobile, mechanized force relies on fast hovercraft to ferry troops quickly beyond enemy defenses into rear areas. Their tactics are simple: disrupt the enemy, thereby ensuring an easier victory for the Dragoons.

Sometimes the Seventh undertakes a mission solely to send a message. After McCarron's Armored Cavalry bloodied the Dragoons on New Valencia and bragged about defeating the mercenaries, Seventh Kommando responded. One night in 3008, every major city on the planet experienced power failures and comm disruptions. The supply depots of all five Cavalry regiments, each in its own city, were destroyed simultaneously. The Cavalry's commander returned to his quarters to find a note stuck to his door with a Seventh Kommando dagger: "Next time we get rough." No one saw anyone enter or depart the premises.

BLACK WIDOW COMPANY [BATTALION POST-3040]

Kerensky's Independent Company was formed in 3014, assembled out of the ragtag MechWarriors "volunteered" by Dragoon battalion commanders, who considered the company an ideal dumping ground for the undesirables in their units—chronic misfits, looters, and other disciplinary hardcases. Kerensky welcomed the challenge. Within months, a combination of harsh, unrelenting discipline, intensive training, and indoctrination pounded Kerensky's Company into a powerful fighting unit. Though scorned at first by other units in the regiment, the company's capabilities and battle history have made an impression not only on the rest of the Dragoons, but on the Inner Sphere at large.

Today they are among the most feared commands in the Inner Sphere; the Widows do not hold back, even against vastly superior forces.

Experience Rating	Elite
Force Composition	1 'Mech company (pre-3040), 1 medium 'Mech battalion (post-3040)
Special Command Abilities	*Berserkers*, *Tactical Adjustments*, *Tactical Expert (Hidden Units)*, Off-Map Movement
Force Building Rules	Starting in 3040, the Black Widow Battalion uses a Clan-style organization of five-'Mech Formations. Post-3040, Lances must have five Units, each of which are counted for the purposes of Formation Requirements and Bonus Abilities.

Captain Natasha Kerensky

The Queen of Spades, The First Lady of Death, and The Black Widow are all names given to Natasha Kerensky, Captain of the Black Widow Company of Wolf's Dragoons. Kerensky is a beautiful but cold, highly professional soldier. Her skill and courage are well-known, and she is regarded as one of the regiment's most daring and resourceful officers. She rules her company with a strong hand and expects absolute loyalty from her troops, and they receive her undying loyalty in return. The Black Widow has no known emotional attachments outside her company, and little, if any, personal life. She is at home only on a battlefield, and her MechWarriors are her family.

CAPTAIN NATASHA KERENSKY									PV: 32 (56)
Unit Type	**Skill**	**TP**	**SZ**	**MV**	**TMM**	**S/M/L**	**OV**	**A/S**	**Specials**
Warhammer WHM-6R	0	BM	3	8	1	3/3/2	1	5/6	
Special Pilot Abilities: Demoralizer, Iron Will, Lucky (1). Kerensky's Iron Will conveys a +3/-3 instead of the standard +2/-2.									

THE BOUNTY HUNTER

Perhaps the most mysterious mercenary in history is the Bounty Hunter. No one knows the true name of the first Bounty Hunter, but it's generally believed that various individuals have assumed the identity throughout the centuries. Sometimes the role is passed down willingly, while others have apparently assumed the identity after killing the previous Bounty Hunter.

The Bounty Hunter often works with a trio of trusted assistants, all elite MechWarriors. The Bounty Hunter himself always pilots a bright green 'Mech with credit symbols scattered over its surface. The Bounty Hunter's 'Mechs are always in perfect condition, sometimes mounting Star League or other advanced technology. The Bounty Hunter's most recent 'Mech, a Marauder, was acquired by shooting Natasha Kerensky out of it. Its extraordinary performance in battle is credited to the Bounty Hunter's skill, but rumors suggest it carries weapons and components more advanced than the Star League ever knew.

The Bounty Hunter only takes on the most challenging contracts offering the most lucrative rewards. The Hunter's appearances in battle are short-lived, and focused on bringing down his target and leaving the field. Any others will be left alone, unless they attack; then the Hunter destroys them with prejudice.

The Bounty Hunter's targets are often traitors or other high-profile targets. Employers are usually House Lords or those of comparable wealth who are able to afford the Hunter's exorbitant rates.

RULES ADDENDUM

The following rules allow players to build Mercenary Forces for their *Alpha Strike* games set in the Late Succession Wars or Early Clan Invasion eras.

Force Building, when used in conjunction with the Alpha Strike Force Building rules (see p. 146, *ASC*), guides players on the assembly of Mercenary Forces ranging from lances to companies to even larger Sub-Commands.

The *Mercenary Special Command Abilities* section expands on the Special Command Abilities (SCAs) from the *Alpha Strike Companion* (see p. 44, *ASC*), and introduces several new abilities.

Two new types of Formations are included in *Mercenary Lances*, along with Standard Lances for players to "grab and go" and field in quick pickup games, or for players who wish to ease into the Force Building rules. In similar fashion, the MechWarriors listed in the *Unaffiliated MechWarriors* section are provided for players to include in their Force, regardless of the Combat Command the choose to field.

The *Technical Readout* provides an overview on a selection of venerable BattleMechs in use by the mercenaries across the Inner Sphere: The *Locust*, *Ostscout*, *Shadowhawk* and *Warhammer*.

FORCE BUILDING

Combat Manual: Mercenaries uses the rules for Force Building as presented in the *Alpha Strike Companion* (see *ASC* pp. 146-157) and adds several new options. In addition to Point Values, Special Command Abilities and Formations (from *Alpha Strike* and the *Alpha Strike Companion*), *Combat Manual: Mercenaries* adds a system for creating a mercenary-specific Force.

When building a Force, the Company Force Sheet (see p. 128) may be used to record each Formation choice. Each sheet covers one company, with overall Force information noted in the upper boxed area. If a Force has multiple companies, a different sheet will be required for each company, and the boxed information would be the same for each company.

FORCE BUILDING TERMS

Unit: During gamplay, a Unit moves and attacks singly and is represented by a separate Unit Card. A Unit is usually a single 'Mech, vehicle, etc., but infantry may include multiple soldiers operating as a single Unit.

Formation: The smallest organization of Units. For most Inner Sphere factions, this is a lance of 4 Units. Formations known as Standard Lances meet certain criteria to fulfill specific roles on the battlefield, and in return grant Bonus Abilities. Standard Lances available to all Factions are listed in *Ground Formation Types* (see p. 150, *ASC*).

Force: The combined Formations fielded by one player in an *Alpha Strike* game. A player may build a larger Force before gameplay begins, such as a Force devised for a campaign, and then select a portion of that Force to meet the requirements of a single scenario. However, the player's Force is the Formations the player is fielding in that game only.

Combat Command: A military group that trains and works together to receive access to Special Command Abilities. Combat Commands are listed in the *Mercenary Combat Commands* chapter.

Sub-Command: A Combat Command is further broken down into Sub-Commands. Formations in a Sub-Command share training so that they can receive the benefits of their Combat Command's Special Command Abilities. As they often share a common history, information for Common Allies and Common Enemies are usually listed under a Combat Command rather than repeating the same information among each of its Sub-Commands.

Era: A group of years defined by the Force Building rules as sharing common technology and historical events. The chosen Era of a Force limits which Units are available to that Force.

Faction: Each *Combat Manual* details at least one Faction. Any Force built using rules contained in *Combat Manual: Mercenaries* are considered members of the Mercenary Faction. Factions may access Units from the general list and their faction-specific list.

Availability List: A collection of Units from which a Force may be selected. An Availability List usually relates to a particular Era, Faction, or Combat Command. The choice of Faction and Combat Command, combined with the Era of play, determines the Availability Lists from which a Force may select Units, and whether or not an associated Faction Points (FPs) cost is required to select a particular Unit.

Faction Points (FPs): Faction Points limit access to Availability Lists from which a Faction would not otherwise be able to select Units. FP could be considered combat salvage, luck, political influence, favors, or simply money that a Force expends to acquire Units not commonly available to their Faction (see *Faction Points*, p. 84).

SELECT POINT VALUE TOTAL

Point Values remain the balancing system for *Alpha Strike*. The rules for Point Values are described in *Alpha Strike* (see *Force Balancing*, p. 24, *AS*). As you add Units to your Force, remember that the base Unit PV may need to be adjusted for the Skill Rating of the Unit (see *Adjusting for Skill*, p. 24, *AS*).

CHOOSE AN ERA

The selection of an Era affects which Factions are available, and also the general tech level and Units available to a Force. *Combat Manual: Mercenaries* lists options for the Late Succession Wars (3025-3049) and Early Clan Invasion (3050-3054) eras.

CHOOSE A FACTION

The Faction is the House or Clan with which the Force is associated, and determines the Force's available equipment and its organization. *Combat Manual: Mercenaries* includes options for the Mercenary Faction. The choice of Faction determines the Standard Lances (see p. 94) and Availability Lists (see p. 84) from which a Force may be assembled.

CHOOSE A COMBAT COMMAND

Every *Alpha Strike* Force belongs to (or may be the entirety of) a Combat Command. These large military organizations are usually regiments, or even brigades consisting of multiple regiments. The choice of Combat Command bestows Special Command Abilities on a Force, and may also dictate the Skill Ratings assigned to Units in later steps (see *Force Composition* below). A Combat Command may also provide special rules for Force Building, such as giving access to or modifying FP costs of Units on certain Availability Lists, or requiring average weights for constituent Formations. A selection of the Inner Sphere's most famous or interesting Mercenary Combat Commands are listed in the *Mercenary Combat Commands* chapter.

Unlisted Mercenaries: A Force may also be fielded from an unlisted Mercenary Combat Command. Doing so does not provide access to non-mercenary Availability Lists or Unique Characters, and any Special Command Abilities must be rolled randomly (see p. 87).

Force Composition: This entry for each Command or Sub-Command lists the organization, Unit types and average Size and Skill of the Command or Sub-Command. With the exception of one Unit per full company, the Skill Rating of each Unit from that Command or Sub-Command should be within one Skill Rating of the average. The one exception can be any Skill Rating.

If the Force has half or more of the number of Units listed for any of the Unit types in the Command or Sub-Command's Force Composition list, then those Units must have an Average Size and Skill matching the Command or Sub-Command's. For example, if a Force Composition lists one 'Mech battalion, and a player's force includes more than 5 'Mech lances (20 of the 40 'Mechs in a battalion with a Command lance), then that Force's 'Mech Units must possess an average Skill Rating and average Size that matches the Combat Command or Sub-Command.

If a Sub-Command's Force Composition does not list a particular Unit type, then that Unit type cannot be added to a Force from that command. (See *Sub-Command Formations*, p. 85 and *Supplemental Formations*, p. 86, for exceptions to this rule.)

Brian is building a Force based on H'Chu's Diggers, a Sub-Command of Cranston Snord's Irregulars, and will field 3 Formations. This is half of the Sub-Command's listed Force Composition (2 'Mech lances and 4 infantry platoons); therefore the final Experience Rating (average Skill Rating) of the Force must be Veteran. There is no average weight (Size) listed for H'Chu's Diggers; however, their Sub-Command entry explicitly states that all 'Mechs must be light and medium (Size 1 and 2). As a result, Brian's Units need to adhere to that restriction, regardless of the number of Formations he fields. Furthermore, Brian would not be able to field more than 2 'Mech Formations, and 4 infantry Formations, as that is the Force Composition of H'Chu's Diggers.

If Brian wished to add aerospace or artillery Formations, he would be able to do so using the rules for Sub-Command Formations and Supplemental Formations (p. 85 and p. 86, respectively).

BASIC REGIMENTAL STRUCTURE

Mercenaries base their Formations on the typical military organization of House militaries. This eases integration of the command alongside the employer's other forces, since consistent terminology eliminates confusion. However, because mercenary resources are often inferior to House militaries, mercenaries are likely to combine disparate Unit types in a single Formation, such as two 'Mech lances and one tank platoon comprising a mercenary company. By comparison, House Formations are usually homogeneous by Unit type. Also, mercenaries are more likely to have reinforced versions of each Formation, since they lack the funds to fully expand to the next Formation size. Reinforced formations usually contain one or two additional elements from the next lower subunit. A reinforced company, for example, may contain one or two additional lances than a normal company. A command unit (such as a command lance) is not usually considered when determining whether a Formation is reinforced, as they see less combat due to their administrative duties.

UNIT ORGANIZATIONS

The Force Composition rules use standard terms to identify the organization of the Force and the Unit types of which it is composed.

BattleMech Organization

BattleMech Formations consist entirely of BattleMechs.

STANDARD MERCENARY BATTLEMECH ORGANIZATION

Unit	Component Formations	Total Strength
Lance	—	4 BattleMechs
Company	3 lances	12 BattleMechs
Reinforced Company	4 lances	16 BattleMechs
Battalion	3 companies + 1 command lance	40 BattleMechs
Reinforced Battalion	4 companies + 1 command lance	52 BattleMechs
Regiment	3 battalions + 1 command lance	124 BattleMechs
Reinforced Regiment	4 battalions + 1 command lance	164 BattleMechs

Aerospace Organization

Aerospace Formations consist entirely of aerospace fighters; however, some mercenaries may field conventional fighters in place of aerospace fighters. They may also include fixed wing support vehicles (support vehicles with the "a" movement type).

STANDARD MERCENARY AEROSPACE ORGANIZATION

Unit	Component Formations	Total Strength
Lance	—	2 aerospace fighters
Squadron	3 lances	6 aerospace fighters
Wing	3 squadrons + 1 command lance	20 aerospace fighters
Reinforced Wing	4 squadrons + 1 command lance	26 aerospace fighters

Armor Organization

Armor Formations can include any combat vehicle or support vehicle as well as conventional fighters. No more than a third of an armor Formation may be conventional fighters.

If any Units in an armor Formation have the Infantry Transport (IT#) special ability, infantry Units may be included in the armor Formation. No more than one-third of the total armor Formation may carry attached infantry Units, and these infantry Units do not count toward the Component Formations of the armor Formation as long as they may be carried by the transport, up to one infantry Unit per transport.

For example, a lance of Goblin Medium Tanks each have IT1. infantry squads (see right) have CAR1. The lance may include the four Goblin Medium Tanks and four infantry squads.

STANDARD MERCENARY ARMOR ORGANIZATION

Unit	Component Formations	Total Strength
Lance	—	4 vehicles
Company	3 lances	12 vehicles
Battalion	3 companies + 1 command lance	40 vehicles
Regiment	3 battalions + 1 command company	132 vehicles
Reinforced Regiment	4 battalions + 1 command company	172 vehicles

Infantry Organization

Infantry Formations can include any infantry (or battle armor if available). They may also include conventional fighters, combat vehicles and support vehicles. No more than a third of the infantry Formation may be non-infantry Unit types.

If the Formation is a mechanized infantry Formation, then combat vehicles or support vehicles with the Infantry Transport special ability (IT#) do not count toward the non-infantry Unit types limit of a Sub-Command or toward the Component Formations of the infantry Formation, as long as the Force includes infantry they have the ability to transport (IT# equal or more than the CAR# rating of the infantry). All of the infantry in a mechanized infantry organization should either be mechanized or motorized infantry, or have vehicles capable of transporting them.

For example, a Maxim Heavy Hover Transport has IT3. A company of mechanized infantry could contain three foot platoons of infantry (CAR3) and three Maxim transports.

STANDARD MERCENARY INFANTRY ORGANIZATION

Unit	Component Formations	Total Strength*
Company	—	3 platoons (120 troops)
Reinforced Company	—	4 platoons (160 troops)
Battalion	3 companies	9 platoons (360 troops)
Reinforced Battalion	4 companies	12 platoons (480 troops)
Regiment	3 battalions	27 platoons (1080 troops)

*Infantry Platoons vary in number of soldiers, so the total number of troops in an infantry Formation will vary depending on the infantry type(s).

INFANTRY SQUADS

Infantry Squads are Conventional Infantry with a Cargo (CAR) Special Ability of 1. They are smaller infantry forces that accompany some combat vehicles as support. Infantry with CAR1 are separate units for gameplay and Point Value costs, but can be treated as part of the combat vehicle (with Infantry Transport IT1) for force building, using only the Combat Vehicle's Role and *Alpha Strike* stats for Formation requirements. Infantry Squads can only be selected for a Force along with the IT1 Unit, they can not be added to a Force on their own.

INFANTRY FOOT SQUADS

Unit Type	TP	SZ	MV	TMM	S/M/L	OV	A/S	PV	Specials
Flamer	CI	1	2f	0	0*/–/–	0	0/1	1	AM, CAR1
MG	CI	1	2f	0	0*/–/–	0	0/1	1	AM, CAR1
Rifle	CI	1	2f	0	0*/–/–	0	0/1	1	AM, CAR1
Laser	CI	1	2f	0	0*/0*/–	0	0/1	2	AM, CAR1
SRM	CI	1	2f	0	0*/0*/–	0	0/1	2	AM, CAR1

REGIMENTAL TABLE OF ORGANIZATION

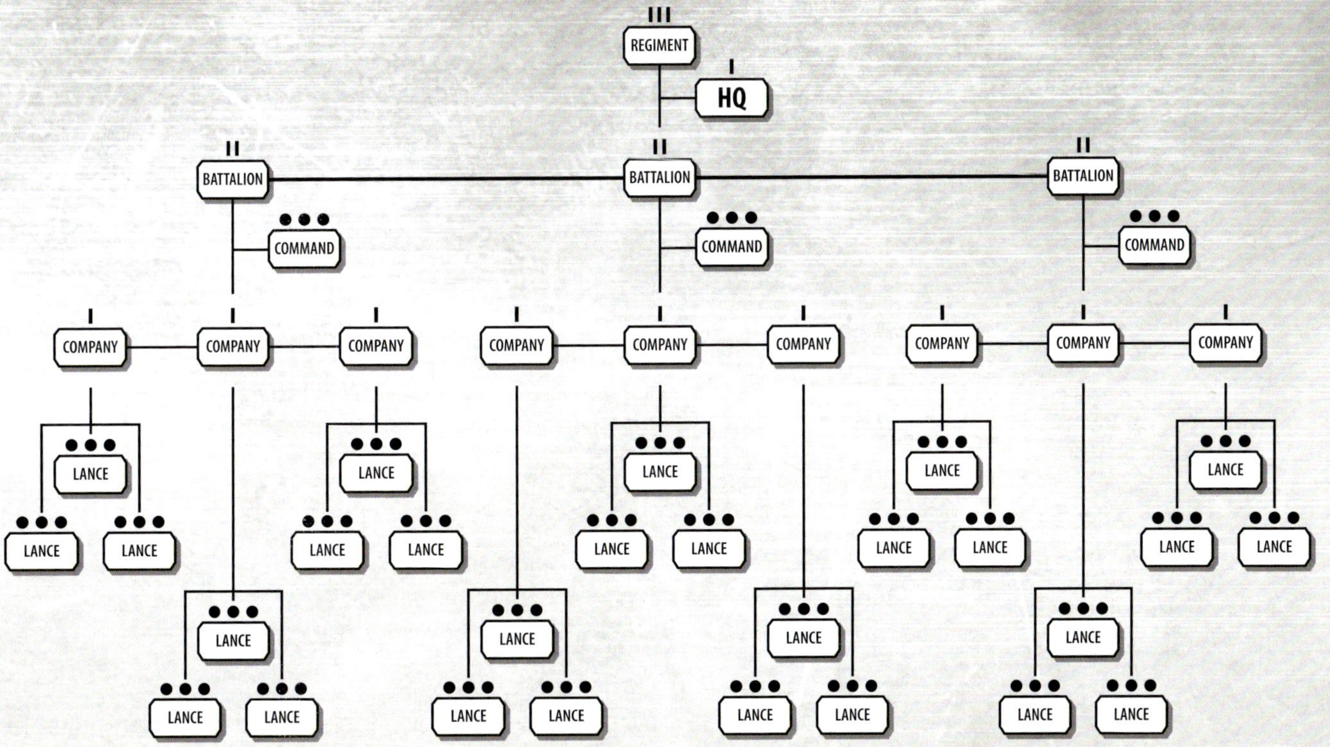

STANDARD MERCENARY ARTILLERY ORGANIZATION		
Unit	**Component Formations**	**Total Strength**
Lance	-	4 artillery Units
Company	3 lances	12 artillery Units
Battalion	3 companies + 1 command lance	36 artillery Units + 4 Units

Artillery Organization

Artillery Formations can include Units with the Artillery special ability (ART). The battalion command lance can be any ground Unit type. Some artillery organizations will include light vehicles or infantry as integrated spotters and recon. These units replace artillery Units in the organization, but no more than one-third of the artillery Formation can be non-artillery units.

STANDARD MERCENARY AVIATION ORGANIZATION		
Unit	**Component Formations**	**Total Strength**
Unit	Component Formations	Total Strength
Lance	-	4 vehicles
Company	3 lances	12 vehicles
Battalion	3 companies + 1 command lance	40 vehicles
Regiment	3 battalions + 1 command company	132 vehicles

Aviation Organization

Aviation Formations are composed of combat vehicles, support vehicles or conventional fighters with the VTOL or Aerospace movement types, but which are not capable of operating in space (do not have the SPC special ability).

BUILD A COMPANY

Multiple Formations in a Force are grouped together as larger Formations, starting with companies. If enough companies are fielded, those are in turn grouped into even larger Formations (see *Force Building Basics*, p. 146, *ASC*). The Company Force Sheet (see p. 128) has space for the Force Building of a single company. Additional sheets are required if building multiple companies. Several Force Building rules are limited per company: Faction Points, Rare Units and multiples of the same variant for 'Mechs only (see *Build Formations* below). Specific Combat Command requirements or limits may occur at organizational levels higher than the company level.

A Force does not need to include complete companies, but at least two complete Formations within a company must be fielded and comply to their Sub-Command's specifications prior to the start of play in order for the Force to benefit from the Sub-Command's Special Command Abilities or Special Rules.

<table>
<tr><th colspan="2">COMPANY COMPOSITION</th></tr>
<tr><td>0-1</td><td>Command Lance</td></tr>
<tr><td>0-2*</td><td>Support Lances</td></tr>
<tr><td rowspan="7">1-4</td><td>Battle Lances</td></tr>
<tr><td>Assault Lances</td></tr>
<tr><td>Striker Lances</td></tr>
<tr><td>Fire Lances</td></tr>
<tr><td>Recon Lances</td></tr>
<tr><td>Pursuit Lances</td></tr>
<tr><td>Security Lances</td></tr>
</table>

*Only 1 Support Lance per 1 core non-Support Lance.

BUILD FORMATIONS

The following steps are repeated for each Formation, which generally consists of three lances per company. A company Formation may include fewer lances, or incomplete lances. However, if a Standard Lance does not include the full number of Units required prior to the start of the game, it does not receive any benefits for a Standard Lance of its type. For example, a lance could include two assault 'Mechs, but it would not receive the Bonus Abilities of the Assault Lance.

STEP 1: CHOOSE FORMATION TYPE

Standard Lances are listed in *Ground Formation Types* (p. 150, *ASC*) and can be used by any Faction. The *Combat Manual* series presents new and variant Standard Lances related to each Faction. (see *New Formation Types*, p. 94). The new Standard Lances follow the same format as those in the *Alpha Strike Companion*. The Units included in Standard Lances must fulfill the requirements for that Formation to receive the Bonus Abilities listed.

STEP 2: CHOOSE UNITS FOR THE FORMATION

There are two methods for filling out your Formation with Units: selecting Units from Availability Lists or using ready-made Standard Lances. A player may mix the two methods, choosing some or all of their Formations from the Standard Lances and then modifying them based on their Faction's Availability Lists.

Standard Lances

Combat Manual: Mercenaries includes a list of Standard Lances with Units already assigned. These Standard Lances include a correct Point Value. If a player selects a Standard Lance and doesn't wish to modify it, they may skip to Step 3 below.

Availability Lists

An Availability List details the Units that are readily available to a specific Faction in a specific Era; for example, the Mercenary Late Succession Wars Availability List is a list of units available to Mercenary Forces in the Late Succession Wars Era.

There are two Availability Lists available to all Mercenaries: General and Mercenary. Mercenary Forces can choose Units from either of these two Availability Lists, published in this *Combat Manual*. If building a Late Succession Wars Force, a player is limited to the Late Succession Wars General and Mercenary Availability Lists. If building an Early Clan Invasion Era Force, they may also use the Early Clan Invasion General and Mercenary Availability Lists.

The Units selected from the Availability Lists must meet any requirements for a Standard Lance, if included in one, as well as any Force Composition Rules for the Combat Command.

Faction Points (FPs): Faction Points are generated and spent at the company level. A player receives 1 FP per Unit in the company, up to 12 FPs. Each Unit has costs 0 or more FPs to add to a Force, based on the Availability List it comes from. A player may not share FPs between different companies. A player cannot exceed 12 FPs per company, but may spend as many or as few FPs per company. A Force with many leftover FPs will clearly appear to belong to its Faction, while a Force that spends all of its FPs will show evidence of prior combat salvage, trade deals, or negotiations. Faction Points are not intended as a Force-balancing system; rather, they help a Force maintain its Faction's "flavor," while allowing some leeway—represented as the Force having acquired odd Units via trade and/or salvage.

SALVAGE, BIRTHRIGHTS AND NEGOTIATION

The armies of the Succession Wars often fielded whatever technology is available. A majority of Units were centuries-old survivors that may have changed hands multiple times. 'Mechs destroyed in battle were fought over and, when possible, repaired and returned to service regardless of who their previous owners were.

MechWarriors handed down their personal 'Mechs as family heirlooms from generation to generation, while family, feudal or national allegiances changed. Allies negotiated agreements to share their military production.

Mercenaries can negotiate access to their employer's military production. Invariably, nearly any Unit could be somewhere in a Great House's army. Faction Points (FP) are a means of maintaining the flexibility of the *BattleTech* universe while still encouraging Faction "flavor." FP costs reflect the general ease or difficulty of acquiring a specific Unit.

WHAT IF I JUST WANT TO START PLAYING?

The Standard Lances (see p. 94 and *ASC*, p. 150) are the quickest way. Just pick a few that match that the desired way to play, or mix and match whatever sounds fun.

Even if players want to hand-pick their Units, there are a few simple points that can help ease Force building.

Faction Points: If Units are chosen from the Mercenary Faction List in the back of this book, ignore Faction Points. They are ONLY needed if Units are added from another faction's Availability List in other *Combat Manuals*. There's no Availability List so expensive that a player can't have at least one Unit per company from any of the Availability List to which they have access. Faction Points are for those wanting to push for a less "pure Faction" force.

Formation Requirements: Most Formations have an Ideal Role. Choosing a Unit with the preferred role can meet Formation requirements for that Unit.

For example, Assault Lances have an Ideal Role of Juggernaut. Select four Juggernauts from the Mercenary Faction List in this book, and that is a legal Mercenary Assault Lance. Pick four Brawlers for a Battle Lance and four Strikers for a Striker Lance, and that is a full Mercenary company. Select Skill ratings to match up with the agreed PV limit, choose Special Command Abilities from the formation's Combat Command, and a complete Mercenary Force is ready to play.

A player should consult the Mercenary Availability Lists Table below for the Era chosen. Each Availability List has a Faction Point Cost associated with selecting a Unit from that list. Units on the General and Mercenary Lists of the current era are generally 0 FP. A player must use FPs to access another Faction's Availability List, representing an alliance, acquisition through trade or enemies, or through salvage. The list of Units belonging to the General and Mercenary Availability Lists for the Late Succession Wars and Early Clan Invasion are found at the end of this book (see *Mercenary Faction Lists*, pp. 110-125). Availability Lists for other Factions can be found in their respective *Combat Manuals*.

The *Mercenary Combat Commands* chapter lists any Common Allies or Enemies for a Force built as part of that Sub-Command. The FP cost of selecting Units from Availability Lists of other Factions is affected if those Factions are Allies or Enemies of a player's Force.

Rare Units: A Unit with an * in the Availability Lists is considered Rare. A player may only have one of any particular Rare Unit in a company. For example, the *Assassin* ASN-21 is rare, as is the *Grasshopper* GHR-5N. A player may include one ASN-21 and one GHR-5N in a single company, but cannot have two ASN-21s in the same company.

Multiple of the Same Variant ('Mech-only): *BattleTech* Forces tend to be ad-hoc, consisting of a mix of whatever Units are available. A company may include more homogenous lances, but at a cost of additional Faction Points (FPs). Each copy of the same Unit in a company costs 1 FP. This applies to specific Unit *variants*—two *Thunderbolt* TDR-5S Units in the same company would cost an additional FP each, but a *Thunderbolt* TDR-5S and a *Thunderbolt* TDR-7M would not. This rule only applies to BattleMechs.

Unique Characters: Unique Characters (as presented in the *Mercenary Combat Commands* chapter or the Unaffiliated MechWarriors section below) do not cost FPs, have a set Skill Rating, an assigned Unit (often a unique Unit with specified stats) and particular Special Pilot Abilities. The Unique Character must be used as-is; the character's Unit, Skill Rating, or Special Pilot Abilities may not be changed. One Unique Character may be included per Force. The Unique Character(s) may only be selected from those listed among a Force's Combat Command, or from the Unaffiliated MechWarriors section (see p. 98).

Sub-Command Formations: Sub-Command Formations are often used to add new Unit types, such as infantry, armor or air Units. Supplemental Formations may be selected from other Sub-Commands within the same Combat Command. Each supplemental Sub-Command Formation must constitute a separate company, but may itself be smaller than a company. For example, a player cannot mix supplemental Sub-Command Formations within a company, but may add only a lance from another Sub-Command and must follow the Force Composition and Force Building Rules of that Sub-Command for that lance. Sub-Command abilities may not be mixed and matched.

For example, a Force includes Formations from two Sub-Commands. One Sub-Command has chosen a Special Command Ability from its Combat Command list, and one from its Sub-Command List. The other Sub-Command must use the same SCA from its Combat Command list, but may choose an SCA from its own Sub-Command list. Likewise, any special rules or other abilities only apply to the Sub-Command for which they are intended.

Supplemental Formations: A Force may add Supplemental Formations from its Faction, defined as Formations that do not belong to its chosen Combat Command or Sub-Commands. These usually represent local militia, garrisons or other attached forces. These Formations may not outnumber a Forces non-supplemental Formations, and they do not benefit from a Force's Special Command Abilities or special rules. These supplemental Formations must be filled with Units from the General or Mercenary Availability Lists (or the Mercenary Standard Lances), as they do not receive Faction Points or access to any other Availability Lists.

ALTERNATE MUNITIONS

The following Alternate Munitions are available during the Late Succession Wars.

Artillery: Flechette, Illumination, Smoke
Autocannon: Flak, Tracer
Bombs: Inferno, Torpedo
LRM/SRM: Heat-seeking, Smoke, Tandem Charge
Mines: Active, Command Detonated, Vibrabomb

In addition to the Late Succession Wars Alternate Munitions, the following become available during the Early Clan Invasion.

Artillery: Arrow IV Homing, Cluster, Copperhead, Thunder (not Active)
Bombs: Arrow IV Homing, Arrow IV Non-Homing, Thunder
LRM/SRM: Thunder

EXPERIENCE RATING / SKILL RATING EQUIVALENCY TABLE

Experience	Skill	Experience	Skill
Wet Behind the Ears	7	Veteran	3
Really Green	6	Elite	2
Green	5	Heroic	1
Regular	4	Legendary	0

MERCENARY AVAILABILITY LISTS TABLE

Late Succession Wars	FP Cost
Mercenary Faction Lists (see pp. 110-125)	
General: Late Succession Wars	0
Mercenaries: Late Succession Wars	0
Allied Lists	
Common Allies for the Combat Command: Late Succession Wars	2
Enemy Lists	
Common Enemies for the Combat Command: Late Succession Wars	3

Early Clan Invasion	FP Cost
Mercenary Faction Lists (see pp. 110-125)	
General: Late Succession Wars, Early Clan Invasion	0
Mercenaries: Late Succession Wars, Early Clan Invasion	0
Allied Lists	
Common Allies for the Combat Command: Late Succession Wars	2
Common Allies for the Combat Command: Early Clan Invasion	3
Enemy Lists	
Common Enemies for the Combat Command: Late Succession Wars	2
Common Enemies for the Combat Command: Early Clan Invasion	3
Common Enemies for the Combat Command: Early Clan Invasion (Clans)	4

STEP 3: SELECT SKILL AND MODIFY PV FOR THE UNIT

For each Unit, select a Skill Rating and adjust the Unit's PV for that Skill Rating, as described in Adjusting for Skill (see p. 24, *Alpha Strike*).

STEP 4: ASSIGN SPECIAL PILOT ABILITIES

Up to one Unit per company may be assigned Special Pilot Abilities (see pp. 50-58, *ASC*). A Unique Character, if any are included, does not count toward this limit. The number of Special Pilot Abilities and the total SPA cost is limited by the Skill rating of that Unit (p. 49, *ASC*).

In addition, Standard Lances often bestow Bonus Special Pilot Abilities that must be assigned during Force building (with the exception of a handful of Formation Bonus Abilities which specifically state that they are assigned during gameplay). Some Combat Command entries include a Force Building Rules section that may affect which SPAs are granted by a Formation's Bonus Ability. For replacement purposes, each 2 points of Lucky (from the Battle Lance Bonus Ability) counts as one SPA.

The Formation is now complete; repeat the above steps for any additional Formations. As companies are completed, the company steps may be repeated until the Point Value maximum is reached.

ASSIGNING SPECIAL COMMAND ABILITIES

Special Command Abilities (see p. 44, *ASC*) apply to the overall Force. They reflect the preferred tactics and specialization training of a Combat Command. The better trained a Force, the more Special Command Abilities the Force can select.

Determine Force Experience Rating

To find a Force's average Experience Rating, add together the Skill ratings for all Units in that Force, divide this sum by the total number of Units, and round the result normally to the nearest whole number. Use that number to determine the Force's final Experience Rating using the Experience Rating / Skill Rating Equivalency Table (p. 86).

For example, a company of 12 'Mechs includes four 'Mechs with a Skill rating of 4, three with a Skill rating of 3, two with a Skill rating of 2, and three more with a Skill rating of 5. The sum of the company's Skill ratings is 44 ([4 x 4] + [3 x 3] + [2 x 2] + [3 x 5] = 44). With 12 units in total, this yields an average Skill Rating of 3.67, which rounds normally to 4. At a rating of 4, the Point Value Skill Rating Table defines the entire Force as having a Regular Experience Rating.

Determine Number of Special Command Abilities

All Forces created to represent Combat Commands listed in the *Mercenary Combat Commands* chapter automatically receive one free Special Command Ability. In addition, middle-grade Forces—those with a Regular Experience Rating—receive one additional, different SCA. Experienced Forces—those rated at Veteran or Elite Experience Ratings—receive two additional, different special SCAs. Truly superior Forces—those with an Experience Rating of Heroic or Legendary—receive three additional, different SCAs. Low-rated Forces—those identified as Green, Very Green, or Wet Behind the Ears—receive no additional Special Command Abilities.

Assign Special Command Abilities

After determining the number of Special Command Abilities a Force possesses, it may choose from either its Combat Command or Sub-Command Special Command Abilities. For example, the 12th Vegan Rangers have *Esprit de Corps* listed at the Combat Command level, so that Special Command Ability is available to any of the 12th Vegan Rangers Sub-Commands, in addition to the Sub-Command's own Special Command Abilities.

Players using an unlisted mercenary Combat Command must roll randomly for each Special Command Ability. For each SCA, roll 2d6 and consult the Special Command Ability Assignment Table below. Reroll duplicate results. Several results require a second 1D6 roll to determine the type of specialization.

SPECIAL COMMAND ABILITY ASSIGNMENT TABLE

2d6 Roll	Special Command Ability
2	Communications Disruption
3	Banking Initiative
4	Overrun Combat
5	Firing Specialization (1-2 Sharp Shooters, 3-4 Brawlers, 5 Anti-Air Specialists, Ground Attack Specialists)
6	Enemy Specialization (1 Mercenary, 2 Davion, 3 Liao, 4 Kurita, 5 Marik, 6 Steiner)
7	Tactical Specialization (1-3 Attack, 4-6 Defense)
8	Environmental Specialists (1 Woods, 2 Water, 3 Winter, 4 Vacuum, 5 Night, 6 Urban)
9	Forcing the Initiative
10	Off-Map Movement
11	Zone of Control
12	Environmental Specialists (1-2 Hot, 3-4 Cold, 5 Low Gravity, 6 High Gravity)

SUPPLEMENTAL MERCENARIES

Many of the big-time mercenary Combat Commands like to maintain their command integrity and fight the battle on their own. But for every Wolf's Dragoons, there are a hundred no-name mercenary outfits willing to fight under any terms that get them paid. Sometimes even Wolf's Dragoons will intentionally dispatch a smaller Force to supplement a House Force—the Black Widow Company being perhaps the most famous example.

If you are building a House Force using one of the House *Combat Manuals*, up to one-third of your Formations may be Mercenaries. The Mercenary Formations are built as if they were their own Force, using the appropriate Availability Lists.

Supplemental Mercenary Forces may not access the House Force's Special Command Abilities. However, they may roll for SCAs—or choose from those listed with Mercenary Combat Commands, if the usual requirements are met—as if they were their own Force, at 1 Experience Rating lower than usual (minimum Wet Behind the Ears/0 SCAs).

Mercenaries fielded as part of a House Force in this fashion receive are discounted 1 PV for every 10 PV spent on them. They are also subject to Morale rules (see pp. 32-33, *ASC*), even if the Morale rules are not in use for the other Forces.

Michael is ready to build a Mercenary Force. His group has set a 400 PV limit, and are playing in the Late Succession Wars. Thus, he has his Point Value total, Era and Faction (400 PV, Late Succession Wars, Mercenary).

Looking over the descriptions in this Combat Manual, *Michael likes the sound (and the lightning) of the Dioscuri (see p. 31). They boast two regiments, Castor and Pollux, and Michael likes the Castor regiment's Special Rules; he selects Castor Regiment of the Dioscuri as his Sub-Command. They are listed at an Experience Rating of Regular. The Dioscuri are a 'Mech regiment, so he will select only 'Mechs for his force. Though not a hard-and-fast rule, the description of the Castor regiment says they field "mostly medium 'Mechs, with a single heavy/assault lance per battalion," so he will keep that in mind. The Force Composition section also states "at least half of the regiment's 'Mechs must be medium (Size 2)," but Michael only needs to adhere to that if he plans to field half a regiment or more (14 lances!) of Castor regiment.*

Michael begins building a company of Dioscuri. There is no mention of an unusual company organization for that Combat Command, so he plans to field three lances of four 'Mechs per lance. The company starts with 12 Faction Points from its 12 units.

The Dioscuri's preference for medium 'Mechs suggests some Standard Lances to use. Striker and Pursuit Lances often include medium 'Mechs, and a Support or Fire Lance might be interesting as well. Michael could apply the "single heavy/assault lance per battalion" to this company, but decides to go with a medium Fire Lance as the third lance instead, wanting to keep his first Dioscuri company a more typical Formation for that Combat Command.

Michael looks over the listing for a Striker Lance, but two of the 'Mechs in that Formation are heavies—so he decides to build the lance himself. With the Federated Suns as their primary employer (Common Allies), Michael can use the General and Mercenary Availability Lists for free, or the Federated Suns Availability List for 2 FPs per Unit. Looking over the IS General list, Michael selects the Enforcer *EF-4R,* Wolverine *WVR-6R,* Vindicator *VND-1R and* Phoenix Hawk *PXH-1. All are included on the General list, and all are 0 Faction Points.*

Next up is the Pursuit Lance. The Standard Lance is a mix of lights and mediums, and Michael likes the provided lineup, so he selects the Formation as-is. All except the Wolfhound *are on the General Availability List and cost 0 FPs. The* Wolfhound *is on the Federated Suns list, so Michael marks down 2 FPs for that 'Mech.*

The last lance of the company is the medium Fire Lance. From the Standard Fire Lance, the Trebuchet *and* Dervish *are medium 'Mechs, so Michael decides to include those. Michael selects the* Griffin *GRF-1N from the General list as the third 'Mech. For the last 'Mech, Michael looks over the Federated Suns list again, and chooses the* Valkyrie *VLK-QA.*

CONTRACT TYPES

There are numerous types of contracts between employers and mercenaries. The type of contract determines what missions and duties are expected from the command and how the employer will support the command. Contracts can roughly be classified as defensive or offensive.

Defensive Contracts

Cadre: The command is hired to train personnel, usually corporate security or planetary militia. This is often paired with a garrison contract.

Garrison: The command is hired to protect one or more specific sites, whether multiple planets or a single factory, from raids or dedicated assaults. Security duty is a subset of garrison duty, in which the command serves as a bodyguard or watchdog for a single person or site.

Retainer: The command is hired to respond to any employer demand for defensive actions for a set period of time. When not called on, the command performs garrison duty.

Relief Duty: The command is hired to support the employer's other forces already under assault by an enemy.

Campaign: The command is hired to engage and delay an enemy assault until the employer's regular forces can be deployed.

Riot Duty: The command is hired to put down social unrest. The Ares Conventions require that such forces only be used to stop rioters threatening a legitimate government and that minimal force be used to quell the unrest.

Michael has only used 4 of his 12 Faction Points, and considers swapping one 'Mech for a Draconis Combine 'Mech (Common Enemies). He likes the look of the Wolverine *WVR-6K, and uses 3 more Faction Points to change the* Wolverine *in the Striker Lance from the general -6R to the Combine -6K variant.*

Michael hadn't intended to use a unique pilot, but he sees Sarah Turner, an Unaffiliated MechWarrior, is a Dervish *pilot and commands a raiding company. He already has a* Dervish *in his Fire Lance, and decides to use Sarah Turner as the captain of his company.*

Michael now calculates the PV of the Units he has selected so far.

Striker Lance: Enforcer *ENF-4R (27),* Wolverine *WVR-6K (32),* Vindicator *VND-1R (28),* Phoenix Hawk *PXH-1 (25). 112 PV.*

Pursuit Lance: Wolfhound *WLF-1 (22),* Clint *CLNT-2-3T (19),* Jenner *JR7-D (20),* Centurion *CN9-A (28). 89 PV.*

Fire Lance: Trebuchet *TBT-5N (27),* Dervish *DV-6M (Sarah Turner) (36),* Griffin *GRF-1N (30),* Valkyrie *VLK-QA (21). 114 PV.*

Michael has only used 315 PV so far. With 85 PV left, Michael has to decide whether to increase the Skill levels of his Units, or add more Units. Michael decides on a mix of both options. While the Castor regiment is entirely 'Mechs, the Dioscuri have infantry support—the Brotherhood—and so Michael decides to add a few detachments of infantry. To deal with heavier forces, Michael selects several platoons of motorized infantry towing Sniper artillery pieces, and several platoons of foot infantry as spotters.

Detachments:

Artillery Lance: 4x Mechanized Infantry (Rifle) w/ towed Thumper (52).

Scout Lance: 4x Foot Infantry (Rifle) (16).

These detachments bring Michael's total to 383 points. He raises the Griffin *(+6),* Wolverine *(+6) and* Wolfhound *(+5) to Skill 3. This makes the final total exactly PV 400.*

One unit per company can be assigned Special Pilot Abilities. Michael chooses the Veteran Griffin *GRF-1N to have the Jumping Jack and Range Master (Long) SPAs. He also makes sure to note Sarah Turner's Jumping Jack and Cluster Hitter special pilot abilities.*

Next, Michael notes the Bonus Abilities received from the Lance Types he chose: two Sniper Special Pilot Abilities available to the Fire Lance (assigned during gameplay, so he puts a note on the Fire Lance itself of "2x Sniper"); for the Pursuit Lance, Michael assigns the Bloodstalker SPA to the Wolfhound, Jenner *and* Centurion*; and in the Striker Lance, the Speed Demon SPAs are assigned to the* Enforcer, Wolverine *and* Vindicator.

Michael is now ready to add the Force's Special Command Abilities. First, he calculates his Force's Experience Rating as Regular (less than half the force was raised in Skill Rating). This gives the force two Special Command Abilities (one for building a Force based on a noted Combat Command, and a second for possessing an Experience Rating of Regular). Castor has just two Command Abilities available, Off-Map Movement and Zone of Control, so Michael marks both down on the Company Force Sheet and is done building his Force.

CONTRACT TYPES [CONTINUED]

Offensive Contracts

Pirate Hunting: The command is hired to track and destroy stateless rogues. These contracts bring excellent wages, salvage, and transport rights. The opposition usually consists of small forces, making these desirable for new and small commands.

Reconnaissance: The command is hired to penetrate enemy territory and determine defensive capabilities. These missions often precede a raid or planetary assault.

Diversionary Raid: The command is hired to lure enemy defenders away from an objective prior to their employer's other forces' arriving to attack that objective.

Objective Raid: The command is hired to penetrate enemy territory and assault a specific target.

Extraction Raid: The command is hired to penetrate enemy territory to capture and return an item, person, or group of persons to the employer.

Planetary Assault: The command is hired to carry out or (more often) support a dedicated invasion of an enemy world. These contracts all but guarantee the heaviest fighting, as taking and holding territory is the primary goal.

Covert Operations: The command is hired to perform missions not publicly acknowledged by the employer. These missions include assassination, kidnapping, guerrilla warfare, sabotage, terrorism, and espionage. These contracts are usually kept secret from the Mercenary Review Board so the employer can maintain plausible deniability. This type of mission places undue weight on the command, and generally offers higher wages than other contract types.

MERCENARY SPECIAL COMMAND ABILITIES

For the purposes of the *Combat Manuals*, several terrains or environmental conditions have been combined into a single Special Command Ability specialization. Players should generally be fairly lenient in deciding whether or not a given map counts for the terrain. For example, a single tree does not constitute Woods, but several small areas (or one large area) of forested terrain should be counted as Woods for the purposes of the SCA specialization.

BATTLETECH

COMPANY FORCE RECORD SHEET

Faction: Mercenary Era: Late Succession Wars PV: 400
Experience Level: Regular
Command Special Abilities: Off-Map Movement, Zone of Control

Combat Command: Dioscuri Sub-Command: Castor Regiment
Company Name: Michael's Company

Lance: Striker Lance Lance Special Abilities:

Unit	Skill	FP (List)	PV	Pilot Special Abilities
Enforcer ENF-4R	4	0 (General)	27	Speed Demon
Wolverine WVR-6K	3	3 (Kurita)	32	Speed Demon
Vindicator VND-1R	4	0 (General)	28	Speed Demon
Phoenix Hawk PXH-1	4	0 (General)	25	

Lance: Pursuit Lance Lance Special Abilities:

Unit	Skill	FP (List)	PV	Pilot Special Abilities
Wolfhound WLF-1	3	2 (Davion)	46	Bloodstalker
Clint CLNT-2-3T	4	0 (General)	34	
Jenner JR7-D	4	0 (General)	33	Bloodstalker
Centurion CN9-A	4	0 (General)	52	Bloodstalker

Lance: Fire Lance Lance Special Abilities: Sniper (2 units/turn)

Unit	Skill	FP (List)	PV	Pilot Special Abilities
Trebuchet TBT-5N	4	0 (General)	27	
Griffin GRF-1N	3	0 (General)	30	Jumping Jack, Ranger Master (Long)
Dervish DV-6M Sarah Turner	3	Unique	36	Jumping Jack, Cluster Hitter
Valkyrie VLK-QA	4	0 (General)	21	

Sub Command / Supplemental

Unit	Skill	FP (List)	PV	Notes
Artillery Detachment				
4X Mechanized Foot Platoon	4	0 (General)	52	(Rifle) w/ towed Thumper
Scout Detachment				
4X Foot Platoon	4	0 (General)	16	(Rifle)

ENVIRONMENTAL SPECIALIZATIONS

Clear: The bonuses for this Special Command Ability work differently than the other Environmental Specializations (see Environmental Specialist (clear) Benefits List, p. 91)

Urban: This specialization includes any pavement, building, or bridge terrain. If this Force chooses the Improved Combat option, attacks from this force halve the Damage Absorption of any buildings (round up).

Woods: This specialization includes Woods (as well as different levels of Woods: Light Woods, Heavy Woods, Ultra-Heavy Woods) and Jungle (and the different levels of Jungle).

Vacuum: This specialization includes Trace Atmosphere.

Winter: This specialization includes Snow, Ice, and Tundra terrain areas, as well as any Cold environment conditions.

Optional Game Setup: Environment Conditions

Environmental Specializations are prominent Command Abilities, yet aren't often used outside of campaigns or detailed scenarios. In order to allow for greater use of Environmental Specializations (or to specifically deny an opponent's use), the following rule may be used. Before setup, each player rolls 2D6 and adds any Initiative bonus their Force would normally receive in play. A result of 10+ allows the side to choose one environmental condition (see *AS*, pp. 92-95) or underlying terrain feature. If both player succeed in their roll, the palyer with the higher result (roll 1D6 to break ties) chooses first. The terrain or environmental condition cannot contradict scenario or campaign conditions, nor can it contradict the choice of a side that rolled higher.

ENEMY SPECIALIZATIONS

Mercenary: In addition to individuals Houses or Clans, Mercenaries may be selected as an Enemy Specialization; this specialization applies against any Force constructed using this *Combat Manual*.

ENVIRONMENTAL SPECIALIST (CLEAR) BENEFITS LIST

Benefit	Rules
Improved Mobility	If a Unit in a Force with this specialization starts its turn in Clear terrain, it may add 2" to its Move for the turn, as long as it also ends its movement in Clear terrain and does not change elevation during the movement.
Improved Combat	If a Unit in a Force with this specialization is attacked while occupying Clear terrain, and there is no Terrain, Environmental or Cover To-Hit Modifier to the attack, the attack receives a +1 To-Hit Modifier as a Terrain Modifier.
Improved Initiative	A Force cannot choose this option with Environmental Specialization (Clear).

NEW SPECIAL COMMAND ABILITIES

The following new Special Command Abilities are available for Mercenary Forces in addition to the existing SCAs.

Berserkers: At the start of any turn, a Force with this ability may elect to go berserk for the rest of the battle. The Force gets a -1 To-Hit Modifier for all attacks, but their Target Movement Modifier is reduced by 1, to a minimum of 0.

Camouflage: Ground Units that are part of a Force with this ability and use the Stand Still movement option receive a +2 Target Movement Modifier, in place of the usual +0. Regardless of the scenario, the Force may place half its starting Units as Hidden Units, even if it is the Attacker. The Force may place Hidden Units even in terrain where 'Mechs cannot usually hide.

Combat Drop Specialists: Units in a Force with this ability always succeed on all Drop rolls (see *Dropping Troops*, p.90, *AS*). The Force receives a +2 Initiative Modifier the turn after making a Combat Drop of at least half its Units.

Esprit de Corps: A Force with this ability is never subject to Forced Withdrawal or Morale checks.

False Flag: This Force must also have the Off-Map Movement Command Ability. It may designate up to one-third of its Units in a scenario as operating under a False Flag. These designated Units are kept off map until they enter the map on the third turn or later. On the turn the controlling player declares the False Flag Units are entering the map, before initiative is rolled, roll 2d6. On an 8+, the Unit has not been discovered as false, and may enter on any map edge, including the opposing player's home edge. In addition, the controlling player receives +2 to their Initiative rolls on the turn the False Flag Forces enter the map. On a 7 or less, the ruse was discovered and the Units must enter from an edge on the half of the map containing their home edge.

Gun it: The Units in this Force may sprint (see *AS*, p. 63) and attack, but do so with a +1 To-Hit penalty and increase their Heat Scale by 1.

Highlander Burial: The Units in a Force with this ability receive a -1 To-Hit Modifier and deal an additional point of damage when making Death From Above attacks.

Hit and Run: At the start of any turn that a Force with the Hit and Run ability is outnumbered, its Units can ignore the To-Hit Modifier for jumping, or receive a -1 To-Hit Modifier if not standing still or immobile.

Rapid Strike: In any scenario in which a Force with this ability is the Attacker, its Units move onto the map as normal, but only half of the opposing Force may deploy at the start of the game or on the first turn. The remaining enemy Units are divided into two equal-sized groups that move onto the map from their home edge on Turns 2 and 3. The group moving onto the map is chosen at random. The controlling player chooses the specific Units that do not deploy in the first turn, as well as the composition of the two undeployed groups.

Savages: All Units get the Blood Stalker SPA. No enemy Unit may be targeted by the Blood Stalker ability by more than one Unit in the force with Savages. If there are not enough enemy Units to target, the remaining Savages Units suffer the penalty for attacking any enemy Unit. When a Unit without a Blood Stalker target activates, and there is an enemy no longer targeted by a Blood Stalker ability, that Unit may then declare a target for its Blood Stalker SPA.

Tactical Adjustments: After turn 3, the opposing Force does not gain any bonuses to their Initiative rolls from Command Abilities or Special Pilot Abilities.

Tactical Experts (Engineers): During setup, this controlling player of the Force with this ability may place light buildings or minefields on the table during setup. The Engineers can place one light building (2" diameter or 1 hex) or five points of minefield density in 1-5 minefields per Lance. The buildings and minefields must be placed on the Engineers' half of the play area.

Tactical Experts (Hidden Units): In any scenario that allows Hidden Units, a Force with this ability may place twice as many Hidden Units (to a maximum of 4 extra Units). If the scenario does not provide for Hidden Units, this force may place up to four Hidden Units on their half of the map, at least 12" away from any enemy Units.

Tactical Experts (Physical): The controlling player of a Force with this ability may choose to have all its Units receive a +1 To-Hit Modifier for weapon attacks in order to receive a -1 To-Hit Modifier for physical and melee attacks. This choice is made in the Combat Phase each turn, before making any attacks.

Tactical Experts (Siege): Units in the command with this Special Command Ability reduce the Damage Absorption rating of buildings by half (round the reduced value down). A non-infantry target in a light building would have a 0 Damage Absorption against an attacker using this Special Command Ability.

PLAYER-GENERATED MERCENARY COMBAT COMMANDS

This rules section allows players to create their own mercenary Combat Command using many of the options available to canon Combat Commands. Different options are given a Combat Command Point cost so that players can choose which options they would like to use.

Combat Command Points (CCPs)

A player-created mercenary Combat Command receives 12 CCPs to create their mercenary Force.

More (or less) prestegious Combat Commands (optional): The default CCPs of 12 for player-created mercenary Combat Commands can be adjusted to fit the players' campaign. 25 or more CCPs and your Force will rival Wolf's Dragoons. 5 CCPs and employers are unlikely to recall who you are even after they hire you.

FORCE COMPOSITION

The player-created mercenary Combat Command must create a force composition, defining its Formations (see p. 82). Each Formation type (armor lance, BattleMech company, aerospace wing, and so on, up to regiment in size) costs 1 CCP. Two Formations may be purchased for 1 CCP total, if they are each under a company in size. Once a BattleMech Formation is purchased, each additional BattleMech Formation costs an extra 1 CCP.

Sub-Commands: If the Combat Command has more than one Formation type, it may designate any or all of them as separate Sub-Commands. If a Combat Command has more than one BattleMech reinforced regiment (or the equivalent amount of smaller 'Mech Formations), each one must be in a seperate Sub-Command. Sub-Commands may have their own Skill Rating and Special Command Abilities (see Skill Rating and Special Command Abilities, below).

EXPERIENCE RATING AND SPECIAL COMMAND ABILITIES

Next, the player must purchase an Experience Rating for each Sub-Command, or for the Combat Command overall if there are no separate Sub-Commands. Expereince Rating of Green costs 0 CCPs, Regular costs 1 CCPs, Veteran costs 2 CCPs and Elite costs 4 CCPs.

A Combat Command selects a number of Special Command Abilities based on its overall Experience Rating (or the largest, best-rated Sub-Command). The Combat Command must choose at least one Special Command Ability for each Experience Rating beyond Green. One for Regular, two for Veteran and three for Elite. The Combat Command may purchase additional command abilities above the number required for its Experience Rating, at the cost of 1 CCP per each additional command ability.

Sub-Commands: If the Combat Command contains more than one Sub-Command, it may choose to split its Special Command Abilities to its Sub-Commands. Each SCA assigned to a Sub-Commands allows each of those Sub-Commands to choose one Special Command Ability. So a Veteran Combat Command with three SCAs may choose one SCA for the overall Combat Command (available to all Sub-Commands) and two SCAs for its Sub-Commands, allowing each of them to select two different SCAs.

AVAILABILITY LISTS

Next, select the Combat Commands Common Allies and Enemies, and which Availability Lists they can access. The Great Houses (Davion, Liao, Kurita, Steiner, Marik) are 1 CCPs each as Common Enemies, 2 CCPs each as Common Allies.

Selecting an Early Clan Invasion Clan Common Enemy costs 3 CCPs. For 4 CCPs, the Combat Command may select Wolf's Dragoons as Common Allies.

Players may use a unique Availability List or Force Building Rules from the mercenaries presented in the Mercenary Combat Commands chapter (such as the Twenty-first Centauri Lancers, Fifteenth Dracon or Snord's Irregulars) at a cost of 4 CCPs. If the unique Availability List or Force Building Rules are only available to a command lance or Sub-Command, this same restriction holds for the player-created mercenary Combat Command.

SPECIAL RULES

A player-created mercenary Combat Command may choose to use the Special Rules of another published Combat Command, at the cost of 2 CCPs. If the Special Rule includes a drawback or penalty (not just a condition, but a negative effect), the special rule costs only 1 CCP.

UNIQUE CHARACTER

A player-created mercenary Combat Command can create one Unique Character. A Unique Character with a Regular Skill Rating does not cost any CCPs. A Veteran Unique Character costs 1 CCP, and an Elite Unique Character costs 2 CCPs. An Heroic Unique Character costs 4 CCPs. The Unique Character may have a custom unit at the cost of 1 additional CCP. The Unique Character's Skill Rating determines how many Special Pilot Abilities they can have, as per the Special Pilot Abilities rule (see p. 49, *ASC*).

MERCENARY OPFOR (OPTIONAL)

This option allows players to randomly roll up an Opposing Force (OpFor) for players to face, without having to build a Force from the ground up each time and allowing for a different composition each battle.

First, determine the mercenary Combat Command. You can either choose a Combat Command from the Mercenary Combat Commands chapter or roll 1D6 and consult the corresponding affiliation tables (at left). Next, roll the number of D6s as indicated on the table and use the listed Combat Command. If the result doesn't seem appropriate for any reason, simply reroll.

1: DAVION

2d6	Combat Command
2	Lindon's Company
3	Grim Determination
4	Blue Star Irregulars
5	12th Vegan Rangers
6	Dismal Disinherited
7	Eridani Light Horse
8	Illician Lancers
9	Lexington Combat Group
10	Screaming Eagles
11	Dioscuri
12	Wylie's Coyotes

2: LIAO

1d6	Combat Command
1	15th Dracon
2	Marshigama's Legionnaires
3-4	Northwind Highlanders
5-6	4th Tau Ceti Rangers

3: MARIK

1d6	Combat Command
1-2	21st Centauri Lancers
3	Langendorf Lancers
4	Fuchida's Fusiliers
5-6	Smithson's Chinese Bandits

4: STEINER

2d6	Combat Command
2	Cranston Snord's Irregulars
3	Crescent Hawks
4	Grave Walkers
5-6	12th Star Guards
7	Hansen's Roughriders
8	Gray Death Legion
9	Kell Hounds
10	The Filthy Lucre
11	Killer Bees
12	Richard's Panzer Brigade

5: KURITA/OTHER

2d6	Combat Command
2	Glory Warriors
3	Ramilie's Raiders
4	Brion's Legion
5	Lone Wolves
6	17th Recon Regiment
7	Simonson's Cutthroats
8	Waco Rangers
9-10	Wolf's Dragoons
11	Derek's Devils
12	Wilson's Hussars

6: RANDOM GENERATION MERCENARY

Experience Rating (1D6)
1: Green; **2-3:** Regular; **4-5:** Veteran; **6:** Elite
Force Composition (1D6)
1-2: 'Mech only; **3:** 'Mechs and Armor; **4:** 'Mechs, Armor, Aerospace; **5:** 'Mechs, Armor, Infantry; **6:** 'Mechs, Armor, Aerospace, Infantry
Availability Lists (1D6; Roll once each for Common Ally and Enemy)
1: Davion; **2:** Liao; **3:** Kurita; **4:** Marik; **5:** Steiner; **6:** None
Special Command Abilities (2D6)
Roll 2D6 and consult the Special Command Ability Assignment Table (p. 87); Roll once for Green, twice for Regular and three times for Veteran or Elite.

SELECT FORMATIONS

Begin building the OpFor by rolling on the Random Formation Type Table. For each Formation rolled, add the corresponding Mercenary Standard Lance to the Force. Next, apply the Combat Command's (or Sub-Command's) Skill Rating to each Unit and adjust PV. Repeat the process until you reach the agreed upon Point Value (PV) limit. If at any point you exceed the PV limit, you may adjust the Skill Rating on a Unit or remove a Unit or Formation all together to drop back below the PV limit.

Once per company you may instead choose the corresponding Standard Lance from one of the Combat Command's Common Allies or Enemies (from other *Combat Manuals*), with the exception of any Clan Common Enemies.

If the Combat Command has a Clan Common Enemy, replace one Unit in the company (after selecting all its Standard Lances) with one Unit from the Clan Availability List. This is in addition to the one non-Clan Common Ally or Common Enemy Standard Lance per company.

Random Skill Ratings (optional): After each Standard Lance is assigned, use the Combat Command's (or Sub-Command's) Skill Rating to roll on the Random Skill Rating Table for each Unit.

Different Unit Types (optional): If the Combat Command has multiple Unit Types, create the first Formation (or whole company) as BattleMechs, then create the next as another Unit Type, and so on until you cycle back to BattleMechs again, or until the PV limit is reached.

For Armor, Aerospace or Infantry Formations, select one Unit from the Availability Lists. The entire Formation is composed of that Unit.

RANDOM FORMATION TYPE TABLE*

2d6 Roll*	Formation	2d6 Roll*	Formation
2-4	Assault	9	Recon
5-6	Fire	10	Pursuit
7	Battle	11	Support
8	Striker	12	Security

*May choose one Command Lance per company instead of rolling.

RANDOM SKILL RATING TABLE

Experience	1D6 Roll Result: Unit Experience Rating (Skill Rating)
Green	**1-4:** Green (5); **5:** Regular (4); **6:** Veteran (3)
Regular	**1:** Green (5); **2-4:** Regular (4); **5:** Veteran (3); **6:** Elite (2)
Veteran	**1-2:** Regular (4); **3-4:** Veteran (3); **5-6:** Elite (2)
Elite	**1:** Regular (4); **2-3:** Veteran (3); **4-5:** Elite (2); **6:** Heroic (1)

MERCENARY LANCES [FORMATIONS]

NEW LANCE [FORMATION] TYPES

In addition to the Standard Lances presented in the *Alpha Strike Companion* (pp. 150-159), the following new Formations may be used.

Security Lance

Mercenary work isn't all glamorous raids and planetary assaults—the bulk of a mercenary's work is garrison duty. Whether protecting something as large as a planet or as small as a manufacturing plant, a good Security Lance knows the lay of the land. Comprised of solid but mobile designs, this Lance has the firepower to ward off raiders as well as pursue them if required.

Requirements: The Formation must have one Scout or Striker and one Sniper or Missile Boat. There can be no more than 1 assault (Size 4) in the Formation.

Bonus Ability: If acting as the Defender in a scenario, 75 percent of the Units in the Formation are assigned a Terrain Master or Environmental Specialist SPA of their choice (must be the same SPA for all units) at the beginning of play. Otherwise, 75 percent of the Units in the Formation are assigned the Speed Demon SPA at the beginning of play.

Demi-Company

A Demi-Company is an ad-hoc formation of six units working together. However, a small number of mercenary commands use Demi-Companies as permanent Formations, with two Demi-Companies comprising one company.

Requirements: Exclusive to the Mercenary Faction. The Formation must have 6 Units. This Formation type modifies another Standard Lance type which must be specified along with the Demi-Company designation. If a Force uses a Demi-Company, all Lances must be Demi-Companies. Two Demi-Companies make up a company instead of three Lances per company. It costs 4 FP to create a Demi-Company.

Ideal Role: Per the Standard Lance being modified.

Bonus Ability: Per the Standard Lance being modified.

STANDARD LANCES

The following mercenary Standard Lances are provided for players who simply want to get straight into the action and not delve into the Force Building rules. Standard Lances are provided for the Late Succession War and the Early Clan Invasion Eras, and all MechWarriors have a base skill of 4 (Regular). Skill Ratings can be adjusted to fine-tune the lance's overall PV within a Force. More adventurous players may swap out one or more Units as long as the Standard Lance's requirements are still met (see pp. 150-159, *ASC*).

STANDARD MERCENARY ASSAULT LANCE

Era	Unit Type	Role	TP	SZ	MV	TMM	S/M/L	OV	A/S	PV	Specials	
LATE SUCCESSION WARS	*Victor* VTR-9B	Juggernaut	BM	4	8j	1	4/4/0	0	6/6	37	AC2/2/-	PV 146
	Hunchback HBK-4G	Juggernaut	BM	2	8	1	4/3/0	0	5/4	28	AC2/2/-	
	Stalker STK-3F	Juggernaut	BM	4	6	1	3/4/2	3	7/7	42	IF1	
	Grasshopper GHR-5H	Skirmisher	BM	3	8j	1	3/4/0.5	0	7/6	39	IF0*	
EARLY CLAN INVASION	*Victor* VTR-9K	Skirmisher	BM	4	8j	1	4/4/2	0	7/6	42	CASE	PV 176
	Catapult CPLT-C1	Missile Boat	BM	3	8j	1	2/3/2	1	5/5	33	IF1,LRM1/1/1	
	Stalker STK-5M	Juggernaut	BM	4	6	1	5/6/2	0	8/7	49	IF1,LRM1/1/1,SNARC,SRM2/2	
	Atlas AS7-S	Juggernaut	BM	4	6	1	5/5/2	0	10/8	52	AC2/2/-,IF1,LRM1/1/1,REAR2/2/-	

STANDARD MERCENARY BATTLE LANCE

Era	Unit Type	Role	TP	SZ	MV	TMM	S/M/L	OV	A/S	PV	Specials	Lance PV
LATE SUCCESSION WARS	*Orion* ON1-K	Brawler	BM	3	8	1	3/3/1	1	8/6	39	IF1	PV 127
	Catapult CPLT-C1	Missile Boat	BM	3	8j	1	2/3/2	1	5/5	33	IF1,LRM1/1/1	
	Vindicator VND-1R	Brawler	BM	2	8j	1	2/2/2	0	5/4	28	IF0*	
	Enforcer ENF-4R	Skirmisher	BM	2	8j	1	3/2/0	0	5/4	27	AC1/1/-	
EARLY CLAN INVASION	*Orion* ON1-M	Brawler	BM	3	8	1	3/4/2	0	7/3	36	CASE,FLK1/1/1,IF1,LRM1/1/1,SNARC	PV 130
	Warhammer WHM-7S	Brawler	BM	3	8	1	5/4/2	1	5/6	36		
	Wolverine WVR-7M	Skirmisher	BM	2	12/10j	2	3/3/2	1	5/3	32		
	Enforcer ENF-5D	Skirmisher	BM	2	10j	2	2/2/2	0	5/2	26	CASE,FLK1/1/1	

STANDARD MERCENARY COMMAND LANCE

Era	Unit Type	Role	TP	SZ	MV	TMM	S/M/L	OV	A/S	PV	Specials	Lance PV
LATE SUCCESSION WARS	*Cyclops* CP-10-Z	Juggernaut	BM	4	8	1	3/3/1	2	5/7	34	AC1/1/-,IF1	PV 113
	Dervish DV-6M	Missile Boat	BM	2	10j	2	2/2/2	1	4/5	30	IF1	
	Quickdraw QKD-4G	Skirmisher	BM	3	10j	2	2/3/1	0	4/5	30	IF1,REAR1/1/-	
	Vulcan VL-2T	Scout	BM	2	12j	2	2/1/0.5	0	3/3	19		
EARLY CLAN INVASION	*Cyclops* CP-11-A	Sniper	BM	4	8	1	4/4/3	0	5/7	38	IF1	PV 127
	Crusader CRD-5S	Missile Boat	BM	3	8	1	3/3/2	1	6/5	34	CASE,IF1,LRM1/1/1,SRM1/1	
	Shadow Hawk SHD-5M	Missile Boat	BM	2	10j	2	2/3/2	0	6/3	33	CASE,IF1	
	Vulcan VT-5M	Striker	BM	2	12j	2	3/2/0	0	3/3	22		

STANDARD MERCENARY FIRE LANCE

Era	Unit Type	Role	TP	SZ	MV	TMM	S/M/L	OV	A/S	PV	Specials	Lance PV
LATE SUCCESSION WARS	*Awesome* AWS-8Q	Sniper	BM	4	6	1	3/3/3	0	8/6	39	ENE	PV 138
	Trebuchet TBT-5N	Missile Boat	BM	2	10	2	2/2/2	1	4/4	27	IF1	
	Dervish DV-6M	Missile Boat	BM	2	10j	2	2/2/2	1	4/5	30	IF1	
	Stalker STK-3F	Juggernaut	BM	4	6	1	3/4/2	3	7/7	42	IF1	
EARLY CLAN INVASION	*Archer* ARC-4M	Missile Boat	BM	3	8	1	3/5/4	0	7/6	45	CASE,IF3,REAR1/1/-	PV 157
	Trebuchet TBT-7M	Missile Boat	BM	2	10j	2	3/3/2	0	4/2	29	CASE,IF1,LRM1/1/1,SNARC	
	Dervish DV-7D	Missile Boat	BM	2	10j	2	3/3/2	0	5/5	34	CASE,IF1,LRM1/1/1	
	Stalker STK-5M	Juggernaut	BM	4	6	1	5/6/2	0	8/7	49	IF1,LRM1/1/1,SNARC,SRM2/2	

STANDARD MERCENARY PURSUIT LANCE

Era	Unit Type	Role	TP	SZ	MV	TMM	S/M/L	OV	A/S	PV	Specials	Lance PV
LATE SUCCESSION WARS	***Wolfhound* WLF-1**	Striker	BM	1	12	2	2/2/0	1	4/3	22	ENE,REAR1/1/-	PV 89
	***Clint* CLNT-2-3T**	Striker	BM	2	12j	2	2/2/1	0	2/3	19		
	***Jenner* JR7-D**	Striker	BM	1	14/10j	3	2/2/0	1	2/3	20		
	***Centurion* CN9-A**	Brawler	BM	2	8	1	2/3/1	0	5/4	28	AC1/1/-,IF1,REAR1/1/0	
EARLY CLAN INVASION	***Wolfhound* WLF-2**	Striker	BM	1	12	2	3/3/1	0	4/3	25	ENE,REAR1/1/-	PV 105
	***Firestarter* FS9-S**	Scout	BM	1	12j	2	1/1/0	0	3/3	22	AMS,HT1/-/-,PRB,RCN,REAR0*/-/-	
	***Wolverine* WVR-7M**	Skirmisher	BM	2	12/10j	2	3/3/2	1	5/3	32		
	***Centurion* CN9-D**	Skirmisher	BM	2	12	2	2/2/2	0	5/2	26	CASE,FLK1/1/1,IF1,REAR1/1/-	

STANDARD MERCENARY RECON LANCE

Era	Unit Type	Role	TP	SZ	MV	TMM	S/M/L	OV	A/S	PV	Specials	Lance PV
LATE SUCCESSION WARS	***Cicada* CDA-2A**	Scout	BM	2	16	3	2/1/0	0	2/3	16	ENE	PV 70
	***Hermes* HER-1A**	Scout	BM	1	18	3	2/1/0	0	2/3	16	ENE	
	***Firestarter* FS9-H**	Scout	BM	1	12j	2	2/1/0	0	3/3	19	HT1/-/-	
	***Vulcan* VL-2T**	Scout	BM	2	12j	2	2/1/0.5	0	3/3	19		
EARLY CLAN INVASION	***Cicada* CDA-3M**	Striker	BM	2	16	3	2/2/1	0	2/2	18	CASE	PV 81
	***Wasp* WSP-1S**	Scout	BM	1	12j	2	2/1/0	0	2/2	15	ENE	
	***Firestarter* FS9-S**	Scout	BM	1	12j	2	1/1/0	0	3/3	22	AMS,HT1/-/-,PRB,RCN,REAR0*/-/-	
	***Phoenix Hawk* PXH-3M**	Skirmisher	BM	2	12j	2	2/2/2	1	4/2	26	AMS,CASE	

STANDARD MERCENARY STRIKER LANCE

Era	Unit Type	Role	TP	SZ	MV	TMM	S/M/L	OV	A/S	PV	Specials	Lance PV
LATE SUCCESSION WARS	***Quickdraw* QKD-4G**	Skirmisher	BM	3	10j	2	2/3/1	0	4/5	30	IF1,REAR1/1/-	PV 114
	***Hermes* II HER-2S**	Scout	BM	2	12	2	2/1/1	0	4/3	21		
	***Vulcan* VL-5T**	Striker	BM	2	12j	2	2/2/0	0	4/3	24		
	***Grasshopper* GHR-5H**	Skirmisher	BM	3	8j	1	3/4/0.5	0	7/6	39	IF0*	
EARLY CLAN INVASION	***Wolverine* WVR-7M**	Skirmisher	BM	2	12/10j	2	3/3/2	1	5/3	32		PV 105
	***Vulcan* VT-5S**	Striker	BM	2	16/12j	3	2/2/1	0	3/2	22	CASE	
	***Ostroc* OSR-3C**	Skirmisher	BM	3	10	2	2/2/0	1	5/5	28	ENE	
	***Hermes* II HER-5S**	Striker	BM	2	12	2	2/2/1	0	4/3	23		

STANDARD MERCENARY SUPPORT LANCE

Era	Unit Type	Role	TP	SZ	MV	TMM	S/M/L	OV	A/S	PV	Specials	Lance PV
LATE SUCCESSION WARS	***Firestarter*** **FS9-H**	Scout	BM	1	12j	2	2/1/0	0	3/3	19	HT1/-/-	PV 107
	JagerMech **JM6-A**	Missile Boat	BM	3	8	1	2/2/2	1	4/5	27	IF1	
	Catapult **CPLT-C1**	Missile Boat	BM	3	8j	1	2/3/2	1	5/5	33	IF1,LRM1/1/1	
	Centurion **CN9-A**	Brawler	BM	2	8	1	2/3/1	0	5/4	28	AC1/1/-,IF1,REAR1/1/0	
EARLY CLAN INVASION	***Firestarter*** **FS9-S**	Scout	BM	1	12j	2	1/1/0	0	3/3	22	AMS,HT1,PRB,RCN,REAR0*/-/-	PV 128
	Thunderbolt **TDR-9SE**	Skirmisher	BM	3	8j	1	3/4/1	0	7/5	39	CASE,IF1	
	Warhammer **WHM-7M**	Brawler	BM	3	8	1	4/4/2	0	5/6	35	AMS	
	Blackjack **BJ-2**	Sniper	BM	2	8j	1	3/3/2	1	5/4	32		

STANDARD MERCENARY SECURITY LANCE

Era	Unit Type	Role	TP	SZ	MV	TMM	S/M/L	OV	A/S	PV	Specials	Lance PV
LATE SUCCESSION WARS	***Firestarter*** **FS9-H**	Scout	BM	1	12j	2	2/1/0	0	3/3	19	HT1/-/-	PV 101
	JagerMech **JM6-A**	Missile Boat	BM	3	8	1	2/2/2	1	4/5	27	IF1	
	Centurion **CN9-A**	Brawler	BM	2	8	1	2/3/1	0	5/4	28	AC1/1/-,IF1,REAR1/1/0	
	Blackjack **BJ-1**	Sniper	BM	2	8j	1	2/2/0.5	1	5/4	27		
EARLY CLAN INVASION	***Firestarter*** **FS9-S**	Scout	BM	1	12j	2	1/1/0	0	3/3	22	AMS,HT1/-/-,PRB,RCN,REAR0*/-/-	PV 132
	Archer **ARC-4M**	Missile Boat	BM	3	8	1	3/5/4	0	7/6	45	CASE,IF3,REAR1/1/-	
	Thunderbolt **TDR-7M**	Brawler	BM	3	8	1	4/4/2	0	7/5	39	CASE,IF1	
	Phoenix **Hawk PXH-3M**	Skirmisher	BM	2	12j	2	2/2/2	1	4/2	26	AMS,CASE	

STANDARD WOLF'S DRAGOONS ASSAULT LANCE

Era	Unit Type	Role	TP	SZ	MV	TMM	S/M/L	OV	A/S	PV	Specials	Lance PV
LATE SUCCESSION WARS	***Cyclops*** **CP-10-Z**	Juggernaut	BM	4	8	1	3/3/1	2	5/7	34	AC1/1/-,IF1	PV 161
	Shogun **SHG-2E**	Missile Boat	BM	4	6j	1	3/3/3	2	8/7	46	CASE,IF2,LRM1/1/2,SRM1/1	
	Awesome **AWS-8Q**	Sniper	BM	4	6	1	3/3/3	0	8/6	39	ENE	
	Stalker **STK-3F**	Juggernaut	BM	4	6	1	3/4/2	3	7/7	42	IF1	
EARLY CLAN INVASION	***Annihilator*** **ANH-2A**	Juggernaut	BM	4	4	0	4/4/3	2	7/8	41	CASE,FLK2/2/3	PV 176
	Shogun **SHG-2F**	Missile Boat	BM	4	6j	1	2/3/2	1	8/7	43	CASE,IF1,LRM(1/1/1),OVL	
	Imp **IMP-3E**	Juggernaut	BM	4	6	1	4/4/3	3	10/4	47	CASE,IF1	
	Marauder **II MAD-5A**	Sniper	BM	4	6j	1	3/3/3	1	10/4	45	FLK1/1/1	

UNAFFILIATED MECHWARRIORS

The following MechWarriors never committed to any one mercenary group, or belonged to one of the many smaller, relatively unknown mercenary commands. They can be used with any Mercenary Combat Command which does not already include a Unique Character.

Mikhail Muller

Mikhail Muller has jumped from one merc group to another, always on the lookout for a big payday. He is a specialist, his *Orion* having swapped out the autocannon and LRMs for a Sniper artillery piece. Mikhail is an expert shot, and has a knack for firing a shell just as the enemy is grouped for maximum effect. But he is also a bit of a diva, and has left several units after complaining they didn't do enough to "keep the enemy off me!"

MIKHAIL MULLER									PV: 42 (58)
Unit Type	**Skill**	**TP**	**SZ**	**MV**	**TMM**	**S/M/L**	**OV**	**A/S**	**Specials**
***Orion* ON1-K** (Muller)	2	BM	3	8	1	1/1/0	1	8/6	ARTS-1
Special Pilot Abilities: Oblique Artilleryman, Combat Intuition									

Lieutenant Fiasal Bukhari

The Bukhari family runs an interstellar trading company based in Tamar, with links through marriage to both the original Tamar brothers and the later ruling Kelswa family. Faisal joined a mercenary command to protect his home and family. He feels betrayed, first by House Steiner in the formation of the Rasalhague Republic, and then by the Federated Commonwealth in its limited defense of Tamar against the Clans.

With the Clan invasion approaching Tamar, Faisal requested and was granted leave to join the defense of Tamar. Fiasal led a lance of fellow mercenaries under a contract with the 26th Lyran Guards, but his *Trebuchet* was destroyed and Faisal was forced to withdraw with the rest of the Lyran Guards. He has made his way back to his former command, where he received a hero's welcome as one of the few with experience versus the Clans.

LIEUTENANT FIASAL BUKHARI									PV: 27 (37) | 29 (41)
Unit Type	**Skill**	**TP**	**SZ**	**MV**	**TMM**	**S/M/L**	**OV**	**A/S**	**Specials**
***Trebuchet* TBT-5N**	2	BM	2	10	2	2/2/2	1	4/4	IF1
***Trebuchet* TBT-7M**	2	BM	2	10j	2	3/3/2	0	4/2	CASE, IF1, LRM1/1/1, SNARC
Special Pilot Abilities: Sniper, Fist Fire									

Captain Sarah Turner

Captain Sarah Turner leads the "Kangaroo" Company, a specialist in raiding. Turner never stands still, whether in a 'Mech or on her own two feet. Outside her 'Mech, she is an avid martial artist, competing in Taekwondo competitions and exhibitions wherever she finds herself.

In the Early Clan Invasion, Turner negotiated an overhaul of her *Dervish*; an upgraded engine and double heat sinks allow her to use all her firepower without overheating.

CAPTAIN SARAH TURNER									PV: 30 (42) | 35 (49)
Unit Type	**Skill**	**TP**	**SZ**	**MV**	**TMM**	**S/M/L**	**OV**	**A/S**	**Specials**
***Dervish* DV-6M**	2	BM	2	10j	2	2/2/2	1	4/5	IF1
***Dervish* DV-6M** (Turner)	2	BM	2	10j	2	3/4/2	0	5/3	LRM1/2/2, IF2
Special Pilot Abilities: Cluster Hitter, Jumping Jack									

Charles Bear

A third-generation MechWarrior descended from Native American ancestors, Bear has served with renowned mercenary commands including the Tau Ceti Rangers, Twenty-first Centauri Lancers, and the Gray Death Legion.

A quiet, somewhat secretive man, Bear does not mix with his fellow MechWarriors. Despite his less-than-friendly manner, he is well-respected for his battlefield prowess and loyalty to his comrades. Younger MechWarriors regard this mysterious, towering man with awe and more than a little fear.

In 3026, Charles Bear enters service with the Gray Death Legion, and from that time on remains exclusively with that mercenary command.

CHARLES BEAR									PV: 38 (54)
Unit Type	**Skill**	**TP**	**SZ**	**MV**	**TMM**	**S/M/L**	**OV**	**A/S**	**Specials**
***Crusader* CRD-3R** (Bear)	2	BM	3	8	1	5/4/0	1	6/5	SRM3/3/-
Special Pilot Abilities: Demoralizer, Lucky (1)									

Captain "El Guapo"

Known only as "El Guapo," the commander of the Errai-based Old Crows Mercenary Company is notorious for his hard drinking and vicious fighting. El Guapo pilots a customized *Banshee*, constantly upgraded since its theft from the Nineteenth Galedon Regulars—an act that precipitated a feud between Guapo's mercs and the Regulars.

CAPTAIN "EL GUAPO"									PV: 38 (62) | 44 (71)
Unit Type	**Skill**	**TP**	**SZ**	**MV**	**TMM**	**S/M/L**	**OV**	**A/S**	**Specials**
***Banshee* BNC-3E**	1	BM	4	8	1	2/2/2	0	8/8	
***Banshee* BNC-3E** (El Guapo)	1	BM	4	8	1	4/4/3	0	10/4	CASE, FLK1/1/1
Special Pilot Abilities: Sniper, Lucky (1)									

TECHNICAL READOUT

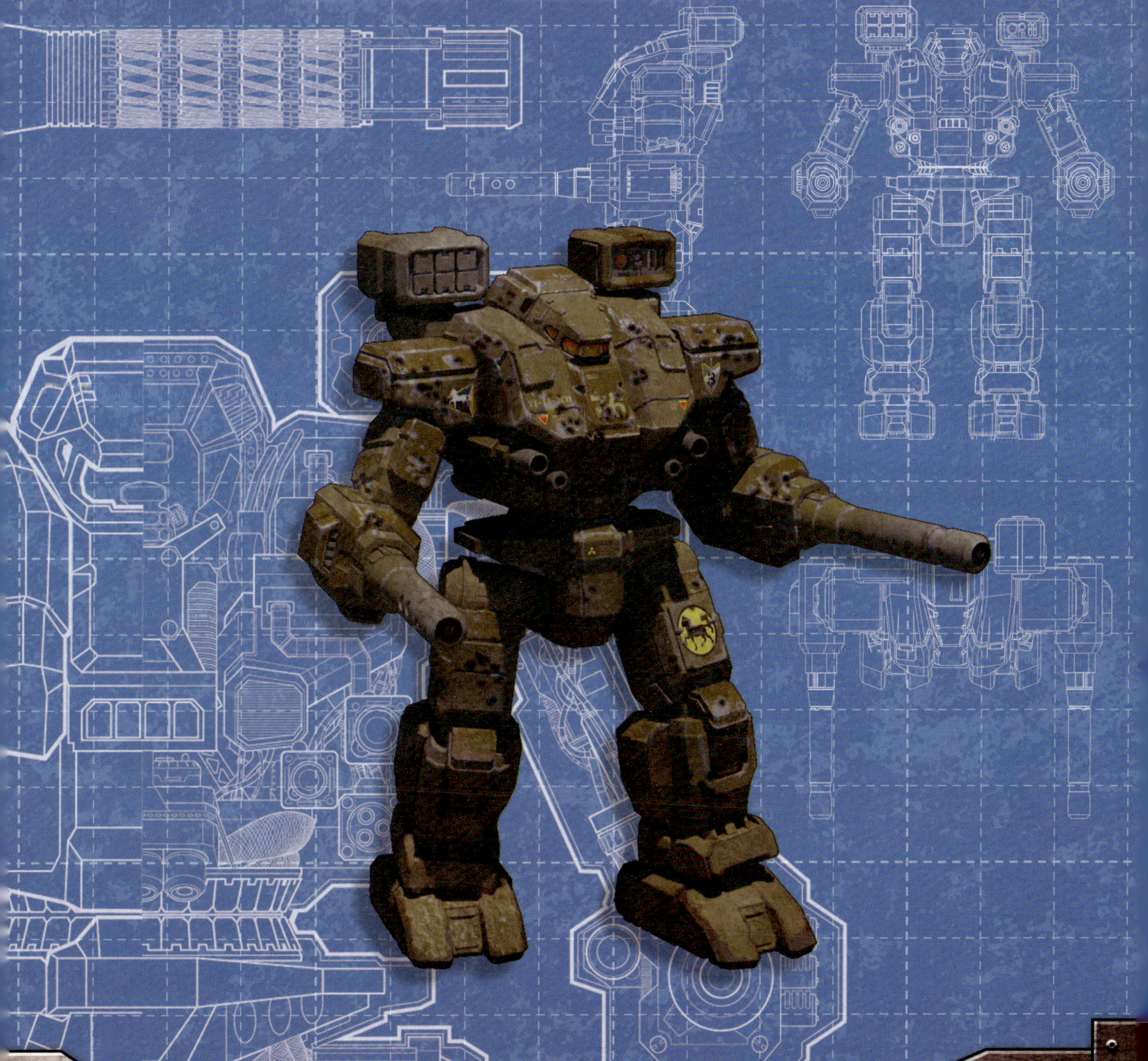

LCT-1V LOCUST

Mass: 20 tons
Chassis: Bergan VII
Power Plant: LTV 160
Cruising Speed: 86 kph
Maximum Speed: 129 kph
Jump Jets: None
Jump Capacity: None
Armor: StarSlab/1
Armament:
1 Medium Martell Laser
2 SperryBrowning Machine Guns
Manufacturer: Bergan Industries, Alliance Defenders Limited, Majesty Metals and Manufacturing
Communications System: Garrett T10-B
Targeting and Tracking System: O/P 911

The *Locust* is among the most common BattleMechs in existence. After five centuries of production, the *Locust* has propagated throughout the entirety of the Inner Sphere; rare is the House or mercenary outfit lacking at least one of these speedy, low-cost scouts. The *Locust* is so ubiquitous, some joke that spare parts can be found at local convenience stores while purchasing snacks and drinks.

CAPABILITIES

For centuries, it was rare to find a 'Mech that could match the *Locust*'s speed. The technological recovery spurred by the Helm Memory Core allows modern 'Mechs to outrun the *Locust*, but only through expensive and sometimes temperamental technology. Very light armor motivates *Locust* MechWarriors to avoid prolonged combat, though the 'Mech carries almost as much as possible. Speed is the *Locust*'s substitute for armor, though its awkward, spindly profile also makes enemies miss their target. Machine guns make the maneuverable *Locust* a terror for infantry.

DEPLOYMENT

In 3042, the Ninth Dieron Regulars uncovered evidence that large depots of materiel stockpiled for the War of 3039 remained on Errai. The Regulars sent a battalion to claim the precious salvage or destroy it and deny it to the hated Davions. The battalion included a recon company led by a lance of *Locusts*. The defending Stirling's Fusiliers of the famed Northwind Highlanders detected the incoming force and immediately sent out skirmishers. Among these was the recon company of Captain Ceallach Munro, also in a *Locust*. The Fusiliers discovered the Ninth's staging area and prepared an ambush, but the sneaky Combine *Locust* lance sniffed out the trap and turned the tables on the Fusiliers. A running battle broke out between the two recon companies. 'Mechs that usually avoid direct combat were now embroiled in it, as neither side was willing to abandon the field of battle. The Fusiliers lured the Regulars into Sangborn Forest on the mountains overlooking the vast ruins of the Maltex Corporation 'Mech factory. Knowledge of the terrain served Munro and his company well, as it became necessary to create small, mostly-controlled avalanches to drive off the Regulars. Holding the high ground allowed the Fusiliers to guide in artillery and air strikes and force the Regulars off Errai.

Lieutenant Bregan Gentry of Second Battalion, First Grave Walkers earned his place in the command's history on Vega in the War of 3039 when he refused the incompetent orders of the Lyran commander and led a guerilla operation. The Second and Fourteenth Legions of Vega were on the brink of breaking Snord's Irregulars in the Carrier Highlands. Gentry's all-energy weapon force, including his LCT-1E *Locust*, harassed the enemy with hit-and-fade attacks for weeks without a break. On 31 July, however, his luck ran out. Gentry's company stumbled into a grand battle between the Legion and the Irregulars and was mistaken for Legion forces when Snord's aerospace forces launched surprise ground attacks. Gentry was killed, though half his command survived to tell of his heroism.

VARIANTS

There are numerous variants of the well-known LCT-1V. Older variants generally replace the machine guns with more effective weapons, often at the cost of precious armor. Modern variants incorporate recovered or newly-developed technology, including components such as ferro-fibrous armor, CASE, streak missiles, triple strength myomer, endo steel skeleton, and anti-missile systems.

NOTABLE UNITS

Captain Ceallach Munro: Captain Munro of Northwind Highlanders' Stirling's Fusiliers has been offered many heavier 'Mechs to replace his ancient *Locust,* but he always demurs. Munro insists he becomes one with his *Locust* and that no other 'Mech can replace it. His ability to weave through forests more than makes up for his 'Mech's lack of jump jets, while his reckless insistence on always traveling at maximum speed makes him a perfect fit for the Fusiliers.

CAPTAIN CEALLACH MUNRO — PV: 14 (17)

Unit Type	Skill	TP	SZ	MV	TMM	S/M/L	OV	A/S	Specials
Locust LCT-1V	3	BM	1	16	3	1/1/0	0	2/2	

Special Pilot Abilities: Terrain Master (Forest Ranger), Melee Specialist

Available To: Northwind Highlanders

OTT-7J OSTSCOUT

Mass: 35 tons
Chassis: Kell/S
Power Plant: VOX 280
Cruising Speed: 86 kph
Maximum Speed: 129 kph
Jump Jets: Ostmann Sct-A
  Jump Capacity: 240 meters
Armor: Durallex Light
Armament:
  1 Tronel II Medium Laser
Manufacturer: Kong Interstellar Corporation
Communications System: Barret 4000
Targeting and Tracking System: TRSS.2L3

The *Ostscout* was the epitome of a scouting unit upon its creation. With few 'Mechs able to match its speed, much less its jump capacity, the *Ostscout* has long been renowned for evading combat after ferreting out enemy positions. The rare 'Mech is not often found among Mercenary forces, as it is hoarded by House militaries. Evading battle has kept most *Ostscouts* in pristine condition despite the depredations of the Succession Wars.

CAPABILITIES

The *Ostscout* was one of the few BattleMechs able to match speeds with a *Locust*, though the addition of jump jets enabled it to exceed that lighter 'Mech's scouting efficacy. Top-of-the-line Star League sensors provided the *Ostscout* with unmatched reconnaissance capability. A nod to self-defense was provided with a single laser, but many *Ostscout* MechWarriors were threatened with Dispossession should they actually engage in combat and risk the precious asset entrusted to them.

DEPLOYMENT

The pursuit of the Black Hat pirates after the Candlemas Massacre of 3016 was greatly aided by the scanning wizardry of an *Ostscout*. Captured on Thule years before by one of Helmar Valasek's raiding parties, the *Ostscout* ranged far and wide on Porthos after the Black Hats were reportedly spotted establishing a base of operations. Valasek didn't care as much about the murdered civilians on Skallevoll—he wanted revenge on those who rebelled against his authority and made off with his money, 'Mechs, and equipment. Seven weeks after beginning its quest, the *Ostscout* located the Black Hat base. Before Santander's Killers could converge on the location, though, the Hats spotted the recon 'Mech and attacked. The Hats had no chance of catching the *Ostscout*, whose pilot, Hondo Jones, openly taunted them over an open comm channel. Before the Hats realized their folly, they were attacked by the Killers, having been led to their staging area by the *Ostscout*.

After Hanse Davion reassigned all Land-Air 'Mechs, one quartet of former LAM pilots were assigned *Ostscouts* in compensation. They formed a rare *Ostscout* lance, assigned to the Third Davion Guards. In the Fourth Succession War, this lance was critical to the Third's successes. On Algol, they enabled the Third to wipe out most of the First Ariana Fusiliers. On Ningpo, they repeatedly detected scouts of McCrimmon's Light Cavalry. On one such occasion, the four *Ostscouts* were so far from friendly lines they elected to engage the enemy rather than allow a potential breakout. The constantly leaping *Ostscouts* evaded enemy fire and slowly forced the Cavalry back into their foothill redoubt through precise concentration of their meager laser fire. On Slocum, the same tactics allowed the Third to destroy the second battalion of the Cavalry. When the Third arrived on Azha, the lance was hardly needed to defeat the poorly-supplied militia that defended the world. The lance came through the war intact, though it was dispersed before the War of 3039. It remains one of few times multiple *Ostscouts* operated in concert.

VARIANTS

The only known variant of the *Ostscout* is the modern refit that removes the medium laser in favor of target acquisition gear. Because the 'Mech is not intended to enter combat, this modification has not been looked upon as unfavorably as casual observers expected.

NOTABLE UNITS

Captain Lupo "Lone Wolf" delVecchio: Captain delVecchio is a well-known recon specialist in the Thirty-second Recon Combat Group. As part of the Lexington Combat Group, delVecchio frequently heads out alone on random patrols, sometimes not returning for days at a time. His *Ostscout* has been with the Thirty-second since the days of the Star League. Despite piloting his *Ostscout* since 3024, delVecchio has never come under enemy fire due to his strong adherence to the spirit of reconnaissance requiring non-engagement. He coaxes greater range from his sensors thanks to intimate familiarity with his 'Mech, as well as greater speed to escape those enemies who have managed to sneak up on him due to modern ECM equipment.

CAPTAIN LUPO "LONE WOLF" DELVECCHIO									PV: 16(19 | 14 (17)
Unit Type	**Skill**	**TP**	**SZ**	**MV**	**TMM**	**S/M/L**	**OV**	**A/S**	**Specials**
Ostscout **OTT-7J**	3	BM	1	16j	3	1/1/0	0	2/3	ENE
Ostscout **OTT-7K**	3	BM	1	16j	3	0/0/0	0	2/3	ENE, TAG
Special Pilot Abilities: Speed Demon, Forward Observer									
Available To: Lexington Combat Group									

SHD-2H SHADOW HAWK

Mass: 55 tons
Chassis: Earthwerks SHD
Power Plant: CoreTek 275
Cruising Speed: 54 kph
Maximum Speed: 86 kph
Jump Jets: Pitban LFT-50
Jump Capacity: 90 meters
Armor: Maximillian 43
Armament:
1 Armstrong J11 Autocannon
1 Holly Long Range Missile 5 Rack
1 Holly Short Range Missile 2 Pack
1 Martel Model 5 Medium Laser
Manufacturer: Earthwerks Incorporated, Majesty Metals and Manufacturing
Communications System: O/P 300 COMSET
Targeting and Tracking System: O/P 2000A

The *Shadow Hawk* is a classic example of a 'Mech built through compromise. It excels at no particular mission, but is able to fulfill myriad roles. It is one of the most familiar 'Mechs in mercenary hands due to its versatility. *Shadow Hawk*s have participated in nearly every major battle for the last five hundred years.

CAPABILITIES

Armchair MechWarriors like to pick out flaw after flaw in the *Shadow Hawk*. Like Land-Air 'Mechs, the Shadow Hawk is considered a jack of all trades, but master of none. For all its supposed shortcomings, the *Shadow Hawk* is a critical component of modern militaries, both House and mercenary. Respectable armor, varied weaponry, and indifference to terrain make it an asset to many commands.

DEPLOYMENT

The Candlemas Massacre on Skallevoll took place in 3016. A rogue lance of Santander's Killers consisting of two *Shadow Hawks*, a TBT-5S *Trebuchet*, and an ancient WTH-1S *Whitworth* fled the pirate's world seeking to establish their own reputation. Calling themselves the Black Hats, the pirates launched a raid on Skallevoll that began well, as the militia was swept aside. Efforts to capitalize on their initial success were stymied by the clever civilian population. While the pirates mauled the militia, valuables were spirited away from the commercial district by the locals. Outraged, the pirates seemingly withdrew from the world. However, they had merely returned to their DropShip to swap their SRMs for Inferno missiles. They returned during the evening of 2 February, while most of the locals were celebrating Candlemas. Seventeen churches and cathedrals were surrounded and set alight, and the 'Mechs blocked all attempts at escape. In addition to the slaughter of innocent worshippers, the pirates also laid waste to three small cities. The Black Hats fled only after word of the atrocity reached Luthien and a company of the Ninth Rasalhague Regulars arrived.

Stellan Whitehorn Sereman achieved a measure of fame during a Capellan raid on Goshen in 3036. The War College cadet became lost during a nighttime patrol when the Capellans landed unexpectedly and a lance of light 'Mechs gathered intelligence on the academy's defenses. Sereman observed the landing and recognized the insignia of Barton's Regiment of McCarron's Armored Cavalry. Realizing he was alone, he radioed in the situation and engaged the enemy. The light 'Mechs scattered as he approached, but not before he lamed the *Locust* with his LRMs. The *Wasp* and *Stinger* flanked him, but he focused his attention on the *Vindicator*. The two exchanged fire while he continued to close the distance. Both 'Mechs were battered by the time Sereman landed a punch that crushed the *Vindicator*'s cockpit. Rather than flee, the fallen warrior's lancemates sought revenge. By the time reinforcements arrived, all five 'Mechs were downed and Sereman was engaged in hand-to-hand combat with the last living invader.

VARIANTS

The most common *Shadow Hawk* variants for centuries were the Davion and Kurita versions. The former traded armor for additional weaponry, while the latter swapped most of the weapons for a PPC and additional heat sinks. Recent variants include a Davion upgrade to streak missiles, and a Marik variant that represents a complete overhaul to incorporate many advanced components and weapons. However, the massive number of *Shadow Hawk*s in mercenary hands should not be expected to conform to standard or variant configurations, due to custom modifications and emergency field replacements.

NOTABLE UNITS

Captain Lori Kalmar-Carlyle: Captain Kalmar-Carlyle is the wife of Gray Death Legion CO Grayson Carlyle. She is the command's executive officer and is part of the command lance. Her *Shadow Hawk*, "Boss Lady," is Carlyle's former 'Mech. Kalmar-Carlyle's expertise is mobile combat, allowing her to serve as the command lance's mobile observation post. Her greatest fear is the element of fire, a phobia which predates an incident in which Carlyle forced her surrender with an Inferno missile. She was the first recruit for what eventually became the Legion.

CAPTAIN LORI KALMAR-CARLYLE									PV: 30 (42)
Unit Type	Skill	TP	SZ	MV	TMM	S/M/L	OV	A/S	Specials
Shadow Hawk SHD-2H	2	BM	2	10/6j	2	2/2/1	0	5/5	IF0*
Special Pilot Abilities: Jumping Jack, Sharpshooter									
Available To: Gray Death Legion									

SHD-2H SHADOW HAWK

WHM-6R WARHAMMER

Mass: 70 tons
Chassis: StarCorps 100
Power Plant: VOX 280
Cruising Speed: 43 kph
Maximum Speed: 64 kph
Jump Jets: None
Jump Capacity: None
Armor: Leviathon Plus
Armament:
 2 Donal PPCs
 2 Martell Medium Lasers
 2 Magna Small Lasers
 1 Holly Short Range Missile 6 Pack
 2 SperryBrowning Machine Guns
Manufacturer: StarCorps Industries, Olivetti Weaponry, Vandenberg Mechanized Industries, Taurus Territorial Industries
Communications System: O/P 3000 COMSET
Targeting and Tracking System: O/P 1500 ARB

The *Warhammer* is one of history's most successful and prolific BattleMechs. StarCorps Industries delivered "a mobile 'Mech with enough firepower to destroy or severely damage any 'Mech of the same weight class or lower," as preference was given to firepower over combat endurance. The *Warhammer* appears in every House military in large numbers, as well as too many mercenary commands to count.

CAPABILITIES

The *Warhammer* mounts an impressive weapons array, a symmetrical load-out save for the missile rack. Enemy MechWarriors rightfully fear the *Warhammer*'s long-range weapons, but its short-range firepower is intended to destroy both enemy 'Mechs and infantry. In some ways, incorporating anti-infantry weapons on such a large "Mech seems superfluous, but the *Warhammer*'s position at the front of an advance often leads it into urban areas where infantry ambushes are likely. Unlike most other heavy 'Mechs, the *Warhammer* sacrifices self-protection in the name of damage infliction. Its light armor has cost many reckless MechWarriors their lives.

DEPLOYMENT

In 3019, Wolf's Dragoons assaulted Hesperus II on the orders of Captain-General Janos Marik. The battle bogged down as the Dragoon regiments failed to break the defensive lines of the Twenty-fourth Lyran Guards, Third Royal Guards, Hsien's Hotheads, and Hansen's Roughriders. Captain Natasha Kerensky in her black *Warhammer*, surprised a lance of defenders in an arroyo and pushed towards the Defiance Industries factory complex. Only the stalwart and desperate effort of Hansen's Roughriders stalled the breakout attack. Kerensky reaped a heavy toll on the Roughriders, tallying more than a dozen kills on Defiance's doorstep as she routinely ignored the *Warhammer*'s commonly-regarded flaws and engaged 'Mechs generally considered superior to her own. Major Cavanaugh "Pinpoint" Striker sought to block her path in his *Awesome* and paid for it with his life. Selfless courage sent a Roughrider medium lance into Kerensky's path; she destroyed a *Phoenix Hawk* and *Griffin* while her command lance took out a *Scorpion*. Only a brave *Shadow Hawk* pilot remained to throw herself against the attackers. Kerensky respected the show of courage and only disabled the brave warrior's 'Mech. That MechWarrior, Celeste Rio, went on to a long and respected career with the Roughriders.

Among the darkest deeds performed by *Warhammers* in combat, McCarron's Armored Cavalry used a lance of their "Hot Hammer" variant to destroy villages and towns on New Valencia in 3007. "The flamers glowed red on New Valencia" was the only recounting the Cavalry offered in reporting the atrocities, but their effort to lure out Wolf's Dragoons did not have the effect the Cavalry might have hoped. Instead of boldly sallying forth from their defensive perimeter, Colonel Jaime Wolf dispatched a lance of *Phoenix Hawks* to locate and ambush the perpetrators. The fast-moving medium 'Mechs outmaneuvered the *Warhammers* in the burning rubble of Paxton, a suburb of Raiteland. Only one of the *Phoenix Hawks* returned to the Dragoons, but none of the *Warhammers* returned to the Cavalry.

VARIANTS

Like most centuries-old BattleMechs, the *Warhammer* has numerous variants. Some are the result of desperation, as the lack of proper replacement parts led to complete weapons changes, while others are rooted in individual nations' preferences. Some add additional heat sinks, while others increase the 'Mech's relatively light armor. New variants are cropping up, too, as the Houses leverage recovered technology to augment a venerable and common 'Mech.

NOTABLE UNITS

Captain Reece McGee: Captain McGee is the grandson of Colonel Andrew McGee, former CO of McGee's Cutthroats. Reece was one of the disaffected members of the command whose calls to leave the Draconis Combine after the Fourth Succession War finally boiled over into open mutiny. Reece was forced to fire upon his own family members during the battle for control of the Cutthroats. When Matthew Simonson's coup was complete, he rewarded the youngest McGee with a company command.

CAPTAIN REECE MCGEE									PV: 32 (38) | 35 (42)
Unit Type	Skill	TP	SZ	MV	TMM	S/M/L	OV	A/S	Specials
Warhammer WHM-6R	3	BM	3	8	1	3/3/2	1	5/6	
Warhammer WHM-7M	3	BM	3	8	1	4/4/2	0	5/6	AMS
Special Pilot Abilities: Dodge, Melee Master									
Available To: Simonson's Cutthroats									

WHM-6R WARHAMMER

GUNS FOR HIRE

Ambermarle's Highlanders

Bad Dream

Black Widow Company

Blackhearts

Blue Star Irregulars

Cranston Snord's Irregulars

Crater Cobras

Crescent Hawks

Derek's Red Devils

The Dioscuri

Filthy Lucre

Fuchida's Fusiliers

11th Fusiliers

Glory Warriors

Grave Walkers

Head Hunters

Helmut's Hermits

Hsien Hotheads

Illician Lancers

Kell Hounds

Brion's Legion

Bullard's Armored Cavalry

Carson's Renegades

21st Centauri Lancers

Clifton's Rangers

Dismal Disinherited

15th Dracon

Dragon's Breath

Eridani Light Horse

Fighting Urukhai

Gray Death Legion

Greenburg's Godzillas

Gregg's Long Striders

Grim Determination

Hansen's Roughriders

Killer Bees

Knights of St. Cameron

The Krushers

Langendorf Lancers

Lexington Combat Group

Lindon's Company

Little Richard's Panzer Brigade

Lone Star Regiment

Lone Wolves

Markson's Marauders

Ramilie's Raiders

17th Recon Regiment

Screaming Eagles

Simonson's Cutthroats

4th Tau Ceti Rangers

Thermo Police

Thumpers

White Witches

Wilson's Hussars

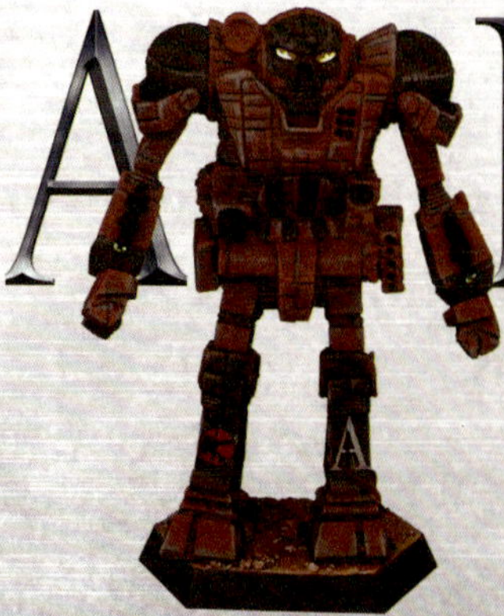
Wolf's Dragoons: Alpha

Wolf's Dragoons: Beta

Marshigama's Legionnaires

Martian Cuirassiers

Mobile Fire

Narhal's Raiders

Northwind Highlanders

Smithson's Chinese Bandits

St. Cyr Heavy Assault Group

12th Star Guards

Stealthy Tigers

Tooth of Ymir

12th Vegan Rangers

Waco Rangers

For additional color schemes visit CAMOSPECS.COM

Wolf's Dragoons: Gamma

Wolf's Dragoons: Delta

Wolf's Dragoons: Epsilon

Wylie's Coyotes

PAINTING A WOLF'S DRAGOONS AWESOME

CamoSpecs artist Michael Holzapfel tackles a Wolf's Dragoons Zeta Battalion *Awesome*.

After cleaning, assembling and priming the model, block out all the metallic areas.

Base Coat the model. Mix flat black with just a small amount of dark green and apply two even coats to all the non-metallic areas. Afterwards apply a thin black wash over the entire model for shading.

Highlights are next. Mix your black with just a small amount of gray green and paint broad strokes on all the edges of the model—make sure to thin your paints. Then, add another small amount of gray green and paint another, smaller, layer around the edges. Repeat lightening and layering as many times until you're satisfied with the result. Here I've painted 6 layers of highlights. **Optional:** at this stage you can give the miniature another black wash to filter the layers and make them uniform.

Optional Chipped Paint: For the red areas I wanted to achieve a chipped paint effect. Use a small piece of sponge or foam, dip in masking fluid, and dab it gently onto the areas to be painted red. Dip a toothpick in masking fluid and set aside for a later step. **Red:** Once dry, block out the red areas with a burgundy or dark red.

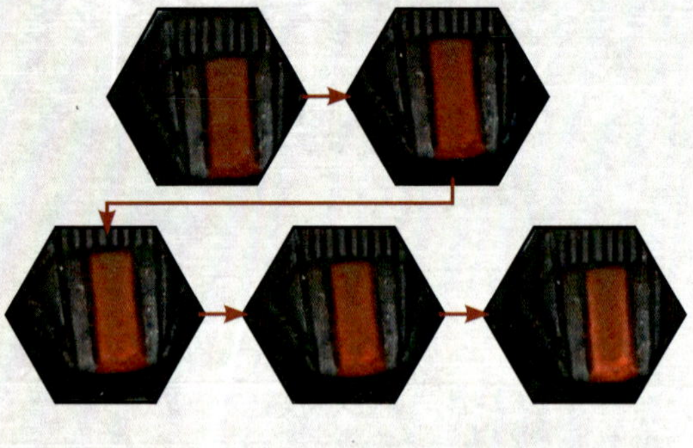

Highlight the red areas using the same layering techniques as the black highlight. Using your base dark red paint, mix in a little bright red and layer on the highlights. For the very final highlight I mixed in a little ivory—not white, as that results in a pink color.

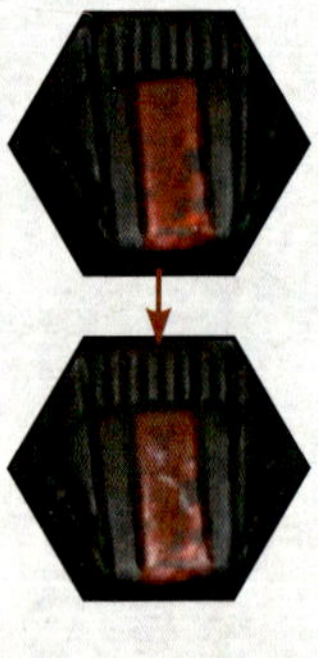

If you opted to try the chipped paint effect, at this point take the toothpick you set aside earlier and rub the red areas gently with the toothpick, revealing random areas of black. This looks good but can be further improved by taking your last red highlight paint and highlighting the areas of the "chips."

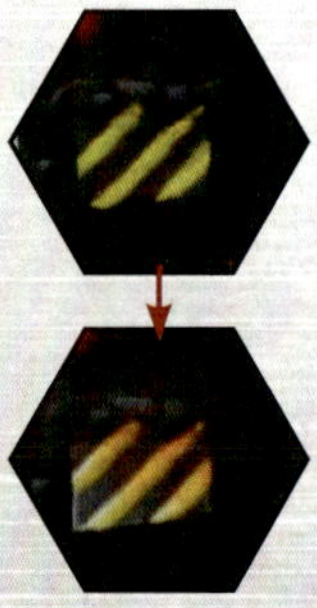

Details: Paint the cockpit using layering techniques again, with dark green while adding bright yellow. Block in yellow warning stripes with a dark yellow, layer on highlights. Wash warning stripes with dark flesh wash.

Final Details: Next, paint some chips and scratches on the black areas by making small marks with black paint on a few select areas, and highlight them with a light gray. Paint the insides of the weapon barrels a dull purple, with a dot of yellow in the center. I carefully painted a number and a Wolf's Dragoons logo on the shoulders, but decals could be used instead.

The Base is meant to evoke an urban battlefield. Base coat is a granite gray color. Highlight with two or three rough layers of progressively lighter grays. Next grab some random greens and browns and add some targeted washes here and there to the base. Follow that with two more controlled layers of even lighter gray highlights. Lastly, paint the edges of the base black.

A Lyran Hatchetman *dances around a* *Filthy Lucre* Stalker*, trying to bring its hatchet to bear.*

This Wolf's Dragoons fire lance—comprised of a Trebuchet*, a* Stalker*, an* Awesome *and a* Dervish*—can lash out with enough firepower to obliterate several city blocks in mere minutes and can do so from a safe distance.*

Rival mercenaries battle at point blank range over meager salvage. The Banshee *hefts a nearby I-beam to gain the advantage over the* Shogun*.*

A Kuritan Avatar*, separated from his lance, comes face to face with a Kell Hounds* Annihilator*.*

Wolf's Dragoons assault 'Mechs ride herd on this captured Davion Sentinel*. The MechWarrior will be ransomed back to his homeland in short order—with or without his BattleMech*

MERCENARY FACTION LISTS

The following Faction Lists are presented in two formats. The first set of tables are grouped by Unit Type, then grouped by Era (with BattleMechs the only Type with an Early Clan Invasion Era Table), and then sorted by Availability and finally listed in alphabetical order. The next format set of Faction Lists group Units by Type and Era, but then sorts by Role and then Point Value (PV).

LATE SUCCESSION WARS: BATTLEMECHS [SORTED BY AVAILABILITY, THEN ALPHABETICAL]

Unit Name	Role	TP	SZ	MV	TMM	S/M/L	OV	A/S	Availability	PV	Specials
Archer ARC-2R	**Missile Boat**	BM	3	8"	1	2/3/3	1	7/6	General	**39**	IF2,LRM1/2/2,REAR1/1/-
Assassin ASN-101	**Scout**	BM	2	14"/10"j	3	2/1/0*	0	2/3	General*	**18**	
Assassin ASN-21	**Scout**	BM	2	14"j	3	1/1/0*	0	2/3	General*	**17**	IF0*
Atlas AS7-D	**Juggernaut**	BM	4	6"	1	5/5/2	0	10/8	General	**52**	AC2/2/-,IF1,LRM1/1/1,REAR1/1/-
Atlas AS7-D-DC	**Juggernaut**	BM	4	6"	1	5/5/1	0	10/8	General	**52**	AC2/2/-,IF1,MHQ1
Atlas AS7-RS	**Juggernaut**	BM	4	6"	1	3/4/1	1	10/8	General	**48**	IF1
Awesome AWS-8Q	**Sniper**	BM	4	6"	1	3/3/3	0	8/6	General	**39**	ENE
Awesome AWS-8R	**Missile Boat**	BM	4	6"	1	2/3/2	0	8/6	General	**38**	IF1,LRM1/1/1
Awesome AWS-8T	**Missile Boat**	BM	4	6"	1	3/3/2	0	8/6	General	**39**	IF1,LRM1/1/1
Awesome AWS-8V	**Sniper**	BM	4	6"	1	3/3/2	0	8/6	General	**39**	IF1
Banshee BNC-3E	**Sniper**	BM	4	8"	1	2/2/2	0	8/8	General	**38**	
Banshee BNC-3M	**Brawler**	BM	4	8"	1	2/2/2	1	8/8	General	**39**	ENE
Banshee BNC-3Q	**Juggernaut**	BM	4	8"	1	3/2/0	0	8/8	General	**37**	AC2/2/-
BattleMaster BLR-1G	**Brawler**	BM	4	8"	1	3/3/1	1	8/7	General	**40**	REAR1/1/-
BattleMaster BLR-1G-DC	**Brawler**	BM	4	8"	1	3/3/1	1	8/7	General	**41**	MHQ1
Black Knight BL-7-KNT	**Brawler**	BM	3	8"	1	3/3/1	2	6/6	General	**34**	ENE
Black Knight BL-7-KNT-L	**Brawler**	BM	3	8"	1	3/3/0	2	6/6	General	**33**	ENE
Blackjack BJ-1	**Sniper**	BM	2	8"j	1	2/2/0*	1	5/4	General	**27**	
Bombardier BMB-10D	**Missile Boat**	BM	3	8"	1	2/2/2	1	7/5	General*	**35**	IF2,LRM1/1/2
Catapult CPLT-C1	**Missile Boat**	BM	3	8"j	1	2/3/2	1	5/5	General	**33**	IF1,LRM1/1/1
Centurion CN9-A	**Brawler**	BM	2	8"	1	2/3/1	0	5/4	General	**28**	AC1/1/-,IF1,REAR1/1/0
Centurion CN9-AH	**Juggernaut**	BM	2	8"	1	3/3/1	0	5/4	General	**29**	AC2/2/-,IF1
Centurion CN9-AL	**Brawler**	BM	2	8"	1	2/2/1	0	6/4	General	**28**	IF1,REAR1/1/-
Charger CGR-1A1	**Scout**	BM	4	10"	2	2/0/0	0	5/6	General	**18**	ENE
Cicada CDA-2A	**Scout**	BM	2	16"	3	2/1/0	0	2/3	General	**16**	ENE
Cicada CDA-2B	**Scout**	BM	2	16"	3	2/1/0	0	2/3	General	**16**	ENE
Cicada CDA-3C	**Scout**	BM	2	14"	3	2/1/1	0	2/3	General	**17**	
Clint CLNT-2-3T	**Striker**	BM	2	12"j	2	2/2/1	0	2/3	General	**19**	
Commando COM-2D	**Striker**	BM	1	12"	2	2/2/0	0	2/2	General	**15**	SRM1/1
Cyclops CP-10-Z	**Juggernaut**	BM	4	8"	1	3/3/1	2	5/7	General	**34**	AC1/1/-,IF1
Dervish DV-6M	**Missile Boat**	BM	2	10"j	2	2/2/2	1	4/5	General	**30**	IF1
Dragon DRG-1N	**Skirmisher**	BM	3	10"	2	2/2/2	0	5/5	General	**30**	IF1,REAR1/1/-
Enforcer ENF-4R	**Skirmisher**	BM	2	8"j	1	3/2/0	0	5/4	General	**27**	AC1/1/-
Firestarter FS9-H	**Scout**	BM	1	12"j	2	2/1/0	0	3/3	General	**19**	HT1/-/-
Grasshopper GHR-5H	**Skirmisher**	BM	3	8"j	1	3/4/0*	0	7/6	General*	**39**	IF0*
Griffin GRF-1N	**Sniper**	BM	2	10"j	2	1/2/2	0	5/5	General	**30**	IF1
Guillotine GLT-4L	**Skirmisher**	BM	3	8"j	1	4/4/0	0	6/6	General	**37**	
Hermes II HER-2S	**Scout**	BM	2	12"	2	2/1/1	0	4/3	General	**21**	
Hunchback HBK-4G	**Juggernaut**	BM	2	8"	1	4/3/0	0	5/4	General	**28**	AC2/2/-
Hunchback HBK-4H	**Juggernaut**	BM	2	8"	1	4/3/0	0	5/4	General	**28**	AC1/1/-
Hunchback HBK-4J	**Missile Boat**	BM	2	8"	1	3/3/2	1	5/4	General	**31**	IF1
Hunchback HBK-4N	**Brawler**	BM	2	8"	1	3/3/2	1	5/4	General	**31**	IF1
Hunchback HBK-4P	**Brawler**	BM	2	8"	1	5/4/0	0	5/4	General	**31**	ENE
Hunchback HBK-4SP	**Brawler**	BM	2	8"	1	4/4/0	0	5/4	General	**30**	SRM2/2
JagerMech JM6-A	**Missile Boat**	BM	3	8"	1	2/2/2	1	4/5	General	**27**	IF1
JagerMech JM6-S	**Sniper**	BM	3	8"	1	3/3/2	0	3/5	General	**26**	AC1/1/1
Javelin JVN-10N	**Striker**	BM	1	12"j	2	2/2/0	0	2/3	General	**18**	SRM2/2
Jenner JR7-D	**Striker**	BM	1	14"/10"j	3	2/2/0	1	2/3	General	**20**	
King Crab KGC-0000	**Juggernaut**	BM	4	6"	1	3/3/1	2	9/8	General	**44**	AC2/2/-,IF1
Locust LCT-1V	**Scout**	BM	1	16"	3	1/1/0	0	2/2	General	**14**	
Longbow LGB-0W	**Missile Boat**	BM	4	8"	1	2/3/3	0	5/7	General	**36**	IF3,LRM1/3/3
Longbow LGB-7Q	**Missile Boat**	BM	4	6"	1	3/4/3	0	8/7	General	**45**	IF3,LRM2/3/3
Marauder MAD-3R	**Sniper**	BM	3	8"	1	2/3/3	1	6/6	General	**35**	

LATE SUCCESSION WARS: BATTLEMECHS [SORTED BY AVAILABILITY, THEN ALPHABETICAL]											
Unit Name	**Role**	**TP**	**SZ**	**MV**	**TMM**	**S/M/L**	**OV**	**A/S**	**Availability**	**PV**	**Specials**
Mongoose MON-66	**Scout**	BM	1	16"	3	2/2/0	0	3/2	General*	**22**	ENE,PRB,RCN
Orion ON1-K	**Brawler**	BM	3	8"	1	3/3/1	1	8/6	General	**39**	IF1
Orion ON1-V	**Brawler**	BM	3	8"	1	3/3/1	2	6/6	General	**35**	IF1
Orion ON1-VA	**Juggernaut**	BM	3	8"	1	4/4/0	0	8/6	General	**39**	AC1/1/-,SRM1/1
Orion ON1-V-DC	**Brawler**	BM	3	8"	1	2/3/1	1	6/6	General	**35**	IF1,MHQ1
Ostroc OSR-2C	**Skirmisher**	BM	3	10"	2	3/3/0	1	5/5	General	**31**	
Ostroc OSR-2D	**Skirmisher**	BM	3	10"	2	4/4/2	0	5/5	General	**35**	
Ostroc OSR-3C	**Skirmisher**	BM	3	10"	2	2/2/0	1	5/5	General	**28**	ENE
Ostscout OTT-7J	**Scout**	BM	1	16"j	3	1/1/0	0	2/3	General	**16**	ENE
Panther PNT-8Z	**Brawler**	BM	1	8"j	1	2/2/0	0	4/3	General	**21**	
Panther PNT-9R	**Brawler**	BM	1	8"j	1	2/2/1	0	3/3	General	**20**	
Phoenix Hawk PXH-1	**Skirmisher**	BM	2	12"j	2	2/2/0	0	4/4	General	**25**	
Quickdraw QKD-4G	**Skirmisher**	BM	3	10"j	2	2/3/1	0	4/5	General	**30**	IF1,REAR1/1/-
Quickdraw QKD-4H	**Skirmisher**	BM	3	10"j	2	2/2/1	1	4/5	General	**29**	IF1,REAR1/1/-
Rifleman RFL-3N	**Sniper**	BM	3	8"	1	2/2/1	2	4/5	General	**26**	
Scorpion SCP-1N	**Skirmisher**	BM	2	12"	2	2/2/1	0	4/5	General	**25**	
Shadow Hawk SHD-2H	**Skirmisher**	BM	2	10"/6"j	2	2/2/1	0	5/5	General	**30**	IF0*
Spider SDR-5V	**Scout**	BM	1	16"j	3	1/1/0	0	2/3	General	**16**	ENE
Stalker STK-3F	**Juggernaut**	BM	4	6"	1	3/4/2	3	7/7	General	**42**	IF1
Stalker STK-3H	**Missile Boat**	BM	4	6"	1	3/4/2	2	7/7	General	**42**	IF2,LRM1/1/2,SRM1/1
Stalker STK-4N	**Juggernaut**	BM	4	6"	1	4/4/1	2	7/7	General*	**41**	IF1,SRM1/1
Stalker STK-4P	**Juggernaut**	BM	3	6"	1	3/4/1	2	7/6	General*	**39**	IF1
Stinger STG-3G	**Scout**	BM	1	12"j	2	1/1/0	0	2/2	General	**14**	ENE
Stinger STG-3R	**Scout**	BM	1	12"j	2	1/1/0	0	2/2	General	**14**	
Thunderbolt TDR-5S	**Brawler**	BM	3	8"	1	3/3/1	1	7/5	General	**36**	IF1
Thunderbolt TDR-5SE	**Skirmisher**	BM	3	8"j	1	3/3/1	0	7/5	General	**37**	IF1
Thunderbolt TDR-5SS	**Brawler**	BM	3	8"	1	3/3/1	1	7/5	General	**35**	
Trebuchet TBT-5J	**Skirmisher**	BM	2	10"j	2	2/3/1	0	4/4	General	**28**	IF1
Trebuchet TBT-5N	**Missile Boat**	BM	2	10"	2	2/2/2	1	4/4	General	**27**	IF1
UrbanMech UM-R60	**Ambusher**	BM	1	4"j	0	2/1/0	0	3/3	General	**12**	AC1/1/-
Victor VTR-9A	**Skirmisher**	BM	4	8"j	1	3/3/0	1	5/6	General	**33**	AC1/1/-
Victor VTR-9A1	**Skirmisher**	BM	4	8"j	1	4/4/0	0	5/6	General	**35**	AC2/2/-
Victor VTR-9B	**Juggernaut**	BM	4	8"j	1	4/4/0	0	6/6	General	**37**	AC2/2/-
Vindicator VND-1R	**Brawler**	BM	2	8"j	1	2/2/2	0	5/4	General	**28**	IF0*
Vulcan VL-2T	**Scout**	BM	2	12"j	2	2/1/0*	0	3/3	General	**19**	
Vulcan VL-5T	**Striker**	BM	2	12"j	2	2/2/0	0	4/3	General	**24**	
Warhammer WHM-6R	**Brawler**	BM	3	8"	1	3/3/2	1	5/6	General	**32**	
Wasp WSP-1A	**Scout**	BM	1	12"j	2	1/1/0	0	2/2	General	**14**	
Whitworth WTH-1	**Missile Boat**	BM	2	8"j	1	2/2/2	1	4/3	General	**26**	IF1
Wolverine WVR-6R	**Skirmisher**	BM	2	10"j	2	2/2/1	0	5/5	General	**29**	
Wyvern WVE-6N	**Skirmisher**	BM	2	8"j	1	2/2/1	1	5/4	General	**29**	IF1
Zeus ZEU-6S	**Sniper**	BM	4	8"	1	3/3/2	0	6/6	General	**35**	IF1,REAR1/1/-
Hornet HNT-151	**Striker**	BM	1	10"j	2	1/1/0*	0	2/2	Mercenary	**14**	IF0*
Merlin MLN-1A	**Brawler**	BM	3	8"j	1	2/2/2	1	6/5	Mercenary	**33**	IF0*
Annihilator ANH-1A	**Juggernaut**	BM	4	4"	0	5/5/0	1	7/8	Wolf's Dragoons	**30**	AC3/3/-
Annihilator ANH-1E	**Juggernaut**	BM	4	4"	0	5/5/4	1	7/8	Wolf's Dragoons	**45**	ENE
Archer ARC-2W	**Missile Boat**	BM	3	8"	1	2/3/3	2	5/6	Wolf's Dragoons	**35**	IF2,LRM1/1/2
Falcon FLC-4N	**Scout**	BM	1	12"j	2	2/1/0	0	3/3	Wolf's Dragoons	**18**	
Firefly FFL-4A	**Striker**	BM	1	10"/8"j	2	2/2/0*	0	3/3	Wolf's Dragoons	**21**	IF0*
Flea FLE-15	**Scout**	BM	1	12"	2	2/1/0	0	2/2	Wolf's Dragoons	**13**	REAR1/-/-
Flea FLE-4	**Scout**	BM	1	12"	2	2/1/0	0	1/2	Wolf's Dragoons	**11**	ENE
Hoplite HOP-4C	**Brawler**	BM	2	8"	1	2/2/0*	0	6/5	Wolf's Dragoons	**28**	AC1/1/-,IF0*
Imp IMP-2E	**Juggernaut**	BM	4	6"	1	4/5/3	1	10/8	Wolf's Dragoons	**53**	IF1
Marauder II MAD-4A	**Juggernaut**	BM	4	6"j	1	3/4/2	0	10/8	Wolf's Dragoons	**50**	ENE
Shogun SHG-2E	**Missile Boat**	BM	4	6"j	1	3/3/3	2	8/7	Wolf's Dragoons	**46**	CASE,IF2,LRM1/1/2,SRM1/1
Shogun SHG-2F	**Missile Boat**	BM	4	6"j	1	2/3/2	1	8/7	Wolf's Dragoons	**43**	CASE,IF1,LRM(1/1/1),OVL
Wasp WSP-1W	**Scout**	BM	1	12"j	2	2/0/0	0	2/2	Wolf's Dragoons	**13**	ENE

EARLY CLAN INVASION: BATTLEMECHS [SORTED BY AVAILABILITY, THEN ALPHABETICAL]

Unit Name	Role	TP	SZ	MV	TMM	S/M/L	OV	A/S	Availability	PV	Specials
Assassin ASN-23	**Striker**	BM	2	14"j	3	1/2/0*	0	2/3	General	**19**	IF0*
Cyclops CP-11-A	**Sniper**	BM	4	8"	1	4/4/3	0	5/7	General	**38**	IF1
Cyclops CP-11-A-DC	**Sniper**	BM	4	8"	1	3/4/3	0	5/7	General	**38**	IF1,MHQ1
Grasshopper GHR-5J	**Skirmisher**	BM	3	8"j	1	3/3/1	0	7/6	General	**38**	AMS
Grasshopper GHR-5N	**Skirmisher**	BM	3	8"j	1	3/4/1	0	7/6	General*	**39**	ENE
Quickdraw QKD-5A	**Skirmisher**	BM	3	10"j	2	3/3/0	0	4/5	General	**29**	REAR1/1/-
Scorpion SCP-1O	**Brawler**	BM	2	12"	2	2/2/1	0	4/5	General*	**25**	
Whitworth WTH-2	**Missile Boat**	BM	2	8"j	1	2/2/2	1	4/3	General	**27**	IF2
Archer ARC-4M	**Missile Boat**	BM	3	8"	1	3/5/4	0	7/6	Mercenary	**45**	CASE,IF3,REAR1/1/-
Atlas AS7-S	**Juggernaut**	BM	4	6"	1	5/5/2	0	10/8	Mercenary	**52**	AC2/2/-,IF1,LRM1/1/1,REAR2/2/-
Awesome AWS-9M	**Brawler**	BM	4	8"	1	4/4/3	1	8/4	Mercenary	**41**	
Bandersnatch BNDR-01A	**Brawler**	BM	3	8"	1	4/5/3	0	6/3	Mercenary	**37**	CASE,FLK1/1/1,IF1,REAR1/1/-
BattleMaster BLR-3M	**Brawler**	BM	4	8"	1	4/4/1	0	8/7	Mercenary	**42**	CASE,REAR1/1/-
Blackjack BJ-2	**Sniper**	BM	2	8"j	1	3/3/2	1	5/4	Mercenary	**32**	
Catapult CPLT-C3	**Missile Boat**	BM	3	8"j	1	2/2/0	0	5/5	Mercenary	**39**	ARTAIS-1
Chameleon TRC-4B	**Scout**	BM	2	12"j	2	2/1/0	1	3/4	Mercenary	**21**	
Cicada CDA-3M	**Striker**	BM	2	16"	3	2/2/1	0	2/2	Mercenary	**18**	CASE
Clint CLNT-2-3U	**Striker**	BM	2	12"j	2	2/2/1	1	2/3	Mercenary	**20**	ENE
Commando COM-5S	**Striker**	BM	1	12"	2	2/2/0	0	2/2	Mercenary	**15**	CASE
Cronus CNS-3M	**Skirmisher**	BM	2	10"j	2	2/2/0	1	6/5	Mercenary	**32**	
Crusader CRD-5M	**Skirmisher**	BM	3	8"j	1	4/4/2	0	6/3	Mercenary	**37**	AMS,CASE,IF1,LRM1/1/1
Dervish DV-7D	**Missile Boat**	BM	2	10"j	2	3/3/2	0	5/5	Mercenary	**34**	CASE,IF1,LRM1/1/1
Firestarter FS9-S	**Scout**	BM	1	12"j	2	1/1/0	0	3/3	Mercenary	**22**	AMS,HT1/-/-,PRB,RCN,REAR0*/-/-
Goliath GOL-3M	**Sniper**	BM	4	8"	1	2/3/3	0	8/4	Mercenary	**37**	CASE,IF1,LRM1/1/1
Griffin GRF-3M	**Sniper**	BM	2	10"j	2	2/3/3	0	5/3	Mercenary	**32**	CASE,IF1,LRM1/1/1
Grim Reaper GRM-R-PR29	**Skirmisher**	BM	2	10"	2	3/3/2	1	6/3	Mercenary	**34**	AMS,CASE,IF1,LRM1/1/1
Guillotine GLT-5M	**Skirmisher**	BM	3	8"j	1	4/4/1	0	6/6	Mercenary	**38**	CASE
Hermes HER-3S	**Scout**	BM	1	22"	4	1/1/0	0	1/3	Mercenary	**16**	ENE,PRB,RCN
Hermes II HER-5S	**Striker**	BM	2	12"	2	2/2/1	0	4/3	Mercenary	**23**	
Hunchback HBK-5M	**Juggernaut**	BM	2	8"	1	3/3/0	0	5/4	Mercenary	**27**	AC2/2/-,CASE
JagerMech JM6-DD	**Sniper**	BM	3	8"	1	3/3/2	1	4/3	Mercenary	**27**	CASE
Javelin JVN-10P	**Striker**	BM	1	12"j	2	2/2/0	0	2/3	Mercenary	**18**	
Locust LCT-3M	**Scout**	BM	1	16"	3	2/1/0	0	2/2	Mercenary	**16**	AMS,CASE
Locust LCT-3S	**Striker**	BM	1	16"	3	2/2/0	0	1/2	Mercenary	**14**	CASE
Marauder MAD-5D	**Skirmisher**	BM	3	8"j	1	4/4/2	1	7/3	Mercenary	**39**	CASE
Marauder MAD-5M	**Skirmisher**	BM	3	8"j	1	4/4/1	0	6/3	Mercenary	**34**	CASE,FLK1/1/1
Merlin MLN-1B	**Brawler**	BM	3	8"j	1	2/3/2	0	6/5	Mercenary	**34**	IF0*
Orion ON1-M	**Brawler**	BM	3	8"	1	3/4/2	0	7/3	Mercenary	**36**	CASE,FLK1/1/1,IF1,LRM1/1/1,SNARC
Ostsol OTL-5M	**Skirmisher**	BM	3	10"	2	4/4/0	0	5/3	Mercenary	**31**	AMS,REAR1/1/-
Phoenix Hawk PXH-3D	**Striker**	BM	2	12"j	2	3/3/2	0	4/2	Mercenary	**28**	AMS
Phoenix Hawk PXH-3M	**Striker**	BM	2	12"j	2	2/2/2	1	4/2	Mercenary	**26**	AMS,CASE
Quickdraw QKD-5M	**Skirmisher**	BM	3	10"j	2	2/2/1	0	5/5	Mercenary	**31**	CASE,IF1,REAR1/1/-
Rifleman RFL-5M	**Brawler**	BM	3	8"	1	4/4/2	0	5/3	Mercenary	**31**	CASE
Shadow Hawk SHD-5M	**Missile Boat**	BM	2	10"j	2	2/3/2	0	6/3	Mercenary	**33**	CASE,IF1
Stalker STK-5M	**Juggernaut**	BM	4	6"	1	5/6/2	0	8/7	Mercenary	**49**	IF1,LRM1/1/1,SNARC,SRM2/2
Stinger STG-5M	**Scout**	BM	1	12"j	2	1/1/0	0	2/2	Mercenary	**15**	AMS
Thunderbolt TDR-7M	**Brawler**	BM	3	8"	1	4/4/2	0	7/5	Mercenary	**39**	CASE,IF1
Thunderbolt TDR-9SE	**Skirmisher**	BM	3	8"j	1	3/4/1	0	7/5	Mercenary	**39**	CASE,IF1
Trebuchet TBT-7M	**Missile Boat**	BM	2	10"j	2	3/3/2	0	4/2	Mercenary	**29**	CASE,IF1,LRM1/1/1,SNARC
Victor VTR-9D	**Skirmisher**	BM	4	8"j	1	4/4/2	0	7/6	Mercenary	**42**	CASE
Vindicator VND-3L	**Brawler**	BM	2	8"j	1	2/2/2	0	5/4	Mercenary	**28**	CASE,IF0*
Vulcan VT-5M	**Striker**	BM	2	12"j	2	3/2/0	0	3/3	Mercenary	**22**	
War Dog WR-DG-02FC	**Brawler**	BM	3	8"	1	4/4/2	0	7/3	Mercenary	**38**	AMS,ECM,REAR0*/-/-
Warhammer WHM-7M	**Brawler**	BM	3	8"	1	4/4/2	0	5/6	Mercenary	**35**	AMS
Wasp WSP-3M	**Scout**	BM	1	12"j	2	1/1/0	0	1/2	Mercenary	**11**	CASE
Wolverine WVR-7D	**Skirmisher**	BM	2	12"/10"j	2	3/3/1	0	6/3	Mercenary	**33**	CASE
Wolverine WVR-7M	**Skirmisher**	BM	2	12"/10"j	2	3/3/2	1	5/3	Mercenary	**32**	
Zeus ZEU-9S	**Sniper**	BM	4	8"	1	3/4/3	0	7/6	Mercenary	**40**	CASE,IF1

EARLY CLAN INVASION: BATTLEMECHS [SORTED BY AVAILABILITY, THEN ALPHABETICAL]

Unit Name	Role	TP	SZ	MV	TMM	S/M/L	OV	A/S	Availability	PV	Specials
Annihilator ANH-2A	**Juggernaut**	BM	4	4"	0	4/4/3	2	7/8	Wolf's Dragoons	**41**	CASE,FLK2/2/3
Archer ARC-5W	**Missile Boat**	BM	3	8"	1	3/4/3	0	7/3	Wolf's Dragoons	**38**	CASE,IF2,LRM1/2/2,SNARC,SRM1/1
Falcon FLC-4P	**Scout**	BM	1	12"/10"j	2	2/1/0	0	3/3	Wolf's Dragoons	**19**	AMS
Firefly FFL-4B	**Striker**	BM	1	10"/8"j	2	2/2/0*	0	3/3	Wolf's Dragoons	**22**	AMS,CASE,IF0*
Firefly FFL-4C	**Striker**	BM	1	10"/8"j	2	3/3/0*	0	3/1	Wolf's Dragoons	**22**	AMS,CASE,IF0*
Flea FLE-17	**Striker**	BM	1	16"	3	2/2/0	0	2/2	Wolf's Dragoons	**17**	ENE,REAR1/-/-
Hoplite HOP-4D	**Sniper**	BM	2	8"	1	1/1/1	0	6/5	Wolf's Dragoons	**25**	FLK1/1/1,IF0*
Hornet HNT-161	**Striker**	BM	1	10"j	2	1/1/0*	0	2/2	Wolf's Dragoons	**14**	CASE
Imp IMP-3E	**Juggernaut**	BM	4	6"	1	4/4/3	3	10/4	Wolf's Dragoons	**47**	CASE,IF1
Marauder II MAD-5C	**Sniper**	BM	4	6"j	1	4/4/3	0	10/4	Wolf's Dragoons	**47**	CASE
Wasp WSP-3W	**Scout**	BM	1	12"j	2	2/0/0	0	1/2	Wolf's Dragoons	**10**	ENE

LATE SUCCESSION WARS: VEHICLES [SORTED BY AVAILABILITY, THEN ALPHABETICAL]

Unit Name	Role	TP	SZ	MV	TMM	S/M/L	OV	A/S	Availability	PV	Specials
AC/2 Carrier	**Sniper**	CV	3	6"t	1	1/1/1	0	2/3	General	**12**	AC1/1/1,EE,SRCH
APC (Hover LRM)	**Missile Boat**	CV	1	20"h	4	0*/0*/0*	0	1/1	General	**9**	EE,IF0*,SRCH
APC (Hover MG)	**Scout**	CV	1	20"h	4	1/0/0	0	1/1	General	**8**	EE,SRCH,TUR(1/-/-)
APC (Hover Sensors)	**Scout**	CV	1	20"h	4	0/0/0	0	1/1	General	**9**	EE,ENE,IT1,RCN,RSD1,SRCH
APC (Hover SRM)	**—**	CV	1	20"h	4	0*/0*/0	0	1/1	General	**8**	EE,IT1,SRCH
APC (Hover)	**—**	CV	1	20"h	4	0*/0/0	0	1/1	General	**7**	EE,IT1,SRCH,TUR(0*/-/-)
APC (Tracked LRM)	**Missile Boat**	CV	1	12"t	2	0*/0*/0*	0	1/1	General	**8**	EE,IF0*,SRCH
APC (Tracked MG)	**Scout**	CV	1	12"t	2	1/0/0	0	1/1	General	**6**	EE,SRCH,TUR(1/-/-)
APC (Tracked SRM)	**Scout**	CV	1	12"t	2	0*/0*/0	0	1/1	General	**7**	EE,SRCH
APC (Tracked)	**—**	CV	1	12"t	2	0*/0/0	0	1/1	General	**6**	EE,IT1,SRCH,TUR(0*/-/-)
APC (Wheeled LRM)	**Missile Boat**	CV	1	12"w	2	0*/0*/0*	0	1/1	General	**7**	EE,IF0*,SRCH
APC (Wheeled MG)	**Scout**	CV	1	12"w	2	1/0/0	0	2/1	General	**8**	EE,SRCH,TUR(1/-/-)
APC (Wheeled SRM)	**—**	CV	1	12"w	2	0*/0*/0	0	2/1	General	**9**	EE,IT1,SRCH,TUR(0*/0*/-)
APC (Wheeled)	**—**	CV	1	12"w	2	0*/0/0	0	2/1	General	**8**	EE,IT1,SRCH,TUR(0*/-/-)
Ballista Self-Propelled Artillery Tank	**Missile Boat**	CV	2	6"t	1	0*/0/0	0	4/3	General	**25**	ARTS-1,EE,REAR0*/-/-
Behemoth Heavy Tank	**Juggernaut**	CV	4	4"t	0	6/6/2	0	7/5	General	**39**	AC2/2/-,EE,IF1,LRM1/1/1,SRCH,SRM2/2, TUR(4/4/-,SRM2/2,AC2/2/-)
Behemoth Heavy Tank (Armor)	**Juggernaut**	CV	4	4"t	0	5/5/2	0	11/5	General	**44**	AC2/2/-,EE,IF1,LRM1/1/1,SRCH,SRM2/2, TUR(4/4/-,SRM2/2,AC2/2/-)
Behemoth Heavy Tank (Flamer)	**Juggernaut**	CV	4	4"t	0	6/5/2	0	7/5	General	**39**	AC2/2/-,EE,HT2,IF1,LRM1/1/1,SRCH, SRM2/2,TUR(4/4/-,SRM2/2,AC2/2/-)
Demolisher Heavy Tank (Defensive)	**Juggernaut**	CV	4	6"t	1	5/4/0	0	4/4	General	**26**	AC4/4/-,EE,SRCH,TUR(4/4/-,AC4/4/-)
Devastator Heavy Tank	**Juggernaut**	CV	4	6"t	1	6/5/0	0	5/4	General	**31**	AC4/4/-,SRCH,TUR(5/4/-,AC4/4/-)
Drillson Heavy Hover Tank	**Striker**	CV	2	18"h	3	2/2/1	0	3/3	General	**21**	IF1,SRCH,TUR(2/2/-)
Drillson Heavy Hover Tank (SRM)	**Striker**	CV	2	18"h	3	3/2/0	0	3/3	General	**20**	SRCH,SRM1/1,TUR(2/2/-)
Heavy Hover APC	**—**	CV	1	16"h	3	0*/0/0	0	2/1	General	**8**	EE,IT6,SRCH
Heavy Hover APC (LRM)	**Scout**	CV	1	16"h	3	1/0*/0*	0	2/1	General	**11**	EE,IF0*,IT3,SRCH
Heavy Hover APC (MG)	**—**	CV	1	16"h	3	1/0/0	0	2/1	General	**9**	EE,IT3,REAR0*/-/-,SRCH
Heavy Hover APC (SRM)	**Scout**	CV	1	16"h	3	1/1/0	0	2/1	General	**11**	EE,IT3,SRCH
Heavy Tracked APC	**—**	CV	1	10"t	2	0*/0/0	0	2/1	General	**5**	EE,IT6,SRCH
Heavy Tracked APC (LRM)	**Scout**	CV	1	10"t	2	1/0*/0*	0	2/1	General	**7**	EE,IF0*,IT3,SRCH
Heavy Tracked APC (MG)	**Scout**	CV	1	10"t	2	1/0/0	0	2/1	General	**6**	EE,IT3,REAR0*/-/-,SRCH
Heavy Tracked APC (SRM)	**Scout**	CV	1	10"t	2	1/1/0	0	2/1	General	**10**	EE,IT3,SRCH
Heavy Wheeled APC	**—**	CV	1	12"w	2	0*/0/0	0	2/1	General	**8**	EE,IT6,SRCH
Heavy Wheeled APC (LRM)	**Scout**	CV	1	12"w	2	1/0*/0*	0	2/1	General	**10**	EE,IF0*,IT3,SRCH
Heavy Wheeled APC (MG)	**Scout**	CV	1	12"w	2	1/0/0	0	2/1	General	**8**	EE,IT3,REAR0*/-/-,SRCH
Heavy Wheeled APC (SRM)	**Scout**	CV	1	12"w	2	1/1/0	0	2/1	General	**10**	EE,IT3,SRCH
Hi-Scout Drone (NapFind)	**Scout**	CV	1	30"h	4	0/0/0	0	0/1	General	**5**	DRO,EE,ENE,SRCH
Hi-Scout Drone (PathTrak)	**Scout**	CV	1	16"t	3	0/0/0	0	0/1	General	**4**	DRO,EE,ENE,SRCH
Hi-Scout Drone Carrier	**—**	CV	3	8"t	1	0*/0*/0	0	3/3	General	**9**	CT15,DCC5,EE,SRCH,TUR(0*/0*/-)
Hunter Light Support Tank	**Missile Boat**	CV	1	10"t	2	1/2/2	0	3/2	General	**18**	IF1,LRM(1/1/1),SRCH
Hunter Light Support Tank (Ammo)	**Missile Boat**	CV	1	10"t	2	1/2/2	0	3/2	General	**18**	IF1,LRM1/1/1,SRCH
Hunter Light Support Tank (LRM10)	**Brawler**	CV	1	10"t	2	3/2/1	0	3/2	General	**19**	IF1,SRCH

LATE SUCCESSION WARS: VEHICLES [SORTED BY AVAILABILITY, THEN ALPHABETICAL]

Unit Name	Role	TP	SZ	MV	TMM	S/M/L	OV	A/S	Availability	PV	Specials
Hunter Light Support Tank (LRM15)	**Missile Boat**	CV	1	10"t	2	2/1/1	0	3/2	General	**16**	IF1,SRCH
J-27 Ordnance Transport	—	CV	1	10"t	2	0*/0/0	0	0/1	General	**2**	CT3,EE,HTC,SRCH,TUR(0*/-/-)
J-27 Ordnance Transport (Armor)	—	CV	1	10"t	2	0*/0/0	0	1/1	General	**4**	CT3,EE,HTC,SRCH,TUR(0*/-/-)
J-27 Ordnance Transport (Fusion)	—	CV	1	10"t	2	0*/0/0	0	0/1	General	**2**	CT3,HTC,SRCH,TUR(0*/-/-)
J-27 Ordnance Transport (Trailer)	—	CV	1	0"t	0	0/0/0	0	1/1	General	**3**	CT8,EE,ENE,HTC,SRCH
Karnov UR Gunship	**Striker**	CV	1	22"v	4	2/0/0	0	1/2	General	**10**	ATMO,EE,SRCH
Karnov UR Transport	—	CV	1	22"v	4	0/0/0	0	1/2	General	**8**	ATMO,CT6,EE,ENE,SRCH
Laser Carrier	**Ambusher**	CV	3	6"t	1	4/4/0	0	2/3	General	**20**	EE,ENE,SRCH
LRM Carrier	**Missile Boat**	CV	3	6"t	1	2/3/3	0	2/3	General	**22**	EE,IF3,LRM(1/3/3),SRCH
M.A.S.H. Truck	—	CV	1	10"w	2	1/0/0	0	2/1	General	**6**	ENE,MASH5,SRCH,TUR(1/-/-)
M.A.S.H. Truck (ICE)	—	CV	1	10"w	2	0/0/0	0	2/1	General	**7**	EE,ENE,MASH5,SRCH
Manticore Heavy Tank	**Brawler**	CV	3	8"t	1	3/3/2	0	6/3	General	**28**	IF1,SRCH,TUR(2/3/2,IF1)
Maxim Heavy Hover Transport	—	CV	2	16"h	3	3/2/1	0	3/3	General	**22**	EE,IF1,IT3,SRCH,SRM1/1,TUR(2/1/-)
Maxim Heavy Hover Transport (SRM2)	—	CV	2	16"h	3	3/2/1	0	3/3	General	**22**	EE,IF1,IT3,SRCH,SRM1/1,TUR(2/2/-,SRM1/1)
Maxim Heavy Hover Transport (SRM4)	—	CV	2	16"h	3	3/2/0	0	3/3	General	**20**	EE,IT3,SRCH,SRM2/2,TUR(2/1/-)
Mobile Headquarters	—	CV	1	12"w	2	1/1/0	0	3/2	General	**20**	CT1,ENE,MHQ7,SRCH,TUR(1/1/-)
Mobile Headquarters (ICE - LL)	—	CV	1	6"w	1	1/1/0	0	1/2	General	**10**	EE,ENE,MHQ2,SRCH
Mobile Headquarters (ICE - LRM)	—	CV	1	10"w	2	1/1/1	0	3/2	General	**17**	CT1,EE,IF1,MHQ2,SRCH,TUR(1/1/1,IF1)
Mobile Headquarters (ICE)	—	CV	1	12"w	2	1/1/0	0	3/2	General	**15**	CT1,EE,ENE,MHQ2,SRCH,TUR(1/1/-)
Mobile Headquarters (LL)	—	CV	1	12"w	2	1/1/0	0	3/2	General	**16**	ENE,MHQ3,SRCH,TUR(1/1/-)
Mobile Headquarters (LRM)	—	CV	1	12"w	2	1/1/1	0	3/2	General	**17**	IF1,MHQ2,SRCH,TUR(1/1/1,IF1)
Mobile Long Tom Artillery LT-MOB-25	**Missile Boat**	CV	2	4"t	0	1/0/0	0	2/3	General	**37**	ARTLT-1,EE,HTC,MHQ2,SRCH
Packrat LRPV PKR-T5	**Scout**	CV	1	14"w	3	1/1/0	0	2/1	General	**10**	IT1,SRCH
Packrat LRPV PKR-T5 (ICE)	**Scout**	CV	1	14"w	3	1/1/0	0	2/1	General	**10**	EE,IT1,SRCH
Partisan Heavy Tank	**Sniper**	CV	4	6"t	1	2/2/2	0	3/4	General	**19**	AC2/2/2,EE,SRCH,TUR(2/2/2,AC2/2/2)
Partisan Heavy Tank (AC2)	**Sniper**	CV	4	6"t	1	2/1/1	0	3/4	General	**16**	AC1/1/1,EE,SRCH,TUR(AC1/1/1)
Partisan Heavy Tank (LRM)	**Missile Boat**	CV	4	6"t	1	3/4/4	0	3/4	General	**30**	EE,IF4,LRM2/4/4,SRCH,TUR(2/4/4,LRM2/4/4,IF4)
Pegasus Scout Hover Tank	**Striker**	CV	1	16"h	3	2/2/0	0	3/2	General	**17**	EE,SRCH,SRM1/1,TUR(2/2/-,SRM1/1)
Pegasus Scout Hover Tank (Missile)	**Striker**	CV	1	16"h	3	3/3/0	0	3/2	General	**20**	EE,SRCH,SRM2/2,TUR(3/3/-,SRM2/2)
Pegasus Scout Hover Tank (Unarmed)	**Scout**	CV	1	16"h	3	0/0/0	0	3/2	General	**11**	CT12,EE,ENE,SRCH
Pike Support Vehicle	**Sniper**	CV	3	6"t	1	1/1/1	0	5/3	General	**18**	EE,SRCH,TUR(1/1/1)
Pike Support Vehicle (AC5)	**Sniper**	CV	3	6"t	1	2/2/1	0	5/3	General	**21**	AC1/1/1,EE,SRCH,TUR(1/1/1,AC1/1/1)
Pike Support Vehicle (Missile)	**Missile Boat**	CV	3	6"t	1	2/3/2	0	5/3	General	**26**	EE,IF2,LRM1/2/2,SRCH,TUR(1/2/2,LRM1/2/2,IF2)
Saladin Assault Hover Tank	**Striker**	CV	1	16"h	3	2/2/0	0	1/2	General	**13**	AC2/2/-,EE,SRCH
Saladin Assault Hover Tank (Armor)	**Striker**	CV	1	16"h	3	2/2/0	0	2/2	General	**15**	AC2/2/-,EE,SRCH
Saracen Medium Hover Tank	**Striker**	CV	1	16"h	3	1/2/1	0	4/2	General	**21**	EE,IF1,SRCH,TUR(1/2/1,IF1)
Schrek AC Carrier	**Sniper**	CV	4	6"t	1	3/2/2	0	5/4	General	**24**	AC1/2/2,EE,SRCH,TUR(2/2/2,AC1/2/2)
Schrek PPC Carrier	**Sniper**	CV	4	6"t	1	3/3/3	0	4/4	General	**25**	ENE,SRCH,TUR(3/3/3)
Schrek PPC Carrier (Anti-Infantry)	**Sniper**	CV	4	6"t	1	3/3/3	0	3/4	General	**23**	SRCH,TUR(3/3/3)
Scimitar Medium Hover Tank	**Striker**	CV	1	16"h	3	1/1/1	0	3/2	General	**15**	EE,SRCH,TUR(1/1/1)
Scimitar Medium Hover Tank (Missile)	**Missile Boat**	CV	1	16"h	3	1/2/1	0	3/2	General	**18**	IF1,SRCH,TUR(1/2/1,IF1)
Scorpion Light Tank	**Brawler**	CV	1	8"t	1	1/1/1	0	2/2	General	**11**	EE,SRCH,TUR(1/1/1)
Scorpion Light Tank (LRM)	**Missile Boat**	CV	1	8"t	1	1/1/1	0	3/2	General	**14**	EE,IF1,SRCH,TUR(1/1/1,IF1)
Scorpion Light Tank (ML)	**Juggernaut**	CV	1	8"t	1	2/2/0	0	2/2	General	**13**	CT1,EE,SRCH,TUR(2/2/-)
Scorpion Light Tank (SRM)	**Juggernaut**	CV	1	8"t	1	2/2/0	0	2/2	General	**13**	EE,SRCH,SRM2/2,TUR(2/2/-,SRM2/2)
SRM Carrier	**Ambusher**	CV	3	6"t	1	6/6/0	0	2/3	General	**26**	EE,SRCH,SRM6/6
Thumper Artillery Vehicle	**Missile Boat**	CV	3	8"w	1	0/0/0	0	6/3	General	**22**	ARTT-1,EE,REAR0*/-/-,SRCH
Vedette Medium Tank	**Brawler**	CV	2	10"t	2	1/1/1	0	3/3	General	**15**	EE,SRCH,TUR(1/1/1)
Vedette Medium Tank (AC2)	**Brawler**	CV	2	10"t	2	1/1/0*	0	3/3	General	**15**	EE,SRCH,TUR(1/1/0*)
Vedette Medium Tank (Liao)	**Striker**	CV	2	10"t	2	2/1/0	0	3/3	General	**15**	EE,SRCH,TUR(1/1/-)
Warrior Attack Helicopter H-7	**Scout**	CV	1	18"v	3	1/1/0*	0	1/1	General	**9**	ATMO,EE,SRCH
Warrior Attack Helicopter H-7A	**Scout**	CV	1	18"v	3	1/1/1	0	1/1	General	**10**	ATMO,EE,SRCH
Warrior Attack Helicopter H-7C	**Sniper**	CV	1	18"v	3	1/2/1	0	1/1	General	**13**	ATMO,EE,IF1,SRCH

LATE SUCCESSION WARS: VEHICLES [SORTED BY AVAILABILITY, THEN ALPHABETICAL]

Unit Name	Role	TP	SZ	MV	TMM	S/M/L	OV	A/S	Availability	PV	Specials
Bulldog Medium Tank	**Brawler**	CV	3	8"t	1	3/2/0	0	3/3	Mercenary	**17**	EE,SRCH,SRM1/1,TUR(2/2/-,SRM1/1)
Bulldog Medium Tank (AC2)	**Brawler**	CV	3	8"t	1	2/2/0*	0	3/3	Mercenary	**17**	EE,SRCH,SRM1/1,TUR(2/2/0*,SRM1/1)
Bulldog Medium Tank (LRM)	**Missile Boat**	CV	3	8"t	1	2/3/2	0	3/3	Mercenary	**21**	EE,IF1,LRM1/1/1,SRCH,SRM1/1,TUR(2/3/2), SRM1/1, LRM1/1/1,IF1)
Condor Heavy Hover Tank	**Striker**	CV	2	16"h	3	2/2/1	0	3/3	Mercenary	**20**	EE,SRCH,TUR(2/2/1)
Condor Heavy Hover Tank (Flamer)	**Striker**	CV	2	16"h	3	3/2/0	0	5/3	Mercenary	**24**	EE,SRCH,TUR(2/2/-)
Hetzer Wheeled Assault Gun	**Ambusher**	CV	2	8"w	1	2/2/0	0	3/2	Mercenary	**15**	AC2/2/-,EE,SRCH
Hetzer Wheeled Assault Gun (AC10)	**Ambusher**	CV	2	8"w	1	1/1/0	0	4/2	Mercenary	**14**	AC1/1/-,EE,SRCH
Hetzer Wheeled Assault Gun (Laser)	**Ambusher**	CV	2	8"w	1	2/2/0	0	4/2	Mercenary	**17**	EE,ENE,SRCH
Hetzer Wheeled Assault Gun (LRM)	**Missile Boat**	CV	2	8"w	1	1/2/2	0	3/2	Mercenary	**18**	EE,IF2,LRM1/2/2,SRCH
Hetzer Wheeled Assault Gun (Scout)	**Ambusher**	CV	2	8"w	1	2/2/0	0	3/2	Mercenary	**15**	AC2/2/-,EE,RSD1,SRCH
Hetzer Wheeled Assault Gun (SRM)	**Ambusher**	CV	2	8"w	1	3/3/0	0	3/2	Mercenary	**18**	EE,SRCH,SRM3/3
J. Edgar Light Hover Tank	**Scout**	CV	1	22"h	4	1/1/0	0	3/2	Mercenary	**16**	SRCH,TUR(1/1/-)
J. Edgar Light Hover Tank (Flamer)	**Scout**	CV	1	22"h	4	1/1/0	0	3/2	Mercenary	**17**	HT1/-/-,SRCH,TUR(1/1/-)
J. Edgar Light Hover Tank (ICE)	**Scout**	CV	1	16"h	3	1/1/0	0	3/2	Mercenary	**14**	EE,SRCH,TUR(1/1/-)
J. Edgar Light Hover Tank (MG)	**Scout**	CV	1	22"h	4	2/1/0	0	3/2	Mercenary	**17**	SRCH,TUR(2/1/-)
Ontos Heavy Tank	**Juggernaut**	CV	4	6"t	1	5/5/1	0	4/5	Mercenary	**31**	EE,IF1,SRCH,TUR(5/5/1,IF1)
Ontos Heavy Tank (Fusion)	**Juggernaut**	CV	4	6"t	1	6/7/2	0	6/5	Mercenary*	**41**	IF1,LRM1/1/1,SRCH,TUR(6/7/2, LRM1/1/1,IF1)
Ontos Heavy Tank (LRM)	**Missile Boat**	CV	4	6"t	1	2/4/4	0	5/5	Mercenary	**33**	EE,IF3,LRM2/3/3,SRCH,TUR(LRM2/3/3,IF3)
Swift Wind Scout Car	**Scout**	CV	1	20"w	4	0/0/0	0	1/1	Mercenary*	**9**	CT1,ENE,MHQ2,SRCH
Swift Wind Scout Car (ICE - Cargo)	—	CV	1	16"w	3	0/0/0	0	1/1	Mercenary*	**6**	CT3,EE,ENE,SRCH
Swift Wind Scout Car (ICE - Speed)	—	CV	1	22"w	4	0/0/0	0	0/1	Mercenary*	**4**	CT3,EE,ENE,SRCH
Swift Wind Scout Car (ICE)	**Scout**	CV	1	20"w	4	0/0/0	0	1/1	Mercenary*	**9**	EE,ENE,MHQ2,SRCH
Badger Tracked Transport A	—	CV	1	12"t	2	1/1/0	0	3/2	Wolf's Dragoons	**14**	IT4,OMNI,SRCH,TUR(1/1/-)
Badger Tracked Transport B	—	CV	1	12"t	2	2/2/2	0	3/2	Wolf's Dragoons	**17**	IT4,OMNI,SRCH,SRM1/1,TUR(1/1/-)
Badger Tracked Transport C	**Missile Boat**	CV	1	12"t	2	0*/1/1	0	3/2	Wolf's Dragoons	**15**	IF1,IT4,OMNI,SRCH,TUR(0*/1/1)
Badger Tracked Transport D	**Striker**	CV	1	12"t	2	3/2/0	0	3/2	Wolf's Dragoons	**18**	ENE,IT4,OMNI,SRCH,TUR(2/2/-)
Badger Tracked Transport E	—	CV	1	12"t	2	3/0/0	0	3/2	Wolf's Dragoons	**14**	ENE,IT4,OMNI,SRCH,TUR(2/-/-)
Badger Tracked Transport Prime	**Striker**	CV	1	12"t	2	2/2/0	0	3/2	Wolf's Dragoons	**19**	IT4,OMNI,SRCH,TUR(2/2/-)
Bandit Hovercraft A	**Scout**	CV	2	18"h	3	1/1/1	0	6/3	Wolf's Dragoons	**23**	ENE,IT4,OMNI,SRCH,TUR(1/1/1)
Bandit Hovercraft B	**Striker**	CV	2	18"h	3	2/2/0	0	6/3	Wolf's Dragoons	**25**	IT4,OMNI,SRCH,SRM1/1,TUR(2/2/- ,SRM1/1)
Bandit Hovercraft C	**Striker**	CV	2	18"h	3	2/2/0	0	6/3	Wolf's Dragoons	**25**	IT4,OMNI,SRCH,SRM1/1,TUR(2/2/- ,SRM1/1)
Bandit Hovercraft D	**Missile Boat**	CV	2	18"h	3	1/1/1	0	6/3	Wolf's Dragoons	**24**	IF1,IT4,OMNI,SRCH,TUR(1/1/1,IF1)
Bandit Hovercraft E	**Missile Boat**	CV	2	18"h	3	1/2/1	0	6/3	Wolf's Dragoons	**26**	IF1,IT4,OMNI,SRCH,TUR(1/1/1,IF1)
Bandit Hovercraft F	**Striker**	CV	2	18"h	3	2/2/0	0	6/3	Wolf's Dragoons	**25**	ENE,IT4,OMNI,SRCH,TUR(1/1/-)
Bandit Hovercraft G	—	CV	2	18"h	3	3/1/0	0	6/3	Wolf's Dragoons	**24**	ENE,IT4,OMNI,SRCH,TUR(1/1/-)
Bandit Hovercraft Prime	**Striker**	CV	2	18"h	3	3/2/0	0	6/3	Wolf's Dragoons	**26**	IT4,OMNI,SRCH,TUR(2/2/-)
Kestrel VTOL	**Scout**	CV	1	24"v	4	0*/0/0	0	1/2	Wolf's Dragoons	**9**	ATMO,EE,IT3,SRCH
Kestrel VTOL (MedEvac)	**Ambusher**	CV	1	24"v	4	1/1/0	0	1/2	Wolf's Dragoons	**14**	AC1/1/-,EE,SRCH
Kestrel VTOL (ML)	**Ambusher**	CV	1	24"v	4	1/1/0	0	1/2	Wolf's Dragoons	**12**	ATMO,CT1,EE,ENE,SRCH
Kestrel VTOL (SL)	**Ambusher**	CV	1	24"v	4	1/0/0	0	1/2	Wolf's Dragoons	**10**	ATMO,EE,ENE,IT1,SRCH
Kestrel VTOL (Scout)	**Ambusher**	CV	1	24"v	4	1/1/0	0	1/2	Wolf's Dragoons*	**14**	AC1/1/-,EE,SRCH
Kestrel VTOL (SRM)	**Ambusher**	CV	1	24"v	4	0*/0/0	0	1/2	Wolf's Dragoons*	**10**	ATMO,EE,IT3,SRCH
Plainsman Medium Hovertank	**Scout**	CV	1	18"h	3	2/2/0	0	3/2	Wolf's Dragoons	**20**	EE,PRB,RCN,SRCH,SRM2/2
Zhukov Heavy Tank	**Juggernaut**	CV	3	6"t	1	3/3/0	0	6/4	Wolf's Dragoons	**26**	AC2/2/-,EE,SRCH,TUR(2/2/-,AC2/2/-)

LATE SUCCESSION WARS: INFANTRY [SORTED BY AVAILABILITY, THEN ALPHABETICAL]											
Unit Name	Role	TP	SZ	MV	TMM	S/M/L	OV	A/S	Availability	PV	Specials
Foot Platoon (Flamer)	**Ambusher**	CI	1	2"f	0	1/0/0	0	2/1	General	**4**	AM,CAR3,HT1/-/-
Foot Platoon (Laser)	**Ambusher**	CI	1	2"f	0	1/1/0	0	2/1	General	**7**	AM,CAR3
Foot Platoon (MG)	**Ambusher**	CI	1	2"f	0	1/0/0	0	2/1	General	**4**	AM,CAR3
Foot Platoon (Rifle)	**Ambusher**	CI	1	2"f	0	1/0/0	0	2/1	General	**4**	AM,CAR3
Foot Platoon (SRM)	**Ambusher**	CI	1	2"f	0	1/1/0	0	2/1	General	**7**	AM,CAR3
Hover Platoon (Flamer)	**Ambusher**	CI	1	8"h	1	1/0/0	0	1/1	General	**6**	CAR20,HT1/-/-
Hover Platoon (Laser)	**Ambusher**	CI	1	10"h	2	1/1/0	0	1/1	General	**9**	CAR20
Hover Platoon (MG)	**Ambusher**	CI	1	8"h	1	1/0/0	0	1/1	General	**5**	CAR20
Hover Platoon (Rifle)	**Ambusher**	CI	1	10"h	2	1/0/0	0	1/1	General	**5**	CAR20
Hover Platoon (SRM)	**Ambusher**	CI	1	8"h	1	1/1/0	0	1/1	General	**9**	CAR20
Jump Platoon (Flamer)	**Ambusher**	CI	1	4"j	1	1/0/0	0	2/1	General	**5**	AM,CAR4,HT1/-/-
Jump Platoon (Laser)	**Ambusher**	CI	1	6"j	1	1/1/0	0	2/1	General	**11**	AM,CAR4
Jump Platoon (MG)	**Ambusher**	CI	1	4"j	1	1/0/0	0	2/1	General	**4**	AM,CAR4
Jump Platoon (Rifle)	**Ambusher**	CI	1	6"j	1	1/0/0	0	2/1	General	**7**	AM,CAR4
Jump Platoon (SRM)	**Ambusher**	CI	1	4"j	1	1/1/0	0	2/1	General	**8**	AM,CAR4
Mechanized Field Artillery (Thumper)	**Missile Boat**	CI	1	2"w	0	1/0/0	0	1/1	General	**11**	ARTT-1,CAR40
Motorized Artillery Platoon (Sniper)	**Missile Boat**	CI	1	2"m	0	1/0/0	0	2/1	General	**15**	ARTS-1,CAR23
Motorized Platoon (Flamer)	**Ambusher**	CI	1	4"m	0	1/0/0	0	2/1	General	**4**	AM,CAR6,HT1/-/-
Motorized Platoon (Laser)	**Ambusher**	CI	1	6"m	1	1/1/0	0	2/1	General	**10**	AM,CAR6
Motorized Platoon (MG)	**Ambusher**	CI	1	4"m	0	1/0/0	0	2/1	General	**4**	AM,CAR6
Motorized Platoon (Rifle)	**Ambusher**	CI	1	6"m	1	1/0/0	0	2/1	General	**6**	AM,CAR6
Motorized Platoon (SRM)	**Ambusher**	CI	1	4"m	0	1/1/0	0	2/1	General	**7**	AM,CAR6
Tracked Platoon (Flamer)	**Ambusher**	CI	1	6"t	1	1/0/0	0	1/1	General	**5**	CAR28,HT1/-/-
Tracked Platoon (Laser)	**Ambusher**	CI	1	6"t	1	1/1/0	0	1/1	General	**8**	CAR28
Tracked Platoon (MG)	**Ambusher**	CI	1	6"t	1	1/0/0	0	1/1	General	**5**	CAR28
Tracked Platoon (Rifle)	**Ambusher**	CI	1	6"t	1	1/0/0	0	1/1	General	**5**	CAR28
Tracked Platoon (SRM)	**Ambusher**	CI	1	6"t	1	1/1/0	0	1/1	General	**8**	CAR28
Wheeled Platoon (Flamer)	**Ambusher**	CI	1	6"w	1	1/0/0	0	1/1	General	**5**	CAR24,HT1/-/-
Wheeled Platoon (Laser)	**Ambusher**	CI	1	8"w	1	1/1/0	0	1/1	General	**9**	CAR24
Wheeled Platoon (MG)	**Ambusher**	CI	1	6"w	1	1/0/0	0	1/1	General	**5**	CAR24
Wheeled Platoon (Rifle)	**Ambusher**	CI	1	8"w	1	1/0/0	0	1/1	General	**5**	CAR24
Wheeled Platoon (SRM)	**Ambusher**	CI	1	6"w	1	1/1/0	0	1/1	General	**8**	CAR24

LATE SUCCESSION WARS: AEROSPACE [SORTED BY AVAILABILITY, THEN ALPHABETICAL]

Unit Name	Role	TP	SZ	MV	S/M/L/E	OV	A/S	TH	Availability	PV	Specials
Lightning LTN-G15	**Dogfighter**	AF	2	6a	4/4/0/0	0	6/3	2	General	**28**	BOMB2,FUEL20,REAR1/1/-,SPC,VSTOL
Centurion CNT-1D	**Interceptor**	AF	1	10a	2/2/0/0	0	4/5	2	Mercenary	**22**	BOMB1, ENE, FUEL20, SPC, VSTOL
Cheetah F-10	**Interceptor**	AF	1	12a	2/1/0/0	0	2/6	1	Mercenary	**19**	BOMB1, ENE, FUEL16, PNT1, SPC, VSTOL
Cheetah F-11-R	**Recon**	AF	1	12a	0*/0/0/0	0	2/6	1	Mercenary	**15**	BOMB1, ENE, FUEL24, PNT1, SPC, VSTOL
Chippewa CHP-W5	**Attack**	AF	3	5a	4/4/2/0	2	4/5	3	Mercenary	**31**	BOMB3,FUEL20,REAR1/-/-,SPC,VSTOL
Chippewa CHP-W7	**Attack**	AF	3	5a	6/7/2/0	1	4/5	2	Mercenary	**38**	BOMB3, FUEL20, REAR1/-/-, SPC, VSTOL
Corsair CSR-V12	**Dogfighter**	AF	2	6a	3/3/0/0	0	7/3	3	Mercenary	**28**	BOMB2, ENE, FUEL20, PNT1, REAR1/-/-, SPC, VSTOL
Eagle EGL-R6	**Dogfighter**	AF	3	6a	4/4/0/0	0	7/4	3	Mercenary	**33**	BOMB3, FUEL20, REAR1/1/-, SPC, VSTOL
Hellcat HCT-213	**Dogfighter**	AF	2	6a	3/3/0/0	2	6/3	2	Mercenary	**26**	BOMB2, ENE, FUEL20, REAR1/1/-, SPC, VSTOL
Lucifer LCF-R15	**Attack**	AF	2	5a	4/3/2/0	0	6/3	2	Mercenary	**29**	BOMB2, FUEL20, PNT2, REAR1/1/-, SPC, VSTOL
Riever F-100	**Attack**	AF	3	5a	6/6/1/0	0	9/5	3	Mercenary	**43**	BOMB3, FUEL20, SPC, VSTOL
Riever F-100A	**Attack**	AF	3	5a	7/7/0/0	0	9/5	3	Mercenary	**45**	BOMB3, FUEL20, SPC, VSTOL
Sabre SB-27	**Interceptor**	AF	1	11a	2/2/0/0	0	2/6	1	Mercenary	**19**	BOMB1, ENE, FUEL20, SPC, VSTOL
Shilone SL-17	**Fire-Support**	AF	2	6a	3/3/2/0	0	6/3	2	Mercenary	**27**	BOMB2, FUEL20, REAR1/1/-, SPC, VSTOL
Sholagar SL-21	**Interceptor**	AF	1	10a	2/2/0/0	0	3/5	1	Mercenary	**20**	BOMB1, FUEL20, SPC, VSTOL
Sholagar SL-21L	**Interceptor**	AF	1	10a	2/2/0/0	0	3/5	1	Mercenary	**20**	BOMB1, ENE, FUEL20, SPC, VSTOL
Slayer SL-15	**Dogfighter**	AF	3	6a	4/4/0/0	0	8/4	3	Mercenary	**34**	BOMB3, FUEL40, REAR1/1/-, SPC, VSTOL
Slayer SL-15B	**Dogfighter**	AF	3	6a	3/4/1/0	0	8/4	3	Mercenary	**34**	BOMB3, FUEL40, REAR1/1/-, SPC, VSTOL
Sparrowhawk SPR-H5	**Interceptor**	AF	1	10a	2/1/0/0	0	4/5	2	Mercenary	**21**	BOMB1, ENE, FUEL20, PNT1, SPC, VSTOL
Stingray F-90	**Dogfighter**	AF	2	6a	3/3/1/0	1	6/3	2	Mercenary	**27**	BOMB2, ENE, FUEL20, SPC, VSTOL
Stuka STU-K5	**Attack**	AF	3	5a	4/5/2/0	1	8/5	3	Mercenary	**40**	BOMB3, FUEL20, REAR1/1/-, SPC, VSTOL
Thrush TR-7	**Interceptor**	AF	1	12a	2/2/0/0	0	1/6	1	Mercenary	**18**	BOMB1, ENE, FUEL20, SPC, VSTOL
Thunderbird TRB-D36	**Attack**	AF	3	5a	4/4/3/0	3	7/5	3	Mercenary	**38**	BOMB3, FUEL20, REAR1/1/-, SPC, VSTOL
Transgressor TR-13	**Dogfighter**	AF	3	6a	4/4/0/0	0	7/4	3	Mercenary	**33**	BOMB3, ENE, FUEL20, REAR1/1/-, SPC, VSTOL
Transgressor TR-14 "AC"	**Dogfighter**	AF	3	6a	4/4/0/0	0	7/4	3	Mercenary	**33**	BOMB3, FUEL20, REAR1/1/-, SPC, VSTOL
Vulcan VLC-5N	**Attack**	AF	3	5a	5/5/0/0	0	7/4	3	Mercenary	**35**	BOMB3, FUEL20, SPC, VSTOL

LATE SUCCESSION WARS: CONVENTIONAL FIGHTERS & AIRBORNE SUPPORT VEHICLES [SORTED BY AVAILABILITY, THEN ALPHABETICAL]

Unit Name	Role	TP	SZ	MV	S/M/L/E	OV	A/S	TH	Availability	PV	Specials
Heavy Strike Fighter Meteor	**Attack**	CF	1	5a	3/3/0/0	0	1/3	1	General	**15**	ATMO,BOMB1,VSTOL
Light Strike Fighter Angel	**Interceptor**	CF	1	10a	1/1/0/0	0	0/5	0	General	**12**	ATMO,BOMB1,VSTOL
Medium Strike Fighter Defender	**Fire-Support**	CF	1	6a	1/1/1/0	0	1/3	1	General	**11**	ATMO,BOMB1,EE,VSTOL
Boomerang Spotter Plane	**Recon**	SV	1	4a	0/0/0/0	0	0/4	0	Mercenary	**5**	ENE,FUEL13,RCN,VSTOL
Dragonfly Spotter Plane	**Recon**	SV	1	4a	0/0/0/0	0	0/4	0	Mercenary	**5**	ENE,FUEL13,RCN,VSTOL
Heavy Strike Fighter Bat Hawk	**Attack**	CF	1	5a	2/2/0/0	0	1/3	1	Mercenary	**12**	ATMO,BOMB1,EE,VSTOL
Hyperion Spotter Plane	**Recon**	SV	1	4a	0/0/0/0	0	0/4	0	Mercenary	**5**	ENE,FUEL13,RCN,VSTOL
Warbler Spotter Plane	**Recon**	SV	1	4a	0/0/0/0	0	0/4	0	Mercenary	**5**	ENE,FUEL13,RCN,VSTOL

LATE SUCCESSION WARS: BATTLEMECHS (SORTED BY ROLE, THEN POINT VALUE)

Unit Name	Role	TP	SZ	MV	TMM	S/M/L	OV	A/S	Availability	PV	Specials
UrbanMech UM-R60	**Ambusher**	BM	1	4"j	0	2/1/0	0	3/3	General	**12**	AC1/1/-
Panther PNT-9R	**Brawler**	BM	1	8"j	1	2/2/1	0	3/3	General	**20**	
Panther PNT-8Z	**Brawler**	BM	1	8"j	1	2/2/0	0	4/3	General	**21**	
Centurion CN9-A	**Brawler**	BM	2	8"	1	2/3/1	0	5/4	General	**28**	AC1/1/-,IF1,REAR1/1/0
Centurion CN9-AL	**Brawler**	BM	2	8"	1	2/2/1	0	6/4	General	**28**	IF1,REAR1/1/-
Vindicator VND-1R	**Brawler**	BM	2	8"j	1	2/2/2	0	5/4	General	**28**	IF0*
Hoplite HOP-4C	**Brawler**	BM	2	8"	1	2/2/0*	0	6/5	Wolf's Dragoons	**28**	AC1/1/-,IF0*
Hunchback HBK-4SP	**Brawler**	BM	2	8"	1	4/4/0	0	5/4	General	**30**	SRM2/2
Hunchback HBK-4N	**Brawler**	BM	2	8"	1	3/3/2	1	5/4	General	**31**	IF1
Hunchback HBK-4P	**Brawler**	BM	2	8"	1	5/4/0	0	5/4	General	**31**	ENE
Warhammer WHM-6R	**Brawler**	BM	3	8"	1	3/3/2	1	5/6	General	**32**	
Black Knight BL-7-KNT-L	**Brawler**	BM	3	8"	1	3/3/0	2	6/6	General	**33**	ENE
Merlin MLN-1A	**Brawler**	BM	3	8"j	1	2/2/2	1	6/5	Mercenary	**33**	IF0*
Black Knight BL-7-KNT	**Brawler**	BM	3	8"	1	3/3/1	2	6/6	General	**34**	ENE
Orion ON1-V	**Brawler**	BM	3	8"	1	3/3/1	2	6/6	General	**35**	IF1
Orion ON1-V-DC	**Brawler**	BM	3	8"	1	2/3/1	1	6/6	General	**35**	IF1,MHQ1
Thunderbolt TDR-5SS	**Brawler**	BM	3	8"	1	3/3/1	1	7/5	General	**35**	
Thunderbolt TDR-5S	**Brawler**	BM	3	8"	1	3/3/1	1	7/5	General	**36**	IF1
Banshee BNC-3M	**Brawler**	BM	4	8"	1	2/2/2	1	8/8	General	**39**	ENE
Orion ON1-K	**Brawler**	BM	3	8"	1	3/3/1	1	8/6	General	**39**	IF1
BattleMaster BLR-1G	**Brawler**	BM	4	8"	1	3/3/1	1	8/7	General	**40**	REAR1/1/-
BattleMaster BLR-1G-DC	**Brawler**	BM	4	8"	1	3/3/1	1	8/7	General	**41**	MHQ1
Hunchback HBK-4G	**Juggernaut**	BM	2	8"	1	4/3/0	0	5/4	General	**28**	AC2/2/-
Hunchback HBK-4H	**Juggernaut**	BM	2	8"	1	4/3/0	0	5/4	General	**28**	AC1/1/-
Centurion CN9-AH	**Juggernaut**	BM	2	8"	1	3/3/1	0	5/4	General	**29**	AC2/2/-,IF1
Annihilator ANH-1A	**Juggernaut**	BM	4	4"	0	5/5/0	1	7/8	Wolf's Dragoons	**30**	AC3/3/-
Cyclops CP-10-Z	**Juggernaut**	BM	4	8"	1	3/3/1	2	5/7	General	**34**	AC1/1/-,IF1
Banshee BNC-3Q	**Juggernaut**	BM	4	8"	1	3/2/0	0	8/8	General	**37**	AC2/2/-
Victor VTR-9B	**Juggernaut**	BM	4	8"j	1	4/4/0	0	6/6	General	**37**	AC2/2/-
Orion ON1-VA	**Juggernaut**	BM	3	8"	1	4/4/0	0	8/6	General	**39**	AC1/1/-,SRM1/1
Stalker STK-4P	**Juggernaut**	BM	3	6"	1	3/4/1	2	7/6	General*	**39**	IF1
Stalker STK-4N	**Juggernaut**	BM	4	6"	1	4/4/1	2	7/7	General*	**41**	IF1,SRM1/1
Stalker STK-3F	**Juggernaut**	BM	4	6"	1	3/4/2	3	7/7	General	**42**	IF1
King Crab KGC-0000	**Juggernaut**	BM	4	6"	1	3/3/1	2	9/8	General	**44**	AC2/2/-,IF1
Annihilator ANH-1E	**Juggernaut**	BM	4	4"	0	5/5/4	1	7/8	Wolf's Dragoons	**45**	ENE
Atlas AS7-RS	**Juggernaut**	BM	4	6"	1	3/4/1	1	10/8	General	**48**	IF1
Marauder II MAD-4A	**Juggernaut**	BM	4	6"j	1	3/4/2	0	10/8	Wolf's Dragoons	**50**	ENE
Atlas AS7-D	**Juggernaut**	BM	4	6"	1	5/5/2	0	10/8	General	**52**	AC2/2/-,IF1,LRM1/1/1,REAR1/1/-
Atlas AS7-D-DC	**Juggernaut**	BM	4	6"	1	5/5/1	0	10/8	General	**52**	AC2/2/-,IF1,MHQ1
Imp IMP-2E	**Juggernaut**	BM	4	6"	1	4/5/3	1	10/8	Wolf's Dragoons	**53**	IF1
Whitworth WTH-1	**Missile Boat**	BM	2	8"j	1	2/2/2	1	4/3	General	**26**	IF1
JagerMech JM6-A	**Missile Boat**	BM	3	8"	1	2/2/2	1	4/5	General	**27**	IF1
Trebuchet TBT-5N	**Missile Boat**	BM	2	10"	2	2/2/2	1	4/4	General	**27**	IF1
Dervish DV-6M	**Missile Boat**	BM	2	10"j	2	2/2/2	1	4/5	General	**30**	IF1
Hunchback HBK-4J	**Missile Boat**	BM	2	8"	1	3/3/2	1	5/4	General	**31**	IF1
Catapult CPLT-C1	**Missile Boat**	BM	3	8"j	1	2/3/2	1	5/5	General	**33**	IF1,LRM1/1/1
Bombardier BMB-10D	**Missile Boat**	BM	3	8"	1	2/2/2	1	7/5	General*	**35**	IF2,LRM1/1/2
Archer ARC-2W	**Missile Boat**	BM	3	8"	1	2/3/3	2	5/6	Wolf's Dragoons	**35**	IF2,LRM1/1/2
Longbow LGB-0W	**Missile Boat**	BM	4	8"	1	2/3/3	0	5/7	General	**36**	IF3,LRM1/3/3
Awesome AWS-8R	**Missile Boat**	BM	4	6"	1	2/3/2	0	8/6	General	**38**	IF1,LRM1/1/1
Archer ARC-2R	**Missile Boat**	BM	3	8"	1	2/3/3	1	7/6	General	**39**	IF2,LRM1/2/2,REAR1/1/-
Awesome AWS-8T	**Missile Boat**	BM	4	6"	1	3/3/2	0	8/6	General	**39**	IF1,LRM1/1/1
Stalker STK-3H	**Missile Boat**	BM	4	6"	1	3/4/2	2	7/7	General	**42**	IF2,LRM1/1/2,SRM1/1
Shogun SHG-2F	**Missile Boat**	BM	4	6"j	1	2/3/2	1	8/7	Wolf's Dragoons	**43**	CASE,IF1,LRM(1/1/1),OVL
Longbow LGB-7Q	**Missile Boat**	BM	4	6"	1	3/4/3	0	8/7	General	**45**	IF3,LRM2/3/3
Shogun SHG-2E	**Missile Boat**	BM	4	6"j	1	3/3/3	2	8/7	Wolf's Dragoons	**46**	CASE,IF2,LRM1/1/2,SRM1/1

LATE SUCCESSION WARS: BATTLEMECHS [SORTED BY ROLE, THEN POINT VALUE]

Unit Name	Role	TP	SZ	MV	TMM	S/M/L	OV	A/S	Availability	PV	Specials
Flea FLE-4	**Scout**	BM	1	12"	2	2/1/0	0	1/2	Wolf's Dragoons	**11**	ENE
Flea FLE-14	**Scout**	BM	1	12"	2	2/1/0	0	2/2	Wolf's Dragoons	**13**	REAR1/-/-
Wasp WSP-1W	**Scout**	BM	1	12"j	2	2/0/0	0	2/2	Wolf's Dragoons	**13**	ENE
Locust LCT-1V	**Scout**	BM	1	16"	3	1/1/0	0	2/2	General	**14**	
Stinger STG-3G	**Scout**	BM	1	12"j	2	1/1/0	0	2/2	General	**14**	ENE
Stinger STG-3R	**Scout**	BM	1	12"j	2	1/1/0	0	2/2	General	**14**	
Wasp WSP-1A	**Scout**	BM	1	12"j	2	1/1/0	0	2/2	General	**14**	
Cicada CDA-2A	**Scout**	BM	2	16"	3	2/1/0	0	2/3	General	**16**	ENE
Cicada CDA-2B	**Scout**	BM	2	16"	3	2/1/0	0	2/3	General	**16**	ENE
Ostscout OTT-7J	**Scout**	BM	1	16"j	3	1/1/0	0	2/3	General	**16**	ENE
Spider SDR-5V	**Scout**	BM	1	16"j	3	1/1/0	0	2/3	General	**16**	ENE
Cicada CDA-3C	**Scout**	BM	2	14"	3	2/1/1	0	2/3	General	**17**	
Assassin ASN-21	**Scout**	BM	2	14"j	3	1/1/0*	0	2/3	General*	**17**	IF0*
Charger CGR-1A1	**Scout**	BM	4	10"	2	2/0/0	0	5/6	General	**18**	ENE
Assassin ASN-101	**Scout**	BM	2	14"/10"j	3	2/1/0*	0	2/3	General*	**18**	
Falcon FLC-4N	**Scout**	BM	1	12"j	2	2/1/0	0	3/3	Wolf's Dragoons	**18**	
Firestarter FS9-H	**Scout**	BM	1	12"j	2	2/1/0	0	3/3	General	**19**	HT1/-/-
Vulcan VL-2T	**Scout**	BM	2	12"j	2	2/1/0*	0	3/3	General	**19**	
Hermes II HER-2S	**Scout**	BM	2	12"	2	2/1/1	0	4/3	General	**21**	
Mongoose MON-66	**Scout**	BM	1	16"	3	2/2/0	0	3/2	General*	**22**	ENE,PRB,RCN
Phoenix Hawk PXH-1	**Skirmisher**	BM	2	12"j	2	2/2/0	0	4/4	General	**25**	
Scorpion SCP-1N	**Skirmisher**	BM	2	12"	2	2/2/1	0	4/5	General	**25**	
Enforcer ENF-4R	**Skirmisher**	BM	2	8"j	1	3/2/0	0	5/4	General	**27**	AC1/1/-
Ostroc OSR-3C	**Skirmisher**	BM	3	10"	2	2/2/0	1	5/5	General	**28**	ENE
Trebuchet TBT-5J	**Skirmisher**	BM	2	10"j	2	2/3/1	0	4/4	General	**28**	IF1
Quickdraw QKD-4H	**Skirmisher**	BM	3	10"j	2	2/2/1	1	4/5	General	**29**	IF1,REAR1/1/-
Wolverine WVR-6R	**Skirmisher**	BM	2	10"j	2	2/2/1	0	5/5	General	**29**	
Wyvern WVE-6N	**Skirmisher**	BM	2	8"j	1	2/2/1	1	5/4	General	**29**	IF1
Dragon DRG-1N	**Skirmisher**	BM	3	10"	2	2/2/2	0	5/5	General	**30**	IF1,REAR1/1/-
Quickdraw QKD-4G	**Skirmisher**	BM	3	10"j	2	2/3/1	0	4/5	General	**30**	IF1,REAR1/1/-
Shadow Hawk SHD-2H	**Skirmisher**	BM	2	10"/6"j	2	2/2/1	0	5/5	General	**30**	IF0*
Ostroc OSR-2C	**Skirmisher**	BM	3	10"	2	3/3/0	1	5/5	General	**31**	
Victor VTR-9A	**Skirmisher**	BM	4	8"j	1	3/3/0	1	5/6	General	**33**	AC1/1/-
Ostroc OSR-2D	**Skirmisher**	BM	3	10"	2	4/4/2	0	5/5	General	**35**	
Victor VTR-9A1	**Skirmisher**	BM	4	8"j	1	4/4/0	0	5/6	General	**35**	AC2/2/-
Guillotine GLT-4L	**Skirmisher**	BM	3	8"j	1	4/4/0	0	6/6	General	**37**	
Thunderbolt TDR-5SE	**Skirmisher**	BM	3	8"j	1	3/3/1	0	7/5	General	**37**	IF1
Grasshopper GHR-5H	**Skirmisher**	BM	3	8"j	1	3/4/0*	0	7/6	General*	**39**	IF0*
JagerMech JM6-S	**Sniper**	BM	3	8"	1	3/3/2	0	3/5	General	**26**	AC1/1/1
Rifleman RFL-3N	**Sniper**	BM	3	8"	1	2/2/1	2	4/5	General	**26**	
Blackjack BJ-1	**Sniper**	BM	2	8"j	1	2/2/0*	1	5/4	General	**27**	
Griffin GRF-1N	**Sniper**	BM	2	10"j	2	1/2/2	0	5/5	General	**30**	IF1
Marauder MAD-3R	**Sniper**	BM	3	8"	1	2/3/3	1	6/6	General	**35**	
Zeus ZEU-6S	**Sniper**	BM	4	8"	1	3/3/2	0	6/6	General	**35**	IF1,REAR1/1/-
Banshee BNC-3E	**Sniper**	BM	4	8"	1	2/2/2	0	8/8	General	**38**	
Awesome AWS-8Q	**Sniper**	BM	4	6"	1	3/3/3	0	8/6	General	**39**	ENE
Awesome AWS-8V	**Sniper**	BM	4	6"	1	3/3/2	0	8/6	General	**39**	IF1
Hornet HNT-151	**Striker**	BM	1	10"j	2	1/1/0*	0	2/2	Mercenary	**14**	IF0*
Commando COM-2D	**Striker**	BM	1	12"	2	2/2/0	0	2/2	General	**15**	SRM1/1
Javelin JVN-10N	**Striker**	BM	1	12"j	2	2/2/0	0	2/3	General	**18**	SRM2/2
Clint CLNT-2-3T	**Striker**	BM	2	12"j	2	2/2/1	0	2/3	General	**19**	
Jenner JR7-D	**Striker**	BM	1	14"/10"j	3	2/2/0	1	2/3	General	**20**	
Firefly FFL-4A	**Striker**	BM	1	10"/8"j	2	2/2/0*	0	3/3	Wolf's Dragoons	**21**	IF0*
Vulcan VL-5T	**Striker**	BM	2	12"j	2	2/2/0	0	4/3	General	**24**	

EARLY CLAN INVASION: BATTLEMECHS [SORTED BY ROLE, THEN POINT VALUE]

Unit Name	Role	TP	SZ	MV	TMM	S/M/L	OV	A/S	Availability	PV	Specials
Scorpion SCP-1O	**Brawler**	BM	2	12"	2	2/2/1	0	4/5	General*	**25**	
Vindicator VND-3L	**Brawler**	BM	2	8"j	1	2/2/2	0	5/4	Mercenary	**28**	CASE,IF0*
Rifleman RFL-5M	**Brawler**	BM	3	8"	1	4/4/2	0	5/3	Mercenary	**31**	CASE
Merlin MLN-1B	**Brawler**	BM	3	8"j	1	2/3/2	0	6/5	Mercenary	**34**	IF0*
Warhammer WHM-7M	**Brawler**	BM	3	8"	1	4/4/2	0	5/6	Mercenary	**35**	AMS
Orion ON1-M	**Brawler**	BM	3	8"	1	3/4/2	0	7/3	Mercenary	**36**	CASE,FLK1/1/1,IF1,LRM1/1/1,SNARC
Bandersnatch BNDR-01A	**Brawler**	BM	3	8"	1	4/5/3	0	6/3	Mercenary	**37**	CASE,FLK1/1/1,IF1,REAR1/1/-
War Dog WR-DG-02FC	**Brawler**	BM	3	8"	1	4/4/2	0	7/3	Mercenary	**38**	AMS,ECM,REAR0*/-/-
Thunderbolt TDR-7M	**Brawler**	BM	3	8"	1	4/4/2	0	7/5	Mercenary	**39**	CASE,IF1
Awesome AWS-9M	**Brawler**	BM	4	8"	1	4/4/3	1	8/4	Mercenary	**41**	
BattleMaster BLR-3M	**Brawler**	BM	4	8"	1	4/4/1	0	8/7	Mercenary	**42**	CASE,REAR1/1/-
Hunchback HBK-5M	**Juggernaut**	BM	2	8"	1	3/3/0	0	5/4	Mercenary	**27**	AC2/2/-,CASE
Annihilator ANH-2A	**Juggernaut**	BM	4	4"	0	4/4/3	2	7/8	Wolf's Dragoons	**41**	CASE,FLK2/2/3
Imp IMP-3E	**Juggernaut**	BM	4	6"	1	4/4/3	3	10/4	Wolf's Dragoons	**47**	CASE,IF1
Stalker STK-5M	**Juggernaut**	BM	4	6"	1	5/6/2	0	8/7	Mercenary	**49**	IF1,LRM1/1/1,SNARC,SRM2/2
Atlas AS7-S	**Juggernaut**	BM	4	6"	1	5/5/2	0	10/8	Mercenary	**52**	AC2/2/-,IF1,LRM1/1/1,REAR2/2/-
Whitworth WTH-2	**Missile Boat**	BM	2	8"j	1	2/2/2	1	4/3	General	**27**	IF2
Trebuchet TBT-7M	**Missile Boat**	BM	2	10"j	2	3/3/2	0	4/2	Mercenary	**29**	CASE,IF1,LRM1/1/1,SNARC
Shadow Hawk SHD-5M	**Missile Boat**	BM	2	10"j	2	2/3/2	0	6/3	Mercenary	**33**	CASE,IF1
Dervish DV-7D	**Missile Boat**	BM	2	10"j	2	3/3/2	0	5/5	Mercenary	**34**	CASE,IF1,LRM1/1/1
Archer ARC-5W	**Missile Boat**	BM	3	8"	1	3/4/3	0	7/3	Wolf's Dragoons	**38**	CASE,IF2,LRM1/2/2,SNARC,SRM1/1
Catapult CPLT-C3	**Missile Boat**	BM	3	8"j	1	2/2/0	0	5/5	Mercenary	**39**	ARTAIS-1
Archer ARC-4M	**Missile Boat**	BM	3	8"	1	3/5/4	0	7/6	Mercenary	**45**	CASE,IF3,REAR1/1/-
Wasp WSP-3W	**Scout**	BM	1	12"j	2	2/0/0	0	1/2	Wolf's Dragoons	**10**	ENE
Wasp WSP-3M	**Scout**	BM	1	12"j	2	1/1/0	0	1/2	Mercenary	**11**	CASE
Stinger STG-5M	**Scout**	BM	1	12"j	2	1/1/0	0	2/2	Mercenary	**15**	AMS
Hermes HER-3S	**Scout**	BM	1	22"	4	1/1/0	0	1/3	Mercenary	**16**	ENE,PRB,RCN
Locust LCT-3M	**Scout**	BM	1	16"	3	2/1/0	0	2/2	Mercenary	**16**	AMS,CASE
Falcon FLC-4P	**Scout**	BM	1	12"/10"j	2	2/1/0	0	3/3	Wolf's Dragoons	**19**	AMS
Chameleon TRC-4B	**Scout**	BM	2	12"j	2	2/1/0	1	3/4	Mercenary	**21**	
Firestarter FS9-S	**Scout**	BM	1	12"j	2	1/1/0	0	3/3	Mercenary	**22**	AMS,HT1/-/-,PRB,RCN,REAR0*/-/-
Quickdraw QKD-5A	**Skirmisher**	BM	3	10"j	2	3/3/0	0	4/5	General	**29**	REAR1/1/-
Ostsol OTL-5M	**Skirmisher**	BM	3	10"	2	4/4/0	0	5/3	Mercenary	**31**	AMS,REAR1/1/-
Quickdraw QKD-5M	**Skirmisher**	BM	3	10"j	2	2/2/1	0	5/5	Mercenary	**31**	CASE,IF1,REAR1/1/-
Cronus CNS-3M	**Skirmisher**	BM	2	10"j	2	2/2/0	1	6/5	Mercenary	**32**	
Wolverine WVR-7M	**Skirmisher**	BM	2	12"/10"j	2	3/3/2	1	5/3	Mercenary	**32**	
Wolverine WVR-7D	**Skirmisher**	BM	2	12"/10"j	2	3/3/1	0	6/3	Mercenary	**33**	CASE
Grim Reaper GRM-R-PR29	**Skirmisher**	BM	2	10"	2	3/3/2	1	6/3	Mercenary	**34**	AMS,CASE,IF1,LRM1/1/1
Marauder MAD-5M	**Skirmisher**	BM	3	8"j	1	4/4/1	0	6/3	Mercenary	**34**	CASE,FLK1/1/1
Crusader CRD-5M	**Skirmisher**	BM	3	8"j	1	4/4/2	0	6/3	Mercenary	**37**	AMS,CASE,IF1,LRM1/1/1
Grasshopper GHR-5J	**Skirmisher**	BM	3	8"j	1	3/3/1	0	7/6	General	**38**	AMS
Guillotine GLT-5M	**Skirmisher**	BM	3	8"j	1	4/4/1	0	6/6	Mercenary	**38**	CASE
Grasshopper GHR-5N	**Skirmisher**	BM	3	8"j	1	3/4/1	0	7/6	General*	**39**	ENE
Marauder MAD-5D	**Skirmisher**	BM	3	8"j	1	4/4/2	1	7/3	Mercenary	**39**	CASE
Thunderbolt TDR-9SE	**Skirmisher**	BM	3	8"j	1	3/4/1	0	7/5	Mercenary	**39**	CASE,IF1
Victor VTR-9D	**Skirmisher**	BM	4	8"j	1	4/4/2	0	7/6	Mercenary	**42**	CASE
Hoplite HOP-4D	**Sniper**	BM	2	8"	1	1/1/1	0	6/5	Wolf's Dragoons	**25**	FLK1/1/1,IF0*
JagerMech JM6-DD	**Sniper**	BM	3	8"	1	3/3/2	1	4/3	Mercenary	**27**	CASE
Blackjack BJ-2	**Sniper**	BM	2	8"j	1	3/3/2	1	5/4	Mercenary	**32**	
Griffin GRF-3M	**Sniper**	BM	2	10"j	2	2/3/3	0	5/3	Mercenary	**32**	CASE,IF1,LRM1/1/1
Goliath GOL-3M	**Sniper**	BM	4	8"	1	2/3/3	0	8/4	Mercenary	**37**	CASE,IF1,LRM1/1/1
Cyclops CP-11-A	**Sniper**	BM	4	8"	1	4/4/3	0	5/7	General	**38**	IF1
Cyclops CP-11-A-DC	**Sniper**	BM	4	8"	1	3/4/3	0	5/7	General	**38**	IF1,MHQ1
Zeus ZEU-9S	**Sniper**	BM	4	8"	1	3/4/3	0	7/6	Mercenary	**40**	CASE,IF1
Marauder II MAD-5C	**Sniper**	BM	4	6"j	1	4/4/3	0	10/4	Wolf's Dragoons	**47**	CASE

EARLY CLAN INVASION: BATTLEMECHS [SORTED BY ROLE, THEN POINT VALUE]

Unit Name	Role	TP	SZ	MV	TMM	S/M/L	OV	A/S	Availability	PV	Specials
Hornet HNT-161	**Striker**	BM	1	10"j	2	1/1/0*	0	2/2	Wolf's Dragoons	**14**	CASE
Locust LCT-3S	**Striker**	BM	1	16"	3	2/2/0	0	1/2	Mercenary	**14**	CASE
Commando COM-5S	**Striker**	BM	1	12"	2	2/2/0	0	2/2	Mercenary	**15**	CASE
Flea FLE-17	**Striker**	BM	1	16"	3	2/2/0	0	2/2	Wolf's Dragoons	**17**	ENE,REAR1/-/-
Cicada CDA-3M	**Striker**	BM	2	16"	3	2/2/1	0	2/2	Mercenary	**18**	CASE
Javelin JVN-10P	**Striker**	BM	1	12"j	2	2/2/0	0	2/3	Mercenary	**18**	
Assassin ASN-23	**Striker**	BM	2	14"j	3	1/2/0*	0	2/3	General	**19**	IF0*
Clint CLNT-2-3U	**Striker**	BM	2	12"j	2	2/2/1	1	2/3	Mercenary	**20**	ENE
Firefly FFL-4B	**Striker**	BM	1	10"/8"j	2	2/2/0*	0	3/3	Wolf's Dragoons	**22**	AMS,CASE,IF0*
Firefly FFL-4C	**Striker**	BM	1	10"/8"j	2	3/3/0*	0	3/1	Wolf's Dragoons	**22**	AMS,CASE,IF0*
Vulcan VT-5M	**Striker**	BM	2	12"j	2	3/2/0	0	3/3	Mercenary	**22**	
Hermes II HER-5S	**Striker**	BM	2	12"	2	2/2/1	0	4/3	Mercenary	**23**	
Phoenix Hawk PXH-3M	**Striker**	BM	2	12"j	2	2/2/2	1	4/2	Mercenary	**26**	AMS,CASE
Phoenix Hawk PXH-3D	**Striker**	BM	2	12"j	2	3/3/2	0	4/2	Mercenary	**28**	AMS

LATE SUCCESSION WARS: VEHICLES [SORTED BY ROLE, THEN POINT VALUE]

Unit Name	Role	TP	SZ	MV	TMM	S/M/L	OV	A/S	Availability	PV	Specials
Kestrel VTOL (SL)	**Ambusher**	CV	1	24"v	4	1/0/0	0	1/2	Wolf's Dragoons	**10**	ATMO,EE,ENE,IT1,
Kestrel VTOL (SRM)	**Ambusher**	CV	1	24"v	4	0*/0/0	0	1/2	Wolf's Dragoons	**10**	ATMO,EE,IT3,
Kestrel VTOL (ML)	**Ambusher**	CV	1	24"v	4	1/1/0	0	1/2	Wolf's Dragoons	**12**	ATMO,CT1,EE,ENE,
Hetzer Wheeled Assault Gun (AC10)	**Ambusher**	CV	2	8"w	1	1/1/0	0	4/2	Mercenary	**14**	AC1/1/-,EE,
Kestrel VTOL (MedEvac)	**Ambusher**	CV	1	24"v	4	1/1/0	0	1/2	Wolf's Dragoons	**14**	AC1/1/-,EE,
Kestrel VTOL (Scout)	**Ambusher**	CV	1	24"v	4	1/1/0	0	1/2	Wolf's Dragoons*	**14**	AC1/1/-,EE,
Hetzer Wheeled Assault Gun	**Ambusher**	CV	2	8"w	1	2/2/0	0	3/2	Mercenary	**15**	AC2/2/-,EE,
Hetzer Wheeled Assault Gun (Scout)	**Ambusher**	CV	2	0"w	1	2/2/0	0	3/2	Mercenary	**15**	AC2/2/-,EE,RSD1,
Hetzer Wheeled Assault Gun (Laser)	**Ambusher**	CV	2	8"w	1	2/2/0	0	4/2	Mercenary	**17**	EE,ENE,
Hetzer Wheeled Assault Gun (SRM)	**Ambusher**	CV	2	8"w	1	3/3/0	0	3/2	Mercenary	**18**	EE,SRM3/3
Laser Carrier	**Ambusher**	CV	3	6"t	1	4/4/0	0	2/3	General	**20**	EE,ENE,
SRM Carrier	**Ambusher**	CV	3	6"t	1	6/6/0	0	2/3	General	**26**	EE,SRM6/6
Scorpion Light Tank	**Brawler**	CV	1	8"t	1	1/1/1	0	2/2	General	**11**	EE,TUR(1/1/1)
Vedette Medium Tank	**Brawler**	CV	2	10"t	2	1/1/1	0	3/3	General	**15**	EE,TUR(1/1/1)
Vedette Medium Tank (AC2)	**Brawler**	CV	2	10"t	2	1/1/0*	0	3/3	General	**15**	EE,TUR(1/1/0*)
Bulldog Medium Tank	**Brawler**	CV	3	8"t	1	3/2/0	0	3/3	Mercenary	**17**	EE,SRM1/1,TUR(2/2/-,SRM1/1)
Bulldog Medium Tank (AC2)	**Brawler**	CV	3	8"t	1	2/2/0*	0	3/3	Mercenary	**17**	EE,SRM1/1,TUR(2/2/0*,SRM1/1)
Hunter Light Support Tank (LRM10)	**Brawler**	CV	1	10"t	2	3/2/1	0	3/2	General	**19**	IF1,
Manticore Heavy Tank	**Brawler**	CV	3	8"t	1	3/3/2	0	6/3	General	**28**	IF1,TUR(2/3/2,IF1)
Scorpion Light Tank (ML)	**Juggernaut**	CV	1	8"t	1	2/2/0	0	2/2	General	**13**	CT1,EE,TUR(2/2/-)
Scorpion Light Tank (SRM)	**Juggernaut**	CV	1	8"t	1	2/2/0	0	2/2	General	**13**	EE,SRM2/2,TUR(2/2/-,SRM2/2)
Demolisher Heavy Tank (Defensive)	**Juggernaut**	CV	4	6"t	1	5/4/0	0	4/4	General	**26**	AC4/4/-,EE,TUR(4/4/-,AC4/4/-)
Zhukov Heavy Tank	**Juggernaut**	CV	3	6"t	1	3/3/0	0	6/4	Wolf's Dragoons	**26**	AC2/2/-,EE,TUR(2/2/-,AC2/2/-)
Devastator Heavy Tank	**Juggernaut**	CV	4	6"t	1	6/5/0	0	5/4	General	**31**	AC4/4/-,TUR(5/4/-,AC4/4/-)
Ontos Heavy Tank	**Juggernaut**	CV	4	6"t	1	5/5/1	0	4/5	Mercenary	**31**	EE,IF1,TUR(5/5/1,IF1)
Behemoth Heavy Tank	**Juggernaut**	CV	4	4"t	0	6/6/2	0	7/5	General	**39**	AC2/2/-,EE,IF1,LRM1/1/1,SRM2/2, TUR(4/4/-,SRM2/2,AC2/2/-)
Behemoth Heavy Tank (Flamer)	**Juggernaut**	CV	4	4"t	0	6/5/2	0	7/5	General	**39**	AC2/2/-,EE,HT2,IF1,LRM1/1/1, SRM2/2,TUR(4/4/-,SRM2/2,AC2/2/-)
Ontos Heavy Tank (Fusion)	**Juggernaut**	CV	4	6"t	1	6/7/2	0	6/5	Mercenary*	**41**	IF1,LRM1/1/1,TUR(6/7/2, LRM1/1/1,IF1)
Behemoth Heavy Tank (Armor)	**Juggernaut**	CV	4	4"t	0	5/5/2	0	11/5	General	**44**	AC2/2/-,EE,IF1,LRM1/1/1,SRM2/2, TUR(4/4/-,SRM2/2,AC2/2/-)

LATE SUCCESSION WARS: VEHICLES (SORTED BY ROLE, THEN POINT VALUE)

Unit Name	Role	TP	SZ	MV	TMM	S/M/L	OV	A/S	Availability	PV	Specials
APC (Wheeled LRM)	**Missile Boat**	CV	1	12"w	2	0*/0*/0*	0	1/1	General	**7**	EE,IF0*,
APC (Tracked LRM)	**Missile Boat**	CV	1	12"t	2	0*/0*/0*	0	1/1	General	**8**	EE,IF0*,
APC (Hover LRM)	**Missile Boat**	CV	1	20"h	4	0*/0*/0*	0	1/1	General	**9**	EE,IF0*,
Scorpion Light Tank (LRM)	**Missile Boat**	CV	1	8"t	1	1/1/1	0	3/2	General	**14**	EE,IF1,TUR(1/1/1,IF1)
Hunter Light Support Tank (LRM15)	**Missile Boat**	CV	1	10"t	2	2/1/1	0	3/2	General	**16**	IF1,
Hetzer Wheeled Assault Gun (LRM)	**Missile Boat**	CV	2	8"w	1	1/2/2	0	3/2	Mercenary	**18**	EE,IF2,LRM1/2/2,
Hunter Light Support Tank	**Missile Boat**	CV	1	10"t	2	1/2/2	0	3/2	General	**18**	IF1,LRM(1/1/1),
Hunter Light Support Tank (Ammo)	**Missile Boat**	CV	1	10"t	2	1/2/2	0	3/2	General	**18**	IF1,LRM1/1/1,
Scimitar Medium Hover Tank (Missile)	**Missile Boat**	CV	1	16"h	3	1/2/1	0	3/2	General	**18**	IF1,TUR(1/2/1,IF1)
Ballista Self-Propelled Artillery Tank	**Missile Boat**	CV	2	6"t	1	0*/0/0	0	4/3	General	**25**	ARTS-1,EE,REAR0*/-/-
Bulldog Medium Tank (LRM)	**Missile Boat**	CV	3	8"t	1	2/3/2	0	3/3	Mercenary	**21**	EE,IF1,LRM1/1/1,SRM1/1, TUR(2/3/2,SRM1/1, LRM1/1/1,IF1)
LRM Carrier	**Missile Boat**	CV	3	6"t	1	2/3/3	0	2/3	General	**22**	EE,IF3,LRM(1/3/3),
Thumper Artillery Vehicle	**Missile Boat**	CV	3	8"w	1	0/0/0	0	6/3	General	**22**	ARTT-1,EE,REAR0*/-/-,
Pike Support Vehicle (Missile)	**Missile Boat**	CV	3	6"t	1	2/3/2	0	5/3	General	**26**	EE,IF2,LRM1/2/2,TUR(1/2/2,LRM1/2/2,IF2)
Partisan Heavy Tank (LRM)	**Missile Boat**	CV	4	6"t	1	3/4/4	0	3/4	General	**30**	EE,IF4,LRM2/4/4,TUR(2/4/4,LRM2/4/4,IF4)
Ontos Heavy Tank (LRM)	**Missile Boat**	CV	4	6"t	1	2/4/4	0	5/5	Mercenary	**33**	EE,IF3,LRM2/3/3,TUR(LRM2/3/3,IF3)
Mobile Long Tom Artillery LT-MOB-25	**Missile Boat**	CV	2	4"t	0	1/0/0	0	2/3	General	**37**	ARTLT-1,EE,HTC,MHQ2,
Badger Tracked Transport C	**Missile Boat**	CV	1	12"t	2	0*/1/1	0	3/2	Wolf's Dragoons	**15**	IF1,IT4,OMNI,TUR(0*/1/1)
Bandit Hovercraft D	**Missile Boat**	CV	2	18"h	3	1/1/1	0	6/3	Wolf's Dragoons	**24**	IF1,IT4,OMNI,TUR(1/1/1,IF1)
Bandit Hovercraft E	**Missile Boat**	CV	2	18"h	3	1/2/1	0	6/3	Wolf's Dragoons	**26**	IF1,IT4,OMNI,TUR(1/1/1,IF1)
Hi-Scout Drone (PathTrak)	**Scout**	CV	1	16"t	3	0/0/0	0	0/1	General	**4**	DRO,EE,ENE,
Hi-Scout Drone (NapFind)	**Scout**	CV	1	30"h	4	0/0/0	0	0/1	General	**5**	DRO,EE,ENE,
APC (Tracked MG)	**Scout**	CV	1	12"t	2	1/0/0	0	1/1	General	**6**	EE,TUR(1/-/-)
Heavy Tracked APC (MG)	**Scout**	CV	1	10"t	2	1/0/0	0	2/1	General	**6**	EE,IT3,REAR0*/-/-,
APC (Tracked SRM)	**Scout**	CV	1	12"t	2	0*/0*/0	0	1/1	General	**7**	EE,
Heavy Tracked APC (LRM)	**Scout**	CV	1	10"t	2	1/0*/0*	0	2/1	General	**7**	EE,IF0*,IT3,
APC (Hover MG)	**Scout**	CV	1	20"h	4	1/0/0	0	1/1	General	**8**	EE,TUR(1/-/-)
APC (Wheeled MG)	**Scout**	CV	1	12"w	2	1/0/0	0	2/1	General	**8**	EE,TUR(1/-/-)
Heavy Wheeled APC (MG)	**Scout**	CV	1	12"w	2	1/0/0	0	2/1	General	**8**	EE,IT3,REAR0*/-/-,
APC (Hover Sensors)	**Scout**	CV	1	20"h	4	0/0/0	0	1/1	General	**9**	EE,ENE,IT1,RCN,RSD1,
Kestrel VTOL	**Scout**	CV	1	24"v	4	0*/0/0	0	1/2	Wolf's Dragoons	**9**	ATMO,EE,IT3,
Swift Wind Scout Car	**Scout**	CV	1	20"w	4	0/0/0	0	1/1	Mercenary*	**9**	CT1,ENE,MHQ2,
Swift Wind Scout Car (ICE)	**Scout**	CV	1	20"w	4	0/0/0	0	1/1	Mercenary*	**9**	EE,ENE,MHQ2,
Warrior Attack Helicopter H-7	**Scout**	CV	1	18"v	3	1/1/0*	0	1/1	General	**9**	ATMO,EE,
Heavy Tracked APC (SRM)	**Scout**	CV	1	10"t	2	1/1/0	0	2/1	General	**10**	EE,IT3,
Heavy Wheeled APC (LRM)	**Scout**	CV	1	12"w	2	1/0*/0*	0	2/1	General	**10**	EE,IF0*,IT3,
Heavy Wheeled APC (SRM)	**Scout**	CV	1	12"w	2	1/1/0	0	2/1	General	**10**	EE,IT3,
Packrat LRPV PKR-T5	**Scout**	CV	1	14"w	3	1/1/0	0	2/1	General	**10**	IT1,
Packrat LRPV PKR-T5 (ICE)	**Scout**	CV	1	14"w	3	1/1/0	0	2/1	General	**10**	EE,IT1,
Warrior Attack Helicopter H-7A	**Scout**	CV	1	18"v	3	1/1/1	0	1/1	General	**10**	ATMO,EE,
Heavy Hover APC (LRM)	**Scout**	CV	1	16"h	3	1/0*/0*	0	2/1	General	**11**	EE,IF0*,IT3,
Heavy Hover APC (SRM)	**Scout**	CV	1	16"h	3	1/1/0	0	2/1	General	**11**	EE,IT3,
Pegasus Scout Hover Tank (Unarmed)	**Scout**	CV	1	16"h	3	0/0/0	0	3/2	General	**11**	CT12,EE,ENE,
J. Edgar Light Hover Tank (ICE)	**Scout**	CV	1	16"h	3	1/1/0	0	3/2	Mercenary	**14**	EE,TUR(1/1/-)
J. Edgar Light Hover Tank	**Scout**	CV	1	22"h	4	1/1/0	0	3/2	Mercenary	**16**	TUR(1/1/-)
J. Edgar Light Hover Tank (Flamer)	**Scout**	CV	1	22"h	4	1/1/0	0	3/2	Mercenary	**17**	HT1/-/-,TUR(1/1/-)
J. Edgar Light Hover Tank (MG)	**Scout**	CV	1	22"h	4	2/1/0	0	3/2	Mercenary	**17**	TUR(2/1/-)
Plainsman Medium Hovertank	**Scout**	CV	1	18"h	3	2/2/0	0	3/2	Wolf's Dragoons	**20**	EE,PRB,RCN,SRM2/2
Bandit Hovercraft A	**Scout**	CV	2	18"h	3	1/1/1	0	6/3	Wolf's Dragoons	**23**	ENE,IT4,OMNI,TUR(1/1/1)

LATE SUCCESSION WARS: VEHICLES [SORTED BY ROLE, THEN POINT VALUE]											
Unit Name	Role	TP	SZ	MV	TMM	S/M/L	OV	A/S	Availability	PV	Specials
AC/2 Carrier	Sniper	CV	3	6"t	1	1/1/1	0	2/3	General	12	AC1/1/1,EE,
Warrior Attack Helicopter H-7C	Sniper	CV	1	18"v	3	1/2/1	0	1/1	General	13	ATMO,EE,IF1,
Partisan Heavy Tank (AC2)	Sniper	CV	4	6"t	1	2/1/1	0	3/4	General	16	AC1/1/1,EE,TUR(AC1/1/1)
Pike Support Vehicle	Sniper	CV	3	6"t	1	1/1/1	0	5/3	General	18	EE,TUR(1/1/1)
Partisan Heavy Tank	Sniper	CV	4	6"t	1	2/2/2	0	3/4	General	19	AC2/2/2,EE,TUR(2/2/2,AC2/2/2)
Pike Support Vehicle (AC5)	Sniper	CV	3	6"t	1	2/2/1	0	5/3	General	21	AC1/1/1,EE,TUR(1/1/1,AC1/1/1)
Schrek PPC Carrier (Anti-Infantry)	Sniper	CV	4	6"t	1	3/3/3	0	3/4	General	23	TUR(3/3/3)
Schrek AC Carrier	Sniper	CV	4	6"t	1	3/2/2	0	5/4	General	24	AC1/2/2,EE,TUR(2/2/2,AC1/2/2)
Schrek PPC Carrier	Sniper	CV	4	6"t	1	3/3/3	0	4/4	General	25	ENE,TUR(3/3/3)
Karnov UR Gunship	Striker	CV	1	22"v	4	2/0/0	0	1/2	General	10	ATMO,EE,
Saladin Assault Hover Tank	Striker	CV	1	16"h	3	2/2/0	0	1/2	General	13	AC2/2/-,EE,
Saladin Assault Hover Tank (Armor)	Striker	CV	1	16"h	3	2/2/0	0	2/2	General	15	AC2/2/-,EE,
Scimitar Medium Hover Tank	Striker	CV	1	16"h	3	1/1/1	0	3/2	General	15	EE,TUR(1/1/1)
Vedette Medium Tank (Liao)	Striker	CV	2	10"t	2	2/1/0	0	3/3	General	15	EE,TUR(1/1/-)
Pegasus Scout Hover Tank	Striker	CV	1	16"h	3	2/2/0	0	3/2	General	17	EE,SRM1/1,TUR(2/2/-,SRM1/1)
Condor Heavy Hover Tank	Striker	CV	2	16"h	3	2/2/1	0	3/3	Mercenary	20	EE,TUR(2/2/1)
Drillson Heavy Hover Tank (SRM)	Striker	CV	2	18"h	3	3/2/0	0	3/3	General	20	SRM1/1,TUR(2/2/-)
Pegasus Scout Hover Tank (Missile)	Striker	CV	1	16"h	3	3/3/0	0	3/2	General	20	EE,SRM2/2,TUR(3/3/-,SRM2/2)
Drillson Heavy Hover Tank	Striker	CV	2	18"h	3	2/2/1	0	3/3	General	21	IF1,TUR(2/2/-)
Saracen Medium Hover Tank	Striker	CV	1	16"h	3	1/2/1	0	4/2	General	21	EE,IF1,TUR(1/2/1,IF1)
Condor Heavy Hover Tank (Flamer)	Striker	CV	2	16"h	3	3/2/0	0	5/3	Mercenary	24	EE,TUR(2/2/-)
Badger Tracked Transport D	Striker	CV	1	12"t	2	3/2/0	0	3/2	Wolf's Dragoons	18	ENE,IT4,OMNI,TUR(2/2/-)
Badger Tracked Transport Prime	Striker	CV	1	12"t	2	2/2/0	0	3/2	Wolf's Dragoons	19	IT4,OMNI,TUR(2/2/-)
Bandit Hovercraft B	Striker	CV	2	18"h	3	2/2/0	0	6/3	Wolf's Dragoons	25	IT4,OMNI,SRM1/1,TUR(2/2/-,SRM1/1)
Bandit Hovercraft C	Striker	CV	2	18"h	3	2/2/0	0	6/3	Wolf's Dragoons	25	IT4,OMNI,SRM1/1,TUR(2/2/-,SRM1/1)
Bandit Hovercraft F	Striker	CV	2	18"h	3	2/2/0	0	6/3	Wolf's Dragoons	25	ENE,IT4,OMNI,TUR(1/1/)
Bandit Hovercraft Prime	Striker	CV	2	18"h	3	3/2/0	0	6/3	Wolf's Dragoons	26	IT4,OMNI,TUR(2/2/-)
J-27 Ordnance Transport	—	CV	1	10"t	2	0*/0/0	0	0/1	General	2	CT3,EE,HTC,SRCH,TUR(0*/-/-)
J-27 Ordnance Transport (Fusion)	—	CV	1	10"t	2	0*/0/0	0	0/1	General	2	CT3,HTC,SRCH,TUR(0*/-/-)
J-27 Ordnance Transport (Trailer)	—	CV	1	0"t	0	0/0/0	0	1/1	General	3	CT8,EE,ENE,HTC,SRCH
J-27 Ordnance Transport (Armor)	—	CV	1	10"t	2	0*/0/0	0	1/1	General	4	CT3,EE,HTC,SRCH,TUR(0*/-/-)
Swift Wind Scout Car (ICE - Speed)	—	CV	1	22"w	4	0/0/0	0	0/1	Mercenary*	4	CT3,EE,ENE,SRCH
Heavy Tracked APC	—	CV	1	10"t	2	0*/0/0	0	2/1	General	5	EE,IT6,SRCH
APC (Tracked)	—	CV	1	12"t	2	0*/0/0	0	1/1	General	6	EE,IT1,SRCH,TUR(0*/-/-)
M.A.S.H. Truck	—	CV	1	10"w	2	1/0/0	0	2/1	General	6	ENE,MASH5,SRCH,TUR(1/-/-)
Swift Wind Scout Car (ICE - Cargo)	—	CV	1	16"w	3	0/0/0	0	1/1	Mercenary*	6	CT3,EE,ENE,SRCH
APC (Hover)	—	CV	1	20"h	4	0*/0/0	0	1/1	General	7	EE,IT1,SRCH,TUR(0*/-/-)
M.A.S.H. Truck (ICE)	—	CV	1	10"w	2	0/0/0	0	2/1	General	7	EE,ENE,MASH5,SRCH
APC (Hover SRM)	—	CV	1	20"h	4	0*/0*/0	0	1/1	General	8	EE,IT1,SRCH
APC (Wheeled)	—	CV	1	12"w	2	0*/0/0	0	2/1	General	8	EE,IT1,SRCH,TUR(0*/-/-)
Heavy Hover APC	—	CV	1	16"h	3	0*/0/0	0	2/1	General	8	EE,IT6,SRCH
Heavy Wheeled APC	—	CV	1	12"w	2	0*/0/0	0	2/1	General	8	EE,IT6,SRCH
Karnov UR Transport	—	CV	1	22"v	4	0/0/0	0	1/2	General	8	ATMO,CT6,EE,ENE,SRCH
APC (Wheeled SRM)	—	CV	1	12"w	2	0*/0*/0	0	2/1	General	9	EE,IT1,SRCH,TUR(0*/0*/-)
Heavy Hover APC (MG)	—	CV	1	16"h	3	1/0/0	0	2/1	General	9	EE,IT3,REAR0*/-/-,SRCH
Hi-Scout Drone Carrier	—	CV	3	8"t	1	0*/0*/0	0	3/3	General	9	CT15,DCC5,EE,SRCH,TUR(0*/0*/-)
Mobile Headquarters (ICE - LL)	—	CV	1	6"w	1	1/1/0	0	1/2	General	10	EE,ENE,MHQ2,SRCH
Badger Tracked Transport A	—	CV	1	12"t	2	1/1/0	0	3/2	Wolf's Dragoons	14	IT4,OMNI,SRCH,TUR(1/1/-)
Badger Tracked Transport E	—	CV	1	12"t	2	3/0/0	0	3/2	Wolf's Dragoons	14	ENE,IT4,OMNI,SRCH,TUR(2/-/-)
Mobile Headquarters (ICE)	—	CV	1	12"w	2	1/1/0	0	3/2	General	15	CT1,EE,ENE,MHQ2,SRCH,TUR(1/1/-)
Mobile Headquarters (LL)	—	CV	1	12"w	2	1/1/0	0	3/2	General	16	ENE,MHQ3,SRCH,TUR(1/1/-)
Badger Tracked Transport B	—	CV	1	12"t	2	2/2/2	0	3/2	Wolf's Dragoons	17	IT4,OMNI,SRCH,SRM1/1,TUR(1/1/-)
Mobile Headquarters (ICE - LRM)	—	CV	1	10"w	2	1/1/1	0	3/2	General	17	CT1,EE,IF1,MHQ2,SRCH,TUR(1/1/1,IF1)
Mobile Headquarters (LRM)	—	CV	1	12"w	2	1/1/1	0	3/2	General	17	IF1,MHQ2,SRCH,TUR(1/1/1,IF1)
Maxim Heavy Hover Transport (SRM4)	—	CV	2	16"h	3	3/2/0	0	3/3	General	20	EE,IT3,SRCH,SRM2/2,TUR(2/1/-)
Mobile Headquarters	—	CV	1	12"w	2	1/1/0	0	3/2	General	20	CT1,ENE,MHQ7,SRCH,TUR(1/1/-)
Maxim Heavy Hover Transport	—	CV	2	16"h	3	3/2/1	0	3/3	General	22	EE,IF1,IT3,SRCH,SRM1/1,TUR(2/1/-)
Maxim Heavy Hover Transport (SRM2)	—	CV	2	16"h	3	3/2/1	0	3/3	General	22	EE,IF1,IT3,SRCH,SRM1/1,TUR(2/2/-,SRM1/1)
Bandit Hovercraft G	—	CV	2	18"h	3	3/1/0	0	6/3	Wolf's Dragoons	24	ENE,IT4,OMNI,SRCH,TUR(1/1/-)

LATE SUCCESSION WARS: INFANTRY [SORTED BY ROLE, THEN POINT VALUE]											
Unit Name	Role	TP	SZ	MV	TMM	S/M/L	OV	A/S	Availability	PV	Specials
Foot Platoon (Flamer)	**Ambusher**	CI	1	2"f	0	1/0/0	0	2/1	General	**4**	AM,CAR3,HT1/-/-
Foot Platoon (MG)	**Ambusher**	CI	1	2"f	0	1/0/0	0	2/1	General	**4**	AM,CAR3
Foot Platoon (Rifle)	**Ambusher**	CI	1	2"f	0	1/0/0	0	2/1	General	**4**	AM,CAR3
Jump Platoon (MG)	**Ambusher**	CI	1	4"j	1	1/0/0	0	2/1	General	**4**	AM,CAR4
Motorized Platoon (Flamer)	**Ambusher**	CI	1	4"m	0	1/0/0	0	2/1	General	**4**	AM,CAR6,HT1/-/-
Motorized Platoon (MG)	**Ambusher**	CI	1	4"m	0	1/0/0	0	2/1	General	**4**	AM,CAR6
Hover Platoon (MG)	**Ambusher**	CI	1	8"h	1	1/0/0	0	1/1	General	**5**	CAR20
Hover Platoon (Rifle)	**Ambusher**	CI	1	10"h	2	1/0/0	0	1/1	General	**5**	CAR20
Jump Platoon (Flamer)	**Ambusher**	CI	1	4"j	1	1/0/0	0	2/1	General	**5**	AM,CAR4,HT1/-/-
Tracked Platoon (Flamer)	**Ambusher**	CI	1	6"t	1	1/0/0	0	1/1	General	**5**	CAR28,HT1/-/-
Tracked Platoon (MG)	**Ambusher**	CI	1	6"t	1	1/0/0	0	1/1	General	**5**	CAR28
Tracked Platoon (Rifle)	**Ambusher**	CI	1	6"t	1	1/0/0	0	1/1	General	**5**	CAR28
Wheeled Platoon (Flamer)	**Ambusher**	CI	1	6"w	1	1/0/0	0	1/1	General	**5**	CAR24,HT1/-/-
Wheeled Platoon (MG)	**Ambusher**	CI	1	6"w	1	1/0/0	0	1/1	General	**5**	CAR24
Wheeled Platoon (Rifle)	**Ambusher**	CI	1	8"w	1	1/0/0	0	1/1	General	**5**	CAR24
Hover Platoon (Flamer)	**Ambusher**	CI	1	8"h	1	1/0/0	0	1/1	General	**6**	CAR20,HT1/-/-
Motorized Platoon (Rifle)	**Ambusher**	CI	1	6"m	1	1/0/0	0	2/1	General	**6**	AM,CAR6
Foot Platoon (Laser)	**Ambusher**	CI	1	2"f	0	1/1/0	0	2/1	General	**7**	AM,CAR3
Foot Platoon (SRM)	**Ambusher**	CI	1	2"f	0	1/1/0	0	2/1	General	**7**	AM,CAR3
Jump Platoon (Rifle)	**Ambusher**	CI	1	6"j	1	1/0/0	0	2/1	General	**7**	AM,CAR4
Motorized Platoon (SRM)	**Ambusher**	CI	1	4"m	0	1/1/0	0	2/1	General	**7**	AM,CAR6
Jump Platoon (SRM)	**Ambusher**	CI	1	4"j	1	1/1/0	0	2/1	General	**8**	AM,CAR4
Tracked Platoon (Laser)	**Ambusher**	CI	1	6"t	1	1/1/0	0	1/1	General	**8**	CAR28
Tracked Platoon (SRM)	**Ambusher**	CI	1	6"t	1	1/1/0	0	1/1	General	**8**	CAR28
Wheeled Platoon (SRM)	**Ambusher**	CI	1	6"w	1	1/1/0	0	1/1	General	**8**	CAR24
Hover Platoon (Laser)	**Ambusher**	CI	1	10"h	2	1/1/0	0	1/1	General	**9**	CAR20
Hover Platoon (SRM)	**Ambusher**	CI	1	8"h	1	1/1/0	0	1/1	General	**9**	CAR20
Wheeled Platoon (Laser)	**Ambusher**	CI	1	8"w	1	1/1/0	0	1/1	General	**9**	CAR24
Motorized Platoon (Laser)	**Ambusher**	CI	1	6"m	1	1/1/0	0	2/1	General	**10**	AM,CAR6
Jump Platoon (Laser)	**Ambusher**	CI	1	6"j	1	1/1/0	0	2/1	General	**11**	AM,CAR4
Mechanized Field Artillery (Thumper)	**Missile Boat**	CI	1	2"w	0	1/0/0	0	1/1	General	**11**	ARTT-1,CAR40
Motorized Artillery Platoon (Sniper)	**Missile Boat**	CI	1	2"m	0	1/0/0	0	2/1	General	**15**	ARTS-1,CAR23

LATE SUCCESSION WARS: AEROSPACE [SORTED BY ROLE, THEN POINT VALUE]

Unit Name	Role	TP	SZ	MV	S/M/L/E	OV	A/S	TH	Availability	PV	Specials
Chippewa CHP-W5	**Attack**	AF	3	5a	4/4/2/0	2	4/5	3	Mercenary	**31**	BOMB3,FUEL20,REAR1/-/-,SPC,VSTOL
Lucifer LCF-R15	**Attack**	AF	2	5a	4/3/2/0	0	6/3	2	Mercenary	**29**	BOMB2, FUEL20, PNT2, REAR1/1/-, SPC, VSTOL
Vulcan VLC-5N	**Attack**	AF	3	5a	5/5/0/0	0	7/4	3	Mercenary	**35**	BOMB3, FUEL20, SPC, VSTOL
Thunderbird TRB-D36	**Attack**	AF	3	5a	4/4/3/0	3	7/5	3	Mercenary	**38**	BOMB3, FUEL20, REAR1/1/-, SPC, VSTOL
Chippewa CHP-W7	**Attack**	AF	3	5a	6/7/2/0	1	4/5	2	Mercenary	**38**	BOMB3, FUEL20, REAR1/-/-, SPC, VSTOL
Stuka STU-K5	**Attack**	AF	3	5a	4/5/2/0	1	8/5	3	Mercenary	**40**	BOMB3, FUEL20, REAR1/1/-, SPC, VSTOL
Riever F-100	**Attack**	AF	3	5a	6/6/1/0	0	9/5	3	Mercenary	**43**	BOMB3, FUEL20, SPC, VSTOL
Riever F-100A	**Attack**	AF	3	5a	7/7/0/0	0	9/5	3	Mercenary	**45**	BOMB3, FUEL20, SPC, VSTOL
Hellcat HCT-213	**Dogfighter**	AF	2	6a	3/3/0/0	2	6/3	2	Mercenary	**26**	BOMB2, ENE, FUEL20, REAR1/1/-, SPC, VSTOL
Corsair CSR-V12	**Dogfighter**	AF	2	6a	3/3/0/0	0	7/3	3	Mercenary	**28**	BOMB2, ENE, FUEL20, PNT1, REAR1/-/-, SPC, VSTOL
Stingray F-90	**Dogfighter**	AF	2	6a	3/3/1/0	1	6/3	2	Mercenary	**27**	BOMB2, ENE, FUEL20, SPC, VSTOL
Lightning LTN-G15	**Dogfighter**	AF	2	6a	4/4/0/0	0	6/3	2	General	**28**	BOMB2, FUEL20, REAR1/1/-, SPC, VSTOL
Eagle EGL-R6	**Dogfighter**	AF	3	6a	4/4/0/0	0	7/4	3	Mercenary	**33**	BOMB3, FUEL20, REAR1/1/-, SPC, VSTOL
Transgressor TR-13	**Dogfighter**	AF	3	6a	4/4/0/0	0	7/4	3	Mercenary	**33**	BOMB3, ENE, FUEL20, REAR1/1/-, SPC, VSTOL
Transgressor TR-14 "AC"	**Dogfighter**	AF	3	6a	4/4/0/0	0	7/4	3	Mercenary	**33**	BOMB3, FUEL20, REAR1/1/-, SPC, VSTOL
Slayer SL-15	**Dogfighter**	AF	3	6a	4/4/0/0	0	8/4	3	Mercenary	**34**	BOMB3, FUEL40, REAR1/1/-, SPC, VSTOL
Slayer SL-15B	**Dogfighter**	AF	3	6a	3/4/1/0	0	8/4	3	Mercenary	**34**	BOMB3, FUEL40, REAR1/1/-, SPC, VSTOL
Shilone SL-17	**Fire-Support**	AF	2	6a	3/3/2/0	0	6/3	2	Mercenary	**27**	BOMB2, FUEL20, REAR1/1/-, SPC, VSTOL
Cheetah F-10	**Interceptor**	AF	1	12a	2/1/0/0	0	2/6	1	Mercenary	**19**	BOMB1, ENE, FUEL16, PNT1, SPC, VSTOL
Thrush TR-7	**Interceptor**	AF	1	12a	2/2/0/0	0	1/6	1	Mercenary	**18**	BOMB1, ENE, FUEL20, SPC, VSTOL
Sabre SB-27	**Interceptor**	AF	1	11a	2/2/0/0	0	2/6	1	Mercenary	**19**	BOMB1, ENE, FUEL20, SPC, VSTOL
Sholagar SL-21	**Interceptor**	AF	1	10a	2/2/0/0	0	3/5	1	Mercenary	**20**	BOMB1, FUEL20, SPC, VSTOL
Sholagar SL-21L	**Interceptor**	AF	1	10a	2/2/0/0	0	3/5	1	Mercenary	**20**	BOMB1, ENE, FUEL20, SPC, VSTOL
Sparrowhawk SPR-H5	**Interceptor**	AF	1	10a	2/1/0/0	0	4/5	2	Mercenary	**21**	BOMB1, ENE, FUEL20, PNT1, SPC, VSTOL
Centurion CNT-1D	**Interceptor**	AF	1	10a	2/2/0/0	0	4/5	2	Mercenary	**22**	BOMB1, ENE, FUEL20, SPC, VSTOL
Cheetah F-11-R	**Recon**	AF	1	12a	0*/0/0/0	0	2/6	1	Mercenary	**15**	BOMB1, ENE, FUEL24, PNT1, SPC, VSTOL

LATE SUCCESSION WARS: CONVENTIONAL FIGHTERS & AIRBORNE SUPPORT VEHICLES [SORTED BY AVAILABILITY, THEN ALPHABETICAL]

Unit Name	Role	TP	SZ	MV	S/M/L/E	OV	A/S	TH	Availability	PV	Specials
Heavy Strike Fighter Bat Hawk	**Attack**	CF	1	5a	2/2/0/0	0	1/3	1	Mercenary	**12**	ATMO,BOMB1,EE,VSTOL
Heavy Strike Fighter Meteor	**Attack**	CF	1	5a	3/3/0/0	0	1/3	1	General	**15**	ATMO,BOMB1,VSTOL
Medium Strike Fighter Defender	**Fire-Support**	CF	1	6a	1/1/1/0	0	1/3	1	General	**11**	ATMO,BOMB1,EE,VSTOL
Light Strike Fighter Angel	**Interceptor**	CF	1	10a	1/1/0/0	0	0/5	0	General	**12**	ATMO,BOMB1,VSTOL
Boomerang Spotter Plane	**Recon**	SV	1	4a	0/0/0/0	0	0/4	0	Mercenary	**5**	ENE,FUEL13,RCN,VSTOL
Dragonfly Spotter Plane	**Recon**	SV	1	4a	0/0/0/0	0	0/4	0	Mercenary	**5**	ENE,FUEL13,RCN,VSTOL
Hyperion Spotter Plane	**Recon**	SV	1	4a	0/0/0/0	0	0/4	0	Mercenary	**5**	ENE,FUEL13,RCN,VSTOL
Warbler Spotter Plane	**Recon**	SV	1	4a	0/0/0/0	0	0/4	0	Mercenary	**5**	ENE,FUEL13,RCN,VSTOL

BATTLETECH

COMPANY FORCE RECORD SHEET

CATALYST game labs

Faction: ______ Era: ______ PV: ______

Experience Level: ______

Command Special Abilities: ______

Combat Command: ______ Sub-Command: ______

Company Name: ______

Lance: ______ Lance Special Abilities: ______

Unit	Skill	FP (List)	PV	Pilot Special Abilities

Lance: ______ Lance Special Abilities: ______

Unit	Skill	FP (List)	PV	Pilot Special Abilities

Lance: ______ Lance Special Abilities: ______

Unit	Skill	FP (List)	PV	Pilot Special Abilities

Sub Command / Supplemental

Unit	Skill	FP (List)	PV	Notes

REGIMENTAL TABLE OF ORGANIZATION

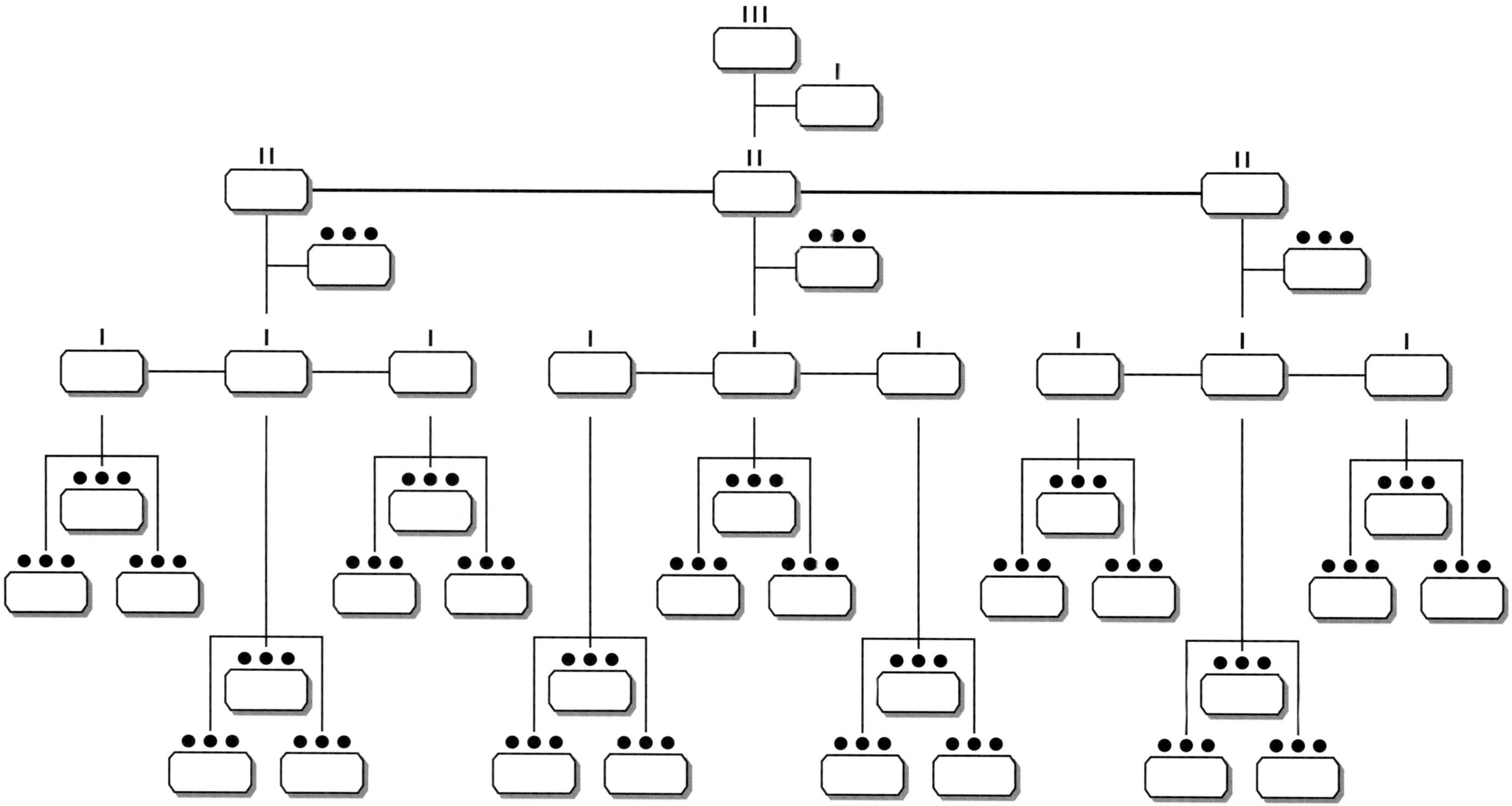

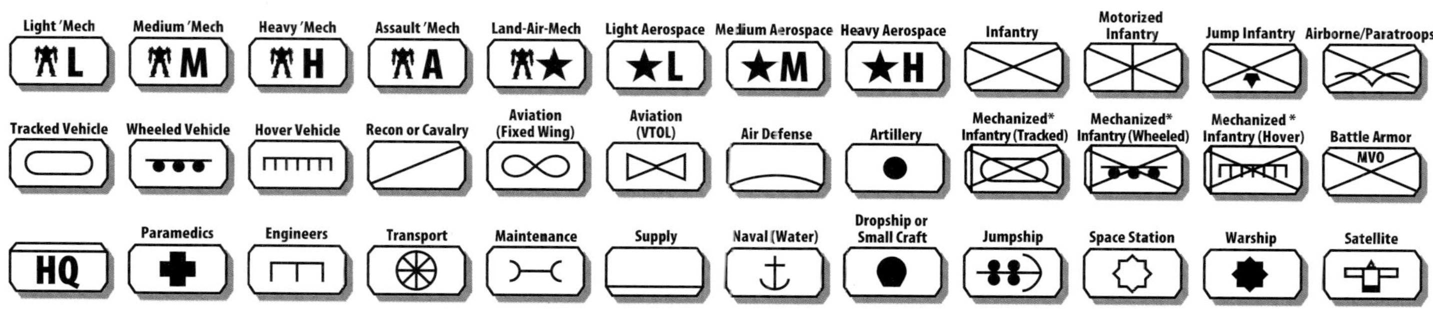

For more information on *BattleTech* Warfare Symbology, see pp. 336-341, *Strategic Operations*.

BATTLETECH MASTER UNIT LIST

WWW.MASTERUNITLIST.INFO

The **Master Unit List** is the free online database that provides *BattleTech* fans with a comprehensive list of game units and their corresponding Battle Values.

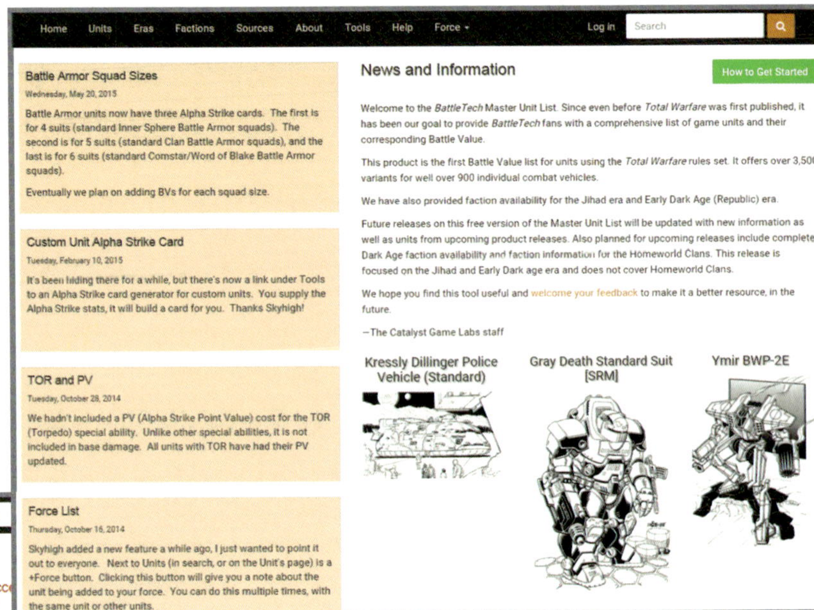

For use with *Total Warfare* and *Alpha Strike* rule sets, it offers more than 3,500 variants for well over 900 individual combat units!

Updates ensure you'll be provided with the latest configurations.

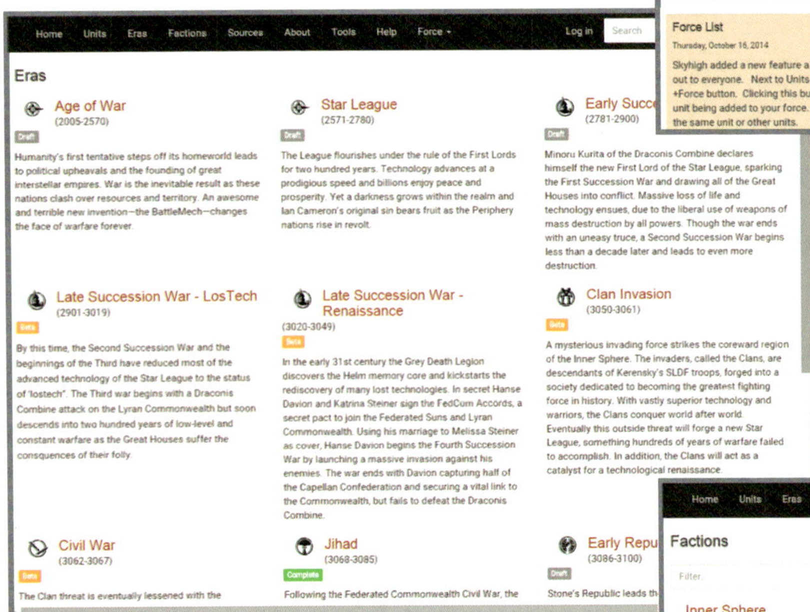

Vast functionality has been incorporated to give you the tools necessary for building accurate and dynamic forces. The database can be sorted by *BattleTech* Eras spanning the history of the game's many rich time periods.

Like the Eras filters, another array of sorting options includes the many *BattleTech* factions—from the Star League, Great Houses, Clans, and of course the Mercenaries and Pirates.

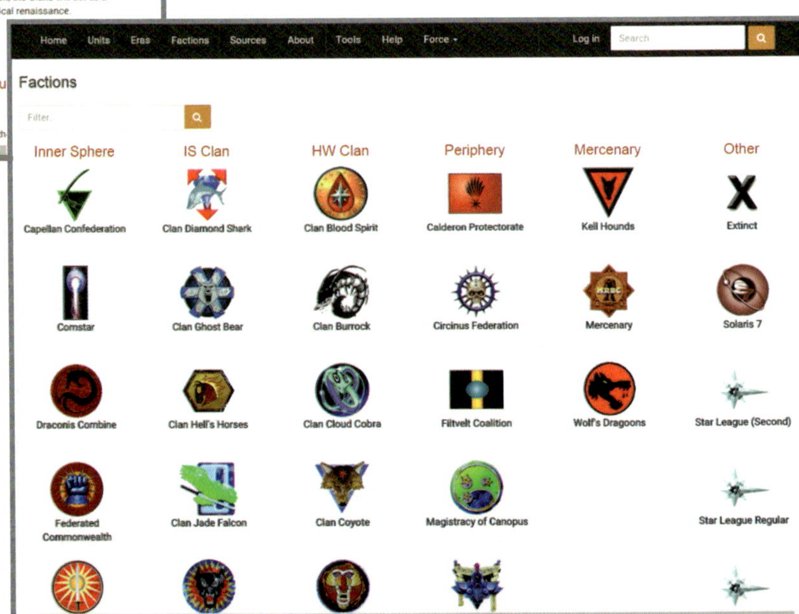

The Master Unit List draws its data from Official Catalyst Game Labs supplements and rulebooks.

MASTER UNIT LIST

THE ONLINE DATABASE

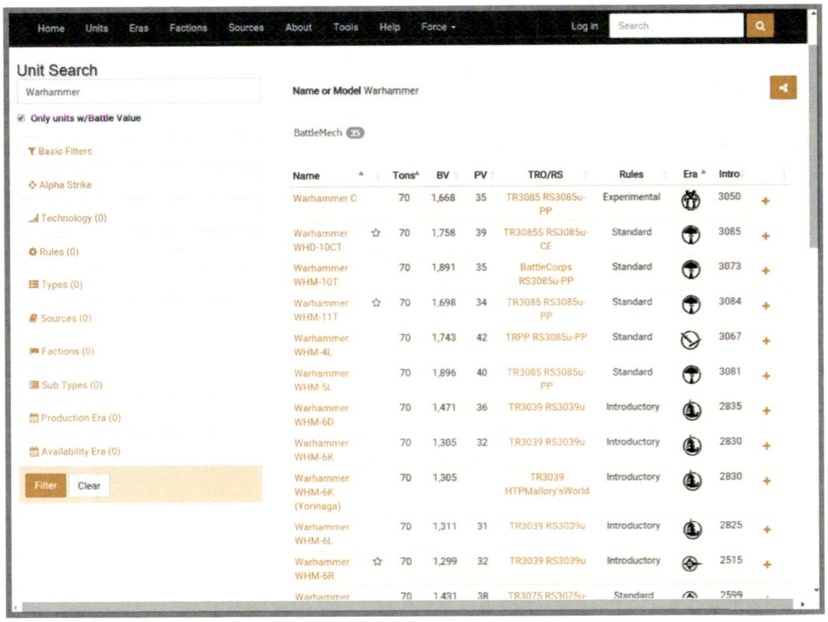

Use the Master Unit List website to build custom *Alpha Strike* forces selecting the war machines you choose. Once selected and added to your force, you can assign pilot skills (adjusting the Point Value accordingly) and even generate a custom PDF that you can download and print. This PDF comes with freshly generated *Alpha Strike Unit Cards* to accompany your force!

That's right, you can download *Alpha Strike Unit Cards* to print out for free!

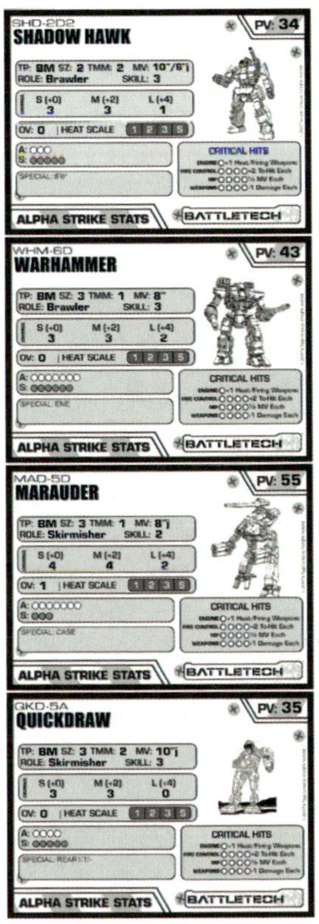

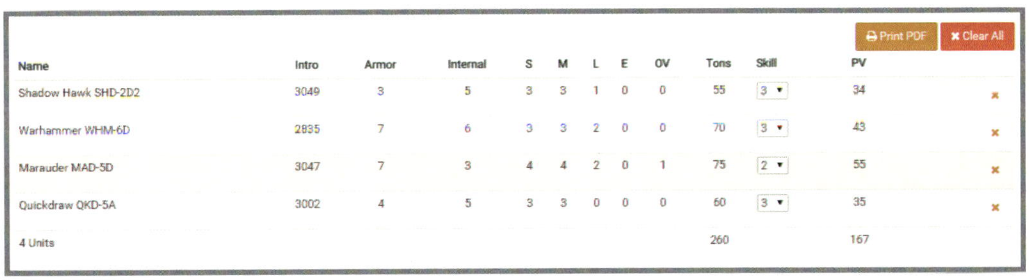

Name	Intro	Armor	Internal	S	M	L	E	OV	Tons	Skill	PV
Shadow Hawk SHD-2D2	3049	3	5	3	3	1	0	0	55	3	34
Warhammer WHM-6D	2835	7	6	3	3	2	0	0	70	3	43
Marauder MAD-5D	3047	7	3	4	4	2	0	1	75	2	55
Quickdraw QKD-5A	3002	4	5	3	3	0	0	0	60	3	35
4 Units									260		167

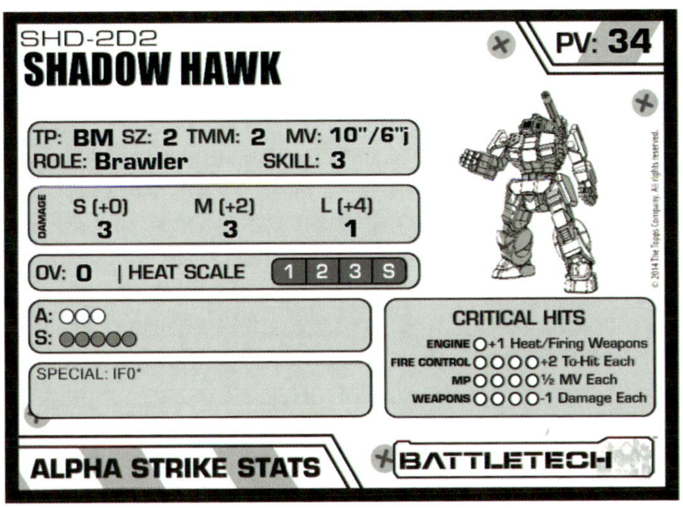

Even more tools are available at the free Master Unit List site. Beyond helpful walkthroughs to get you started, you'll find dice roll aids for cluster hits, force balanced assignment tables, Battle Value skill options can be calculated, and you can even generate random planet systems.

Visit WWW.MASTERUNITLIST.INFO today!

BATTLETECH™

BattleTech: Alpha Strike

Stock #: CAT35600

For centuries the Great Houses fought to reclaim the glory of the fallen Star League, sending regiments of their elite MechWarriors into battle across hundreds of worlds as humanity slid inexorably toward a new Dark Age. The coming of the Clans—descendants of the lost Star League army—did little to stem the slaughter. It only raised the stakes.

Alpha Strike is the new, fast-playing form of the *BattleTech* game of futuristic, armored combat. Developed for the modern tabletop miniatures wargamer, complete with sample armies and a ready-to-play campaign system, all you need besides this book are dice, miniatures, and tabletop terrain to fight for control over the Inner Sphere—one world at a time!

BattleTech: Alpha Strike Companion

Stock #: CAT35670

Alpha Strike Companion adds legions of new rules and expanded options for *Battletech: Alpha Strike*. With this expansion, players will unlock new tactical abilities, special warrior options, design quirks, and unit types. But more than that, players will find within these pages an expanded abstract aerospace system that will enable them to wage war from planet to jump point, while a handy conversion system opens the path to translating the stats for any *BattleTech* unit to its fast-playing *Alpha Strike* equivalent.

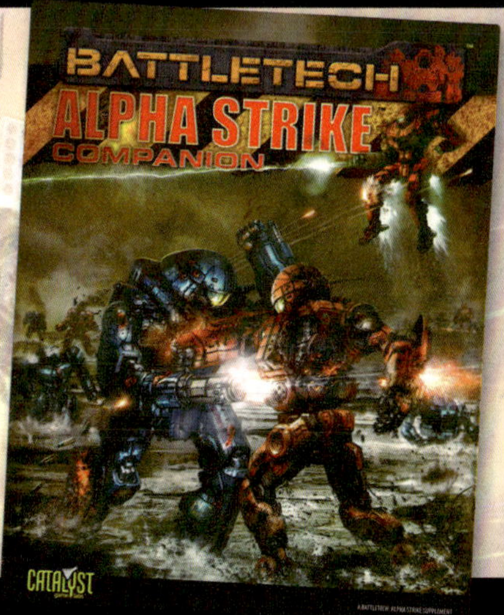

CATALYST game labs™

WWW.CATALYSTGAMELABS.COM

BATTLETECH FICTION

EMBERS OF WAR

PRINT PREORDER AND EPUB AVAILABLE NOW

For Ezra Payne and the Stealthy Tiger mercenaries, professionalism is everything. Hired to assist in the bitter, bloody fighting on the planet Hall, they quickly earn a decisive victory for their employer.

But their respite does not last. More mercenaries, hired by the Allied Mercenary Command itself, land on Hall.

As a new conflict erupts, will the Stealthy Tigers' BattleMechs be enough to save them? Or will the looming threat of renewed war engulf them in its fiery embrace?

Embers of War CAT35820

AVAILABLE NOW

The entire back catalog of print classic BattleTech novels is making its way to epublication. A half a dozen are available, with more on the way!

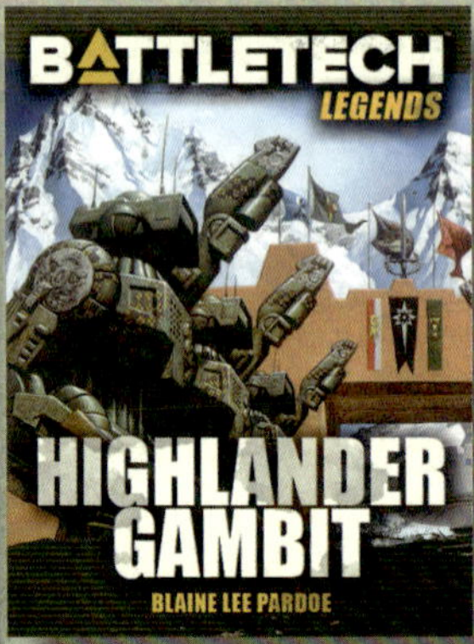

WWW.CATALYSTGAMELABS.COM